Horatio King

Sketches of travel

Twelve months in Europe

Horatio King

Sketches of travel
Twelve months in Europe

ISBN/EAN: 9783337210236

Printed in Europe, USA, Canada, Australia, Japan

Cover: Foto ©Andreas Hilbeck / pixelio.de

More available books at **www.hansebooks.com**

GARDEN OF THE TUILERIES, PARIS.

OR

TWELVE MONTHS IN EUROPE.

By HORATIO KING,

Ex-Postmaster General of the United States.

An honest tale speeds best, being plainly told.—*Shakspeare.*

WASHINGTON CITY:
PUBLISHED BY J. BRADLEY ADAMS.
"SCHOOL OF MUSIC" PRESS.
1878.

Entered according to Act of Congress, in the year 1878,

BY HORATIO KING,

In the office of the Librarian of Congress, at Washington.

Printed at the "School of Music,"
707 8th street, N. W.,
Washington, District of Columbia.

PREFACE.

WRITING A BOOK is one of the last things I ever contemplated; and it was not until nearly a year after our return from Europe that I even thought of penning, for weekly publication, this running account of our pleasant trip. Otherwise I should have taken much fuller notes and have had to depend less upon my memory and books of reference. In all essential particulars, what I have taken from other writers is indicated by quotation marks. I have never set up any claim to literary merit. I make no such claim now. I have not strained after originality, but have only sought to give a plain, unpretending sketch of our travels. It takes now the form of a book on the advice and expressed desire of many friends. I hope it may prove fortunate.

H. K.

CONTENTS.

CHAPTER I.

Departure from New York — Sensations of a First Ocean Trip — Welcome to a Land Bird — Original Ocean Hymn — Ode to an Iceberg — Warning Signals — Hour Bells — Literary Reunion — Arrival at Queenstown 1

CHAPTER II.

Incidents on Landing — Appearance of Queenstown — Cork — Blarney Castle and the "Blarney Stone" 7

CHAPTER III.

Lakes of Killarney — Dunloe Gap — Muckross Abbey — Meeting of the Waters — "Sweet Innisfallen" — Old Castle at Mallow . 10

CHAPTER IV.

Dublin — Trinity College — Burke and Goldsmith — Dublin Castle — Bank of Ireland — Houses of the Irish Parliament — St. Patrick's Cathedral — Park and Botanical Gardens — Belfast — Port Rush — Ride in a Jaunting Car — Giant's Causeway . . . 13

CHAPTER V.

Glasgow — St. George's Square — The Cathedral — Necropolis — Kelvin Grove Park — Museum — Birth-place and Tomb of Burns — Alloway Kirk — Tam O'Shanter and Souter Johnny — Brig o' Doon — Eglinton Castle 20

CHAPTER VI.

Lochs Lomond and Katrine — The Trosachs — Stirling Castle — Mary, Queen of Scots — John Knox — Cemetery — Wallace Monument — Edinburgh Castle — Heart of Mid Lothian — The old Tolbooth — John Knox's House — The Canongate — Lady Stair's Close 24

CHAPTER VII.

Edinburgh — Roslin Castle — Calton Hill — Sir Walter Scott's Monument — Canongate Churchyard — White House Inn — Dr. Johnson — Gallery of Paintings — Museum — Horatius Bonar — Holyrood Palace — Queen Mary and Lord Darnley — The Assassination of Rizzio — Arthur's Seat — St. Anthony's Well and Chapel — Jennie Deans — Antiquarian Museum . . . 31

CHAPTER VIII.

Melrose and Dryburgh Abbeys — Abbottsford — Leamington — Kenilworth Castle — Warwick Castle — Stratford-on-Avon — Shakspeare's House — His Place of Burial — Interesting Particulars — Oxford University and Museum 37

CHAPTER IX.

London — Westminster Abbey — Poets' Corner — Monuments and Inscriptions — Shakspeare — Addison — Milton — Livingstone — Sir John Franklin — Many others, including Major André — His Letter to General Washington 34

CHAPTER X.

London — Hyde Park — Wellington and Albert Monuments — The Thames Embankment — Richmond — Kew Gardens — Albert Hall Concert — Mansion House — Zoölogical Gardens — Kensal Green Cemetery — Madame Tussaud's — British Museum — Hampton Court 51

CHAPTER XI.

London — State Dinner of the Clothworker's Company — The Loving Cup 58

CHAPTER XII.

London — South Kensington Museum — National Picture Gallery — East India Museum — Trafalgar Square — Charing Cross — Tower of London — Windsor Castle — Eton College — Gray's Elegy . 63

CHAPTER XIII.

London — St. Paul's — Temple Church and Temple Bar — Dean Stanley in Westminster Abbey and at his House — Rev. Mr. Spurgeon 70

CHAPTER XIV.

London — House of Commons — House of Lords — Parliament Buildings — Guy Fawkes — Westminster Hall — United States Legation — Newgate Prison — Bonhill-field Burying-ground — Cheapside to Queen's Road — Wat Tyler — Jack Cade . . 76

CHAPTER XV.

Crossing the Channel — Rotterdam — The Hague — Queen's House in the Woods — Houses of Lords and Commons — National Museum — Amsterdam — Royal Palace — Museum — Zoölogical Gardens — Antwerp — Its fine Churches — Rubens . . . 83

CHAPTER XVI.

Brussels — Royal Celebration at the Cathedral of St. Gudule — National and Wurtz Galleries of Fine Arts — Grand Military Review — Cologne — Its great Cathedral — Up the Rhine — Old Castles — Ehrenbreitstein — Mouse Tower — Bingen . . 91

CHAPTER XVII.

Frankfort — Dannecker's Ariadne — Goethe and Schiller Monuments — Palmer Gardens — The Römer — Jewish Quarter — House of the Rothschilds — Homburg — Nuremberg — Chamber of Inquisition — Houses of Albert Dürer and Hans Sachs — Cemetery — Churches of St. Lawrence and St. Sebald — Gallery of Paintings . 99

CHAPTER XVIII.

Ratisbon — Walhalla — Eger — A Pleasant Traveling Companion — Leipsic — Women and Cows at Work in the Fields — Battle of Leipsic 107

CHAPTER XIX.

Berlin — King's Palace — Unter den Linden Strasse — Brandenburg Gate — National Monument — Statue of Frederick the Great — Musenm — Beer Garden — Charlottenburg — Potsdam — Its Palaces, Gardens, etc.. 112

CHAPTER XX.

Dresden — Picture Galleries — Military Museum — Museum of Natural History — Green Vaults — German Social Life . . 120

SKETCHES OF TRAVEL.

CHAPTER XXI.

Vienna — Scenes and Incidents on the Way — Imperial Painting Gallery — Armor Historical Gallery — Schönbrunn — Cathedrals — Laxenburg — Mödling 128

CHAPTER XXII.

Salzburg — Castle — Lake Königs — Visit to the Hallein Salt Mines — Novel Experience . . . . . . - 135

CHAPTER XXIII.

Munich — Grand Military Review — Cathedrals — Museum — Glyptothek — Pinakothek — Art Exhibition — Royal Palace — Royal Foundry — Statue of Bavaria . . . . . - 140

CHAPTER XXIV.

Zürich — Lake Constance — Consul Byers — Interesting Relics — Odd Sights — Ragatz — Dr. Schleiden — Tamini Gorge . . 148

CHAPTER XXV.

Lucerne — Thorwaldsen's Lion — Excursion to Fluelen . - 155

CHAPTER XXVI.

Interlachen — Brunig Pass — Giesbach Falls — Thun . . 160

CHAPTER XXVII.

Berne — Bear Dens — Federal Palace — Old Clock Tower — Singular Sight — Freiburg — Great Organ 165

CHAPTER XXVIII.

Lake Leman — Lausanne — Ouchy — M. Thiers — Vevay — Castle of Chillon — Gorge du Trient   173

CHAPTER XXIX.

Martigny — Col de Balme — Chamouni — Mont Blanc — Mer de Glace — Mont Brevent 181

CHAPTER XXX.

Argentière — Old Mountain Guide — Chamouni to Geneva — Description — A good Pun 189

CHAPTER XXXI.

Geneva — Mr. Consul Upton — Ferney — Voltaire's House — M. Taine — Père Hyacinthe — The Cathedral Church of St. Peter — John Calvin — Rath Museum — Touching Incident . . 196

CHAPTER XXXII.

Mont Cenis Tunnel — Turin — Description — Royal Palace . . 202

CHAPTER XXXIII.

Milan — Painting of the Last Supper — Leonardo da Vinci — The Cathedral — Picture Gallery — Lake Como — Varenna to Verona 209

CHAPTER XXXIV.

Verona — Protestant Mission — The Roman Catholics — Juliet's Tomb — Tombs of the Scaligers — Cathedral . . . 215

CHAPTER XXXV.

Venice — Churches — Campanile 222

CHAPTER XXXVI.

Venice — Bridges — Gondolas — Funeral Procession — Palace of the Doges — Academy of Fine Arts — Bridge of Sighs — Prison — St. Mark's Square — The Doves . . . 227

CHAPTER XXXVII.

Padua — Ferrara — Bologna — Love Story — A Fright on the Train — Florence — The Misericordia 234

CHAPTER XXXVIII.

Florence — Santa Maria Novella — Artists' Studios — Pitti Palace — Museum of Natural History — Protestant Cemetery . . 241

CHAPTER XXXIX.

Florence — San Lorenzo — Medicean Chapel — Sagrestia Nuovo — Assassination — The Duomo — Baptistery and Bronze Doors — Fiesole 248

CHAPTER XL.

Florence — Uffizi and Pitti Galleries — Michael Angelo's House — La Certoza 253

CHAPTER XLI.

Florence — Story of Genevra — Thanksgiving Day — Singular Superstition — Freedom of Worship — Santa Croce — Piazza della Signoria, etc. - - - - - - - 259

CHAPTER XLII.

Rome — Scenes by the Way — First Impressions - - - 266

CHAPTER XLIII.

Rome — St. Peter's — The Vatican — Sistine Chapel - - 272

CHAPTER XLIV.

Rome — Vespers at St. Peter's and Trinità de' Monti — Mr. Van Meter's Schools — Borghese Picture Gallery — Tomb of Augustus — Fountain of Trevi — Church of the Capuchins - - 278

CHAPTER XLV.

Rome — Farnese Palace — San Pietro in Montorio — Trajan and Roman Forums — Appian Way — Footprints of our Saviour — Temple of Bacchus — Ancient Relics — Sculptors' Studios — Barberini Palace — Beatrice Cenci - - - - 284

CHAPTER XLVI.

Rome — Father Chatard — Pincian Hill — Vatican Sculpture Gallery — The Pantheon — St. Paul's House - - - - 290

CHAPTER XLVII.

Rome — Visit to Pius IX — Santa Maria Maggiore — A Call from Father Chatard — Interesting Account - - - - 296

CHAPTER XLVIII.

Rome — Palace of the Cæsars — Tarpeian Rock — Coliseum — Roman Forum - - - - - - - 303

CHAPTER XLIX.

Rome — Christmas at St. Peter's — Church of St. Paul — Arch of Janus — Tomb of Caius Cestius — Graves of Shelley and Keats — Marmetine Prisons — St. Pietro in Vincoli — St. Giovanni Laterano — The Santa Scala - - - - - 311

CHAPTER L.

Rome — Santa Croce in Gerusalemme — Santa Maria in Araceli — The Bambino — Corsini Palace — St. Onofrio — Tasso — Garibaldi — Colonna Palace 318

CHAPTER LI.

Naples — Virgil's Tomb — National Museum — Italian Beggars — Villa Reale 325

CHAPTER LII.

Naples — Castellamare — Sorrento — Pompeii . . . 331

CHAPTER LIII.

Naples — Trip to Baiæ — Grotto of Posilido — Pozzuoli — Crater of Solfatara — Lake Avernus — Royal Palace — Vesuvius — Lava Beds 338

CHAPTER LIV.

Rome — Capitoline Museum — Interesting Excursion — Names of the Seven Hills — Church of St. Augustine — Baths of Caracalla — Catacombs — William and Mary Howitt . . . 345

CHAPTER LV.

Rome to Geneva — Pisa — The great Cathedral, Baptistery, Leaning Tower, and Campo Santo — Spezzia — Genoa — A Fright — View of the City 352

CHAPTER LVI.

Geneva — Coppet — Madame de Staël — Geneva to Paris — Strange Sight — Nice — Toulon — Marseilles — Arles — Nismes — Avignon — Lyons — Dijon — Fontainebleau . . . 359

CHAPTER LVII.

Paris — Versailles — Palace — St. Cloud — Sèvres — Garden of the Tuileries — Churches of St. Étienne du Mont, Nôtre Dame, and the Madeleine — The Louvre — Tomb of Napoleon — Hôtel des Invalides 366

CHAPTER LVIII.

Paris — Place de la Concorde — Place du Carousal — Place Napoleon Place and Column of Vendôme — Column of July — Place de la Bastile — Place du Trône — Champs Élysées — Siege of Paris — Arc de Triomphe — Portes St. Martin and St. Denis — Tour St. Jacques — Palais Royal . . . . . . - 375

CHAPTER LIX.

Paris — Destruction from the War — Reception of the Emperors of Russia and Austria and King of Prussia in 1867 — Emperor and Empress of France — Père La Chaise — Abélard and Héloïse — Jardin des Plantes — Pantheon — St. Roche — Palace and Garden of the Luxembourg — Hôtel Cluny . . - 383

CHAPTER LX.

Paris to London — The Thames — London to Liverpool — Ocean Passage — Home Again . . . . . . - 391

LIST OF ILLUSTRATIONS.

PARIS — GARDEN OF THE TUILERIES.
EDINBURGH — EDINBURGH CASTLE AND SCOTT MONUMENT.
LONDON — WESTMINSTER ABBEY.
AMSTERDAM.
POTSDAM — SANS SOUCI.
MUNICH — BAVARIAN STATUE AND HALL OF FAME.
VENICE — COURT OF THE PALACE OF THE DOGES.
FLORENCE.
ROME — COLISEUM OF VESPASIAN.
FONTAINEBLEAU — GARDEN AND PALACE.
VERSAILLES — PALACE.
PARIS — HÔTEL DES INVALIDES.
PARIS — PLACE VENDÔME.
PARIS — TOUR DE ST. JACQUES DE LA BOUCHERIE.
PARIS — LUXEMBOURG PALACE.

SKETCHES OF TRAVEL,

OR

TWELVE MONTHS IN EUROPE.

CHAPTER I.

IN undertaking to give some sketches of travel in Europe, it may be as well to start from New York, although there is hardly anything more monotonous than an ocean trip on a smooth sea; and as we (myself and wife,) had fine weather the most of the way, our passage over was without any remarkable incident. We sailed the 12th of May, 1875, a good time to start, on the Cunard steamship "Scotia," commanded by Captain LEITCH, a first-rate officer. We chose this ship because she has side wheels. The number of passengers did not exceed eighty—all strangers to us except Horatio Stone, the sculptor, who was on his way to Rome never to return. He had formerly resided there a considerable length of time, and in reference to our apprehensions of danger in visiting that city, he ridiculed the idea of its being any more sickly there than in any other city. Whether or no he contracted there the disease which carried him off, we are not advised; but, on reaching Geneva, in September, we heard with sorrow that he had died sometime in July or August, at Carrara, the place of fine Italian marble quarries.

Our departure from New York was marked by the

usual crowd and excitement—friends come to bid farewell—the hurrying to and fro between ship and shore—and finally, as our great vessel moved slowly from her moorings, the casting of pennies into the water as a means of appeasing the evil spirits of the deep—the waving of handkerchiefs and other demonstrations of affection—the earnest looking to catch the last view of friends—any one who has ever started on such a voyage knows all about this. Byron has truly said:

> "It is an awkward sight
> To see one's native land receding through
> The growing waters; it unmans one quite,
> Especially when life is rather new."

He means, we imagine, when "life is rather new" in such experiences. A first ocean trip, surely, gives rise to sensations never before felt; but the effect on all persons is not always the same. For ourselves, we are free to admit that we were keenly sensible to the truth of the remarks of Madame de Staël, that "it becomes a much more serious matter to quit one's country, when in going away it is necessary to cross the sea. Everything," she says, "is solemn in a voyage of which the ocean marks the first steps; it seems that an abyss opens behind you, and that the return may be forever impossible. Moreover, the sight of the sea always makes a profound impression; it is the image of the Infinite which attracts the soul incessantly, and in which, without cessation, the soul appears to lose itself."

If not deadened by nausea, on finding one's self on the broad bosom of the ocean in a fair day, one experiences a feeling of exhilaration not easy to describe; but nausea "unmans one quite," and any intellectual effort while in that state should be regarded with lenity, as it no doubt generally is, at least on shipboard. Hence, any little squib or original poetical effusion, after the dull monotony of a few days at sea, is quite likely to be received and passed around kindly; and it often serves, too, to open the way to acquaintanceship among the passengers. We secured some of these trifles which were perpetrated on our ship, and we will venture to reproduce them. In the afternoon of the day of embarkation the sea became rather rough, and it was less agreeable on the following day, which was raw, drizzly, and cold. We were now far out of sight of land, and the only cheerful sight during the day was a little land bird which alighted on one of the yard-arms of the vessel. With somewhat of homesickness and disagreeable premonitions of another kind of malady not more pleasant, it was not surprising that the passengers were touched by the following impromptu lines to our sweet visitor:

> Welcome, dear birdie! welcome, I say!
> Tell me, dear birdie, com'st thou to stay?
> Tidings, what tidings bring'st thou to me,
> Of friends, our dear friends, far over the sea?
> Backward, fly quickly to where they all dwell,
> And tell them you saw us all sailing on well.

The next was the following hymn, composed near the end of the week—our sailing day was Wednesday—and it was sung to the tune of "God save the Queen," as a part of the religious services on Sunday:

> Father of Light and Love,
> High on Thy throne above,
>   Give us Thine ear.
> All weak and powerless, we,
> Thy children on the sea,
> Would turn our thoughts to Thee,
>   And nothing fear.

O, God, in Thee we trust,
In Jesus' bosom must
   Our safety be;
Then would we ever rest
Our heads upon His breast —
The haven e'er the best,
   On land or sea.

O, take us safe to shore,
Thy guidance we implore
   From day to day;
To Thee our thanks we bring,
Give us all hearts to sing
The praises of our King,
   His will obey.

One day, when the ocean was perfectly smooth, we were gratified with the sight of an iceberg of respectable dimensions, covering, say, four or five acres in extent, not over a mile off; and we could just discern several others, not probably as large, in the distance. Whereupon was produced this impromptu

ODE TO AN ICEBERG.

Cold, silent sentinel of the vasty deep,
Self-anchored on the great highway of life —
"Life on the ocean wave" — what mean'st thou
By thy stern, stolid look? and in thy rear
Yet other glaciers, as if in reserve
To serve the purpose of thine own intent.
Cam'st thou in threat'ning guise and day serene
To warn of dangers still ahead at night,
O'ercast by cloud and storm? or standest thou
As mark expressive of all danger past?
Silent and cold thou art, and yet methinks
I do discern in thy more softened air,
As in review we take our leave of thee,
That thou art really a sentinel of love.

There was something in this which seemed to interest the first officer of the ship, for we observed that he procured a copy of it. Such "silent sentinels" may well be the terror of "all that go down to the sea in ships;" and the wonder is that more vessels are not lost by coming in contact with them in the darkness of night and dense fogs such as one seldom fails to encounter in crossing the Atlantic. There is no doubt that many a ship with all on board is thus suddenly sent to the bottom of the ocean, while the cause of its loss remains forever unknown. It is during such nights when one feels that at any moment he may be engulfed, that he hears at short intervals, in almost breathless silence, the fearful screeching of the steam-whistle and the sound of the bells which are kept ringing as an additional warning to other vessels to keep out of the way. On the other hand, there is a sensation of relief when, late in the night, the sound of the hour-bell strikes the ear, with the cheerful cry of the watchmen, "All's well." It was in response to this feeling, doubtless, that the following lines were penned, likewise by one of our passengers:

"ALL'S WELL."

List to the sound of bells,
As on the air it swells,
And in the darkness tells
   The hour of night;
Then hear the watchmen's cry —
On lookout to espy
All dangers far and nigh —
   That all is right.

The cheering words, "All's well,"
All nervous fears dispel,
And to our senses tell
   That safety reigns.
Then sink we into rest,
Lulled by the foamy crest
Upon the ocean's breast,
   In somnous strains.

> Now, when life's end is near,
> And all seems dark and drear,
> We breathless list to hear
>   The last hour-bell;
> O, may the joyful word
> In silver tones be heard —
>   "ALL'S WELL."

Well, it must be admitted that this is dealing pretty extensively in rhymes, not to call them poetry; but how is one better to indite an ocean epistle than to present a view of such small things as transpire in the monotony of the voyage? True, all this would be omitted in an account of a stormy and dangerous trip, where fearful exposure and hairbreadth escapes were the order of the day as well as night; but, happily, we were spared this experience. Toward the end of the trip, when the passengers began to get acquainted with one another, we had a sort of literary reunion, two or three evenings, in the dining saloon, where, we remember, we listened to pleasant speeches from Horatio Stone, Mr. Wanamaker, the celebrated Sunday School teacher from Philadelphia, and others; and we had charming singing, also, by a Spanish Countess, as well as by Miss Edith Abell, who, with her mother, was on her way to Italy to study music, and of whose achievements in singing we have since heard very favorable accounts. Then, again, there were some quoit and other active games on deck during the day, and some card-playing among a few in the evening.

All were delighted, when, on the early morning of the 21st of May, land was espied on the coast of Ireland, and by five o'clock of the same day we ourselves and a few other passengers were safely landed at Queenstown, rejoiced to be once more on *terra firma*. The mails and some freight having also been transferred to the tender, bearing the British and American flags, our good ship, with most of our *compagnons de voyage*, immediately proceeded on her way to her destined port of Liverpool — a sail of some eighteen hours.

CHAPTER II.

QUEENSTOWN, MAY 21. — What a rest to be on land again! and what a pleasant sight was the little village of Queenstown and its adjacent fields as we sailed into her snug harbor and waited for the tender to come and take us on shore. The land rises abruptly from near shore, and the village is situated on the sides of the hills facing the harbor. Much of the land seems fitted only for pasturage, covered here and there with patches of gorse, or furze, a thick, prickly shrub, now in full bloom, its flowers being of a bright yellow color. From a distance the contrast between the deep green of the early grass and the yellow of these flowers was very striking, and with the white-painted houses of the scattered villages on the one hand and the strong fortification on the other, presented a landscape which has doubtless commanded the pencil of more than one artist.

The custom-house officers were on the tender, and the luggage of the passengers was passed with little ceremony, so that soon after our arrival at the wharf we were ready to proceed directly to the railroad station, a distance of some thirty rods, where the train was shortly ready to take us to Cork. A number of Irish beggars, old and young, of both sexes, were ready on the wharf with their pressing appeals for alms, which, judging from their appearance, they were sadly in need of, for they were without shoes or stockings, and the few clothes they had on were extremely mean.

We hurried on to the station, where we settled with the porters for bringing our luggage, and although we thought their charge rather high, we supposed it to be all right until one of our ship companions from New Orleans, a native or former resident of Dublin, made his appearance, and knowing the legal rates for this service, informed us that we and all the passengers with us who had preceded him had been overcharged. He at once denounced the porters as rascals, when a police officer took the matter up and they made no hesitation in returning what they knew they had no right to charge.

We were told that far the pleasantest way to Cork was by the steamboat on the river Lee, along which the scenery is said to be very beautiful; but there was to be no boat this evening, and we, therefore, took the cars, which, in a half hour's time, brought us to the city. Fine as the scenery may be on the river, it can hardly be more charming than on some parts of the route by rail. The country through which we passed is very fertile, and appeared to be in the highest state of cultivation. We saw several beautiful residences, the grounds of which were laid out in the most elegant manner.

CORK, MAY 22.—Cork is situated on the north and south branches of the river Lee, which is spanned by many fine bridges. It presented a more cheerful aspect in every point of view than we expected to see. We anticipated seeing here large numbers of that poverty-stricken class of Irish people, so many of whom emigrate from Southern Ireland to the United States, but of such we saw comparatively few (there might have been many in the suburbs,) while the great mass of citizens appeared to be well off and to enjoy life without complaint. Judging from what we saw in the short time we remained in the city, we came to the conclusion that every branch of trade was active and prosperous, as much so as in other seaport towns. We visited some of the churches, in one of which we saw a remarkable statue of Christ. One was the church of the Holy Trinity, a handsome Gothic building, founded by Father Mathew, to whose memory a monument has been erected here, being a statue of himself upon a raised pedestal, and presenting an excellent likeness of him as we remember him on the occasion of his visit to Washington.

In company with six of our fellow passengers we made a visit to Blarney Castle by private carriages, going by one road and returning by another, the distance being about six miles—a most pleasant trip, affording charming views of Queen's College, Black Rock, the Heights of Glenmire and the Groves of Blarney. The ruins of the famous Blarney Castle consist mainly of a large square structure or tower one hundred and twenty feet in height, completely covered with ivy. The "Blarney Stone" is situated twenty feet below the summit in a detached position not easily reached, yet all visitors, ambitious to do a foolish thing, usually try to kiss it. If there is any merit in the act, it is perhaps in the courage shown to accomplish it; for without some person to assist you in maintaining your balance as you lie stretched at full length to reach the stone, you would be in danger of falling and breaking your neck. However, the feat is attempted, oftener than otherwise, no doubt, "for the fun of the thing;" and for the timid there is on the ground floor another stone, easy of access, and said to possess all the wonderful qualities of the more noted block.

CHAPTER III.

LAKES OF KILLARNEY, MAY 24.—We came here in three hours, by rail, from Cork, on Saturday evening, the 22d. Our hotel is beyond the village of Killarney, on the margin of the principal lake. The situation is charming, but we have found the weather a little too cool to make the tour of the lakes. Sunday was to us a welcome day of rest, following so soon after our ten days on the ocean; but on Monday forenoon we rode eight miles, to Dunloe Gap and back, passing the ruins of Aghadoe and Dunloe Castle, which is in good repair. We rode into the Gap to the end of the carriage road, followed by horsemen with their horses and saddles for hire through the Gap. Near the end of our journey, too, several brawny girls, barefoot and in short clothes, ran with the speed of a deer to keep up with our carriage, urging us in the most persistent manner to buy their bunches of wild flowers. Here, also, we were proffered "mountain dew" and goat's milk by the granddaughter of a celebrated character named Kate Kearney, who used to ply the same trade, and lived in a stone and mud house, which still serves as a shelter for her worthy descendant. Sufficiently toned up by the sharp mountain air which came down powerfully through the Gap, we were constrained to decline indulging in any of her "poteen;" nor did we patronize the two or three native artillerymen who were stationed here, with small cannon, which, for a trifling fee, they fire with remarkable effect in respect to the echoes of the report in the mountains.

In the afternoon we rode eight or ten miles through the beautiful grounds of Lord Kenmare and the Hon. Mr. Herbert, M. P., to the "Meeting of the Waters," where "the picturesque Dinish Island divides the stream. This spot is said to have been warmly admired by Sir Walter Scott when he visited the lakes." There is a small inn or half-way house on the island, where refreshments can be obtained, and where fishing implements are kept for the use of visitors. On our way back we visited Muckross Abbey, a photograph of which is among our collection, and from the back of which we copy: "The well-known ruins of Muckross Abbey are situated in the beautiful demesne of Muckross, the property of Colonel Herbert, about two miles from the town of Killarney, and to the antiquary, as well as the general visitor, present considerable attractions. The Abbey was erected by the McCarthys, Princes of Desmond, for Franciscan friars, A. D. 1340. In 1602 it was reëdified, and though ruin has resumed its sway, is still in a good state of preservation. The cloisters are the most perfect portion of the ruins, and consist of semi-circular and twelve-pointed arches, overshadowed by the foliage of an immense yew tree, planted at the time of the erection of the Abbey, and whose trunk measures upward of ten feet in circumference. The chancel contains a fine east window, the tracery of which is still perfect. Here were also interred the remains of the O'Sullivans, the O'Donoughues, and the MacCarthy More, founder of the Abbey." We brought away with us, as keepsakes, some of the leaves of this famous old yew tree, which we regarded with special interest, not unmixed with a sort of reverence inspired by age.

Killarney, with its lake and mountain scenery, and the highly-adorned estates of Lord Kenmare, Hon. Mr. Herbert, and other wealthy landlords, must be a charming summer resort. The lake—there is really only one—is in three parts; the lower and largest being six miles long and three wide. The upper lake is four miles long and two broad. On the side of one of the mountains is O'Sullivan's cascade, which has a fall of seventy feet, and opposite to this is Innisfallen Island, immortalized by Moore:

>"Sweet Innisfallen, fare thee well—
> May calm and sunshine long be thine;
> How fair thou art let others tell,
> While but to feel how fair be mine.
>
> "Sweet Innisfallen, long shall dwell
> In memory's dream that sunny smile
> Which o'er thee on that evening fell
> When first I saw thy fairy isle."

DUBLIN, MAY 25.—Leaving Killarney at 7 A. M., we have made good time to reach Dublin, one hundred and eighty-six miles, at 5½ P. M., considering that we stopped two hours at Mallow for the connecting train from Cork. These two hours were agreeably passed in a walk through the town and a visit to the ruins of an old castle in the vicinity, the history of which we did not learn. It was once the stronghold, no doubt, of some lord of the manor; but its crumbling walls are now covered with ivy, and the crows and other birds seemed to hold possession.

The crows especially appear to be quite at home all along the route, and are very tame compared with their American cousins. Evidently they are ignorant of the smell of gunpowder, or they would be more shy. It was a satisfaction to observe how freely and contentedly they appeared to enjoy life. The buoyant opening of spring, looking from a human point of view, may have conduced somewhat toward this happy state of feeling; for in the words of Shelley—

> " 'T is now the season when the earth upsprings
> From slumber; as a shepherd angel's child,
> Shadowing its eyes with green and golden wings."

CHAPTER IV.

BELFAST, MAY 28, 8 o'clock P. M.—We are now on the steamer about to convey us to Greenock, where we are to take the cars for Glasgow. To go back to the solid-looking old city of Dublin, through the center of which runs the river Liffey, which is navigable only for small vessels,—Kingstown, six miles distant, is the principal harbor of Dublin, and the two cities are connected by a railroad. We reached Dublin on the 25th, and stopped until the morning of the 27th, visiting the principal places of interest, including some of the large mercantile houses famous for their poplins and Irish linens. We made two visits to Trinity College and its spacious lawns, where the students were flitting from one point to another in their square caps and long gowns, dreaming, no doubt, of distinguishing themselves—

some in one way and some in another—hereafter. They were very polite to us in giving any information we desired. The college buildings are so arranged as to form a large open square, in the center of which is the bell tower. In answer to a remark by us that it was a pity such fine buildings should look so dingy—for they are almost black—one of the students replied, "Oh, no, we wish they had a still older look." Connected with the college are fine play-grounds, where, after their daily studies, we saw large numbers of the students playing at ball, pitching quoits, and otherwise stirring their blood and strengthening their muscles by athletic exercises. At the main entrance to the college stand statues of Burke and Goldsmith, who were students here at the same time—about 1746. Oliver was rather a wild youth, and graduated without honors. It was in retaliation for some jocular epitaphs written upon him by his literary associates long afterward that he wrote on his college companion:

> "Here lies our good Edmund, whose genius was such
> We scarcely can praise it or blame it too much;
> Who, born for the universe, narrow'd his mind,
> And to party gave up what was meant for mankind."

In the college library are busts of many distinguished Irish characters, among them Dean Swift's and those of some of his contemporaries. We saw here the first English Bible brought into Ireland. The museum is filled with interesting objects, of which we took note particularly of the harp of Brian Boru, of Irish fame, the charter-horn of King O'Kavanagh, and the writing desk of Charles Lever, the novelist.

The castle, which, like Trinity College, was founded by Queen Elizabeth, is another establishment of great interest as the residence of the Lord Lieutenant of Ireland. In the grand entrance hall we found a company of soldiers with their muskets stacked, and the walls were covered with swords and other weapons arranged in ornamental style, various battle-flags, etc. We went into the different state apartments, where, in the winter season, the Lord Lieutenant and his lady give splendid entertainments. The chapel, too, with its beautiful stained-glass windows, was well worth visiting. Represented upon these windows are the different arms of all the Lord Lieutenants of Ireland.

The Bank of Ireland, formerly the Irish House of Parliament, is the most imposing structure, perhaps, in Dublin. It is situated in College Green, near Trinity College. The House of Lords remains unchanged, save that in the place of the throne there is a statue of George III. On either side of the hall is a large picture—the one representing the Battle of Boyne Water, and the other the Siege of Derry. The House of Commons is used for one of the offices of the bank.

Of the churches we visited, St. Patrick's Cathedral was the most interesting, as containing numerous monuments to distinguished persons. Here rest the ashes of Dean Swift and of the "Stella" of his poetry —Mrs. Johnson. This cathedral was built in 1190, and dedicated to St. Patrick, who, in 448, himself erected a church on the same site where the cathedral now stands. It is related that while engaged in his mission of preaching to the Irish people he baptized the first converts to the Christian faith at a well which is still shown in the south transept of the cathedral.

In company with two of our steamer companions,

a jolly ride in a jaunting car to Phœnix Park and the Botanical Gardens took us through a good part of the city and by the monumental columns erected to Nelson and Daniel O'Connell, whose brother's beautiful estate we forgot to say we saw on our way between Cork and Killarney. Phœnix Park is a royal inclosure at the west end of the city, and embraces an area seven miles in circumference. Situated therein is the villa of the Viceroy, or Lord Lieutenant, the residence of the principal secretary, an obelisk to Wellington, two hundred feet high, the Hibernian schools, a salute battery, and the ammunition magazine. It is regarded as one of the most beautiful parks in the United Kingdom. We were delighted with our ride and what we saw. A jaunting car is a curious vehicle — not seen, we imagine, anywhere out of Ireland. It is a box on two wheels, the seats for passengers running lengthwise over the wheels, with foot-boards to rest the feet upon. These seats each accommodate two persons, who, of course, must ride sideways, and there is room for one person with the driver in front. The only place for luggage, we believe, is on top between the passengers' seats. If you go for a carriage, look to be addressed something in this wise: "I see yer honor and herself have a lanin' for the ould style; shure it's illigant and dacent, not like that baste of a furrin conthrivance beyant. Begorra, sir, I could lep over the likes of it wid this little mare — an' maybe I'd thry!"

We had another long ride of one hundred and eighty-six miles from Dublin, by Belfast, to Port Rush, on the 27th. On a good part of the way the country had much the appearance of hilly New England. It lacked only stone and post and rail fences, in place of the hedge fences, and more forests, to make the comparison quite perfect. On the low, swampy grounds workmen were engaged in spading up great quantities of peat, cutting it into pieces about the size and shape of a brick, and piling it up to dry. This serves for a large portion of the fuel consumed in Ireland. From the bog-wood found in these peat beds many articles of merchandise, such as canes, brooches, finger-rings, etc., are manufactured. They are quite ornamental—just as good, perhaps, while they last, but not quite as durable as silver and gold.

After an indifferent *table d' hôte* dinner we rested over night at the "Antrim Arms," lulled by the waves of the Northern Sea—for we were now almost at the extreme northern point of Ireland. Next morning we took a jaunting car for Giant's Causeway, a distance of six miles, where we spent several hours and returned in time to take the train back to Belfast at 3½ P. M. We had for our driver a witty Irishman, who said he had lived in the United States; and as he was well posted, he proved a very acceptable guide, pointing out and giving to us a history of all the prominent objects on the way. He appeared quite proud of having—I think the year before—had the honor of driving in his jaunting car over this route General Sherman and his aids, Colonels Audenreid and Fred. Grant. He was particularly delighted with the General's amiable condescension in so freely conversing with him—saying that he talked all the way. Among other things, he said the General was enthusiastic in pointing out the manner in which Port Rush might, by a short breakwater from a group of islands off the coast to the main land, be made a most excellent harbor, capable of floating all the vessels in the world. The coast all along our road is very rocky, and with the ocean in full view one can hardly imagine a more romantic ride than we enjoyed. Two miles from the Causeway we passed near the ruins of the Castle of Dunluce, which stands upon an isolated rock one hundred feet above the level of the sea, and is connected with the main land by a bridge only some twenty inches wide. It was founded no one knows at what date, but is known to have once been the residence of the McQuillans, who claimed to trace their family back three thousand years, and to the city of Babylon, whence they left for Scotland. Although these ruins are spoken of as the most picturesque in the United Kingdom, we consider the Giant's Causeway as the one great sight of Ireland. Here is a promontory extending one thousand feet or more into the sea, and at low tide one may walk over the heads of basaltic pillars, numbering, it is said, not less than forty thousand. They are variously shaped — from triangular to nonagon, or nine sided — and are arranged side by side with such perfect uniformity that one might fancy them to be the work of ingenious artificers; still it is questionable whether the art of man could rival the nicety with which each piece is fitted to the other. In one place there is what they call the Wishing Chair — the projection of the pillars being such as to form a complete seat with back and arms. We were assured by an elderly Irish woman, who urged us to buy some of her "mountain dew," with a small quantity of water from the Giant's Well, another natural curiosity near by, that any wish made by us while sitting in this chair was certain to be granted! We accordingly tried it (not the mountain dew,) and, wonderful to tell, her assurance in our own case was most happily verified! Consequently, it would be very unbecoming in us, to say the least, to suggest any doubts on the subject. Other singular formations were pointed out to us — the Amphitheater Gateway, Chimney-tops, the Pulpit, etc. In the side of a hill, further in shore, there is a series of pillars so arranged as to present the appearance, and they take the name, of the Giant's Organ; and near these is the "Giant's Grandmother, who was petrified for having three husbands at the same time." In the vicinity of the Causeway there are wonderful caves — one forty-five feet high and three hundred and fifty feet in length, and another seventy feet in height and six hundred feet long. They can be entered only by row-boats from the sea. A horse pistol discharged therein makes a report equal to that of a small field-piece in open space.

We have seen little of Belfast, except what came within our view in going from the railroad dépôt to the steamboat landing, stopping at the Post Office, a fine building, in the anxious but disappointed hope of hearing from home. We saw enough, however, to satisfy us of what we already knew, that it is a handsome city, full of life and business activity. For two pence, the regular fee, the baggage-master at the dépôt took care of our trunk while we made our trip to the Giant's Causeway.

CHAPTER V.

GLASGOW, JUNE 1.—After a quiet night on the steamer from Belfast we arrived in Glasgow at six o'clock on the morning of the 29th ultimo, having come by land from Greenock, where we took the railroad cars. We are pleased with everything about this city except the smoke, clouds and rain, which give it a decidedly gloomy character. We have scarcely had a sight of the sun here, and we are told that there is hardly a day in certain seasons of the year when it does not rain. The smoke from the furnaces on the Clyde constantly floats in thick volumes over the city, enveloping it in semi-darkness even when there are no other clouds to obscure the sun's rays. The city has a very solid appearance, the buildings generally looking as though they were built for all time. Most of the streets are of good width, and there is an abundance of pure water, brought through tunnels and aqueducts thirty-four miles from Loch Katrine, to keep it clean. The first steamer in Europe, we are told, was launched here in 1812. This is the native place of James Watts, who first demonstrated the power of steam, and in St. George's Square, a spacious and beautiful park, there is a bronze statue of him in a sitting posture and meditative mood. Here also are equestrian statues of Prince Albert and Queen Victoria, statues of Lord Clyde, Richard Moore, Sir Robert Peel, and a lofty monument to Sir Walter Scott. On Sunday we attended church at the great Cathedral, which was founded in the twelfth century, and which is one of the grandest in Europe, being, perhaps, unsurpassed in respect especially to its stained-glass windows. After church we took a walk through the adjacent cemetery, called the Necropolis, which rises in terraces to a considerable elevation, and is beautifully laid out. It is the burying-place of many distinguished persons, containing numerous costly monuments—the most conspicuous of which is one to John Knox, the reformer. On Monday we walked to Kelvin Grove Park and Museum in the west end of the city. This Park, containing some forty acres, is very beautiful, and facing it are some of the finest residences. In the Museum we saw a letter written by Lord Nelson, ordering dinner and wine, several letters from the Duke of Wellington, and one written by Robert Burns. Without favors to ask, we called on our consul, whose name, curiously enough, is Samuel L. Glasgow, and he and his wife returned our call at the Queen's Hotel. We found in them all we could desire as representatives of our country abroad —unaffected courtesy, ample knowledge of what they were required to do, and a willingness to give advice or to communicate any desired information.

Of course, we have been to Ayr, which is forty miles by railroad from Glasgow. This took all of one day, which was full of enjoyment. Our route led us through Paisley, famous for its shawls of that name. Burns' cottage is two miles from the village of Ayr. We entered it with alacrity, devouring with our eyes every object that had ever met the vision of the rustic poet. Here, in a little recess in the side of the kitchen, just large enough to admit a bed, the immortal bard first drew breath. Here, too, were the candle-stand chairs, and the old-fashioned dresser, plates and dishes, which were used by him. An old clock, the case of which reaches from floor to ceiling, likewise remains here, still counting the expiring hours since the moment when it noted the last beat of the poet's pulse. The window by the whitewashed dresser consists of only four seven-by-nine squares of glass, and the front window is but double that size, while the fire-place is large and high enough to hold an eighth of a cord of wood. The other room of the original cottage was also shown to us. This was the parlor or sitting-room, and here, also, some of the old furniture is yet preserved. The old one-story Alloway Kirk is situated about two miles from the cottage. Only the four walls, with bell-tower and bell, remain standing. It is in a cemetery, flanked on both sides by grave-stones — some of which mark the graves of Burns' father, mother, and sister; and here, too, we were assured, rest the ashes of jolly Tam O'Shanter and Souter Johnny.

> "O, *Tam*, had'st thou but been sau wise
> As ta'en thy ain wife *Kate's* advice!
> She tauld thee weel thou wast a skellum,
> A blethering, blustering, drunken blellum;
> That frae November till October
> Ae market day thou was nae sober;
> That ilka melder wi' the miller
> Thou sat as lang as thou had siller;
> That ev'ry naig was ca'd a shoe on,
> The smith and thee gat roaring fou on;
> That at the Lord's house, ev'n on Sunday,
> Thou drank wi' Kirkton Jean till Monday.
> She prophesy'd that, late or soon,
> Thou would be found deep drown'd in *Doon;*
> Or catch'd wi' warlocks i' the mirk
> By *Alloway's* auld haunted Kirk."

Near by the Kirk we stopped at the well "where Mungo's mither hang'd hersel';" and proceeding a short distance from the cemetery we came to the handsome monument erected to the memory of

Burns. It is about sixty feet high, surrounded by nine Corinthian columns, thirty feet high, supporting a cupola which is surmounted by a gilt tripod. It is within an inclosure charmingly ornamented with trees, shrubs, vines, and flowers, and there is an admission, fee of one or two pence. Here we were shown a portrait of Burns, the Bible he presented to his Highland Mary, and a snuff-box made from the wood of Alloway Kirk. Here, too, are kept for sale various articles constructed from wood grown in the vicinity; and no visitor, we imagine, departs without securing some of these choice mementos. In a grotto here we saw Thom's famous statues of Tam O'Shanter and Souter Johnny, which were exhibited to admiring crowds in the United States about forty years ago. Nothing could more truthfully represent this scene:

> "Ae market night
> Tam had got planted unco right,
> Fast by an ingle, bleezing finely,
> Wi' reaming swats, that drank divinely;
> And at his elbow Souter Johnny,
> His ancient, trusty, drouthy crony;
> Tam lo'ed him like a vera brither;
> They had been fou for weeks thegither.
> The night drave on wi' sangs and clatter;
> And ay the ale was growing better:
> The landlady and Tam grew gracious,
> Wi' favours secret, sweet, and precious:
> The Souter tauld his queerest stories:
> The landlord's laugh was ready chorus:
> The storm without might rair and rustle,
> Tam did na mind the storm a whistle."

Hard by are "the banks and braes o' bonnie Doon," and we watched its rippling waters from the "auld brig o' Doon," whose substantial stone abutments and arch look as though they might defy the ravages of time. The "two brigs," also immortalized by the poet, are nearer the village of Ayr, on our way to which, near Paislèy, an ancient oak was pointed out to us as the one under which Wallace is said to have hid from the English forces. We also passed Eglinton Castle; but the great interest of our trip to-day centers in Burns and the place where he lived and died. An indefinable charm seems to be imparted even to the leaves gathered as keepsakes from under the window of his humble cottage and around his tomb. As we walked over the same ground he used to tread, imagination carried us back fourscore and ten years to the time of his death, and we felt like exclaiming with Roscoe:

> "Rear high thy bleak, majestic hills,
> Thy sheltered valleys proudly spread,
> And, Scotia, pour thy thousand rills,
> And wave thy heaths with blossoms red;
> But, ah! what poet now shall tread
> Thy airy heights, thy woodland reign,
> Since he, the sweetest bard, is dead,
> That ever breathed the soothing strain?"

CHAPTER VI.

EDINBURGH, JUNE 2.—Sending our baggage direct by mail from Glasgow to this city, we started yesterday morning on the northern route, by the way of the lakes—the Trosachs and Stirling—and reached here the same day about 10 o'clock P. M., at which hour we could still see to read easily by twilight. We came first by train thirty miles to Ballock, at the foot of Loch Lomond, where we took the steamer Rob Roy, and sailed nearly the length of the lake, in which there are thirty-three islands, to Inversnaid, where a huge coach, ascended by a ladder, was in waiting to take us five miles over a romantic road to Stronachlacher, on Loch Katrine. Here is a small inn, and as we had a half hour before the steamer could return to take us over the lake, we strolled into the pasture among the ferns and heather to obtain a near view of Rob Roy's house, which stands back a little distance from the lake. Here in these highlands was his stronghold, better than a fortress. From this point the steamer was about one hour in going to the eastern end of the lake, where, passing near Ellen's Isle, we landed in a sort of rustic arbor charming to behold. We were fortunate in having a pleasant day for this trip. The lakes were almost as smooth as glass, and, mirror-like, reflected the landscape so perfectly that it was sometimes impossible to discover the dividing line between the real and the shadow. The view from the steamer of the rugged mountains of Ben Lomond and Ben Venue to the north could not have been better. Another coach ride of eight or ten miles through the Trosachs and along by Loch Vennachar brought us to Callander, the terminus of the railroad from Stirling. Our driver was dressed in a red coat and white silk hat, so that he was not likely to be taken for one of the passengers, of whom there were enough—all English but ourselves —to fill the coach. As on the previous coach, we were all seated on top, the inside being for luggage; and as we were driven through the woods up over the heath-covered highlands, where flocks of sheep were quietly grazing, the picture thus presented was worthy of the pencil of an artist. Taking the cars at Callander, which is a small village scattered for a mile or more along the highway, we were soon at Stirling, where we stopped two hours to see the old Castle, cemetery, and other objects of interest. This Castle is famous as the ancient residence of the Kings of Scotland, and of Mary, Queen of Scots. It is now used as a barrack for soldiers, and we had for our guide an old veteran who told us all about it. He took us into the room in which James II. assassinated William, Earl of Douglas, because he had refused to cease his opposition to him, and the King's attendants threw his body out of the window. Next to this is the small room, called the Secret Chamber, which we also entered, where witnesses were secreted to listen and betray. We likewise visited the Chapel connected with the Castle, where Mary was crowned Queen of Scots; and from the top of the Castle we looked through a hole in the wall where she used to sit concealed and witness the feats of the Knights of the Round Table in their tournaments on the lawn below. This lawn, laid out for some game, is still kept in that shape. From the walls of the Castle we could see the field where the great battle of Bannockburn was fought, and eleven other battle-fields. In one room we saw the pulpit, chair, and communion-table of John Knox, a Bible two hundred years old, and in another room some of the old crown jewels and many other interesting relics. The old church in which James VI. was crowned, and John Knox preached his coronation sermon, was likewise an object of special interest. This is at the entrance of the cemetery, through which we wandered, reading the curious inscriptions on the tombstones and monuments. One of these monuments consists of a marble group of three figures on a circular pedestal covered with glass. One of the figures represents a maiden, seated with the Bible in her lap; at her feet sits a more youthful maiden, and behind them stands an angel—with wings, of course. From this very unique monument we copied the following:

"Margaret, Virgin martyr of the ocean wave, with her like-minded sister Agnes.

"Through Faith, Margaret Wilson, a youthful maiden, chose rather to depart and be with Christ than to disown His holy cause and covenant to own Erastian Usurpation and conform to Prelacy enforced by cruel laws. Bound to a stake within flood-mark of the Solway tide, she died a Martyr's death, on 11th May, 1685.

"Love many waters cannot quench — God saves
His chaste, impearled One! in covenant true.
O, Scotia's Daughters! camest scan the Page
And prize this Flower of Grace, blood-bought for you."

On an eminence called the Abbey Craig, three hundred feet high, near the city of Stirling, and near where the battle of Stirling was fought in 1297, stands a handsome monument to Wallace. This monument, being two hundred and twenty feet in height above its base, is seen from a long distance. From Stirling to Edinburgh one may go either by steamer or rail; and as the more speedy mode we chose the latter.

Through the kind introduction and advice of our consul at Glasgow, we find ourselves at a nice private boarding-house, 22 York place, kept by the Misses Thompson, and where our consul for Edinburgh. John T. Robeson, Esq., also boards. It is in a central position, a short distance only from Princess street — which is the Broadway of Edinburgh — and the Scott monument. We prefer it to a hotel. To-day we have visited the Edinburgh Castle, which is on a high ledge, so precipitous that it is accessible only from the eastern side. On one occasion, however, in 1313, history tells us that it was recovered from the English by the Earl of Moray, assisted by thirty men, who, in the darkness of night, scaled the western precipice, guided by one of their number, "who had been in the habit of descending and reascending the cliff surreptitiously to pay court to his mistress." In the crown room, within a grated inclosure, we saw the insignia of Scottish royalty, consisting of a crown, scepter, and sword of state, and with them is the Lord Treasurer's rod of office—all which had been concealed in an oak chest in 1707, and not discovered until 1818. The most attractive point here is Queen Mary's room, where her son, James VI., was born, and when only six days old was let down from a window of his room in a basket, to be taken to a place of greater safety. It makes one dizzy to look from this window to the ground. A remarkable portrait of Queen Mary hangs in this room, and on the wall, surmounted by the Scottish arms, is the following inscription:

> "Lord Jesu Chryst that crounit was with Thornes,
> Preserve the Birth, quhais Badgie Heir is borne,
> And send Hir Sonne successione, to Reigne stille,
> Lang in this Realme, if that it be Thy will.
> Als grant, O Lord, quhat ever of Hir proceed,
> Be to Thy Honer, and Praise sobied.
> 19th IVNII, 1566."

In this chamber Queen Mary's bedstead, and one of her chairs in which we had the honor of sitting, still remain.

On the bomb battery lies dismounted a gigantic cannon, called "Mons Megs," capable of discharging a twenty-inch ball. It was made of thick iron bars hooped together, at Mons, in Brittany, and was employed at the siege of Norham Castle, in 1513. In 1684 it was removed to the Tower of London, where it was regarded as a most interesting relic until 1829, when it was restored to the Castle. It burst in 1682, while being used in firing a salute to the Duke of York.

On our way from the Castle we gazed with strange interest upon the "Heart of Mid Lothian"—the form of a heart set in the cobble-stone pavement on the spot where stood the old Tolbooth, in which Effie Deans was incarcerated, and where the Porteous mob, so vividly described in Scott's "Heart of Mid Lothian," took place. A little further on, in a lower part of the city, we came to the house of John Knox, which is a very old and odd-looking affair; but three rooms—the sitting-room, bed-room and study—are all that are shown to visitors. It was provided for him when he was elected Minister of Edinburgh in 1559, and he occupied it, with some interruptions, from 1560 until his death in 1572. Over the door is the following inscription:

    LUFE.GOD.ABOVE.ALL.AND.YOUR.
    NEIGHBOUR.AS.YOUR.SELF.

Under the window, from which it is said he used to address the populace, is an effigy of him in the attitude of speaking.

Continuing our walk along this part of the old town, called "The Canongate," we came to the house now, or lately, used as a printing office, in which Boswell, the biographer of Johnson, resided, and in which he received Johnson in 1773. Opening from Longmarket street is a narrow alley called "Lady Stair's Close," in which is laid the scene of Sir Walter Scott's romantic story, "My Aunt Margaret's Mirror." Over the doorway of the house described in the story is the inscription: "Fear the Lord and depart from evil."

EDINBURGH CASTLE AND SCOTT MONUMENT.

CHAPTER VII.

EDINBURGH, JUNE 8.—We have had a week's delightful enjoyment in old Edinburgh and vicinity, going one day a few miles out of town to visit Roslin Castle, only the ruins of which remain. The Chapel near by, however, has been preserved, and is much admired for its exquisite architecture, including what is called the "Apprentice's Pillar," which has been reproduced in plaster in the South Kensington Museum, London. Nothing could be more charming than the scenery surrounding the Castle, and through Hawthornden, the home of the poet Drummond in the the time of Shakspeare.

> "Here, too, are labyrinthine paths
> To caverns dark and low,
> Wherein, they say, King Robert Bruce
> Found refuge from his foe."

Edinburgh is conspicuous not only for its solid stone edifices, but also for its monuments. In Parliament Square is a fine equestrian statue of Charles II. In one street are statues of Pitt, George IV., John, the fourth Earl of Hoptonn, and a column, one hundred and thirty-six feet in height, to Lord Melville, surmounted with his statue; and, then, on Calton Hill are Nelson's monument, two hundred feet in height, Dugald Stewart's monument, and an unfinished national monument, after the style of the Parthenon, erected in honor of the heroes of Waterloo. Besides these monuments on Calton Hill, which overlooks the city, there is an observatory from which a splendid view is had of the surrounding country, embracing Arthur's Seat, Lammermoor, and Pentland Hills.

"Traced like a map the landscape lies
 In cultured beauty stretching wide;
There Pentland's green acclivities,
 There ocean with its azure tide,
There Arthur's Seat — and, gleaming through
 The eastern wing, Dun Edin blue;
While in the orient Lammer's daughters —
 A distant giant range — are seen
North Berwick Law, with cone of green,
 And bass amid the waters."

But the most graceful monument, perhaps, in Europe is that to Sir Walter Scott in Princess street garden. It takes two hundred and eighty-seven steps to reach its top. Under the canopy is a statue of Sir Walter in a sitting posture, his faithful dog by his side. The niches are filled from characters in Scott's novels, such as Prince Charles, Meg Merrilies, the Lady of the Lake, and the Last Minstrel. At a short distance from this monument is a bronze statue of John Wilson, (Christopher North,) and a little further on is a white marble statue of Allan Ramsay.

In the Canongate churchyard we saw the stones that mark the graves of Adam Smith, author of the "Wealth of Nations," Dugald Stewart, David Allan, artist, and Ferguson, the poet. That over the grave of Ferguson was erected by Robert Burns, "to remain forever sacred to the memory of Robert Ferguson, born September 5, 1751, died October 16, 1774," to which record are added these lines:

"No sculptured marble here, nor pompous lay;
 No storied urn, nor animated bust —
This simple stone directs pale Scotia's way
 To pour her sorrow o'er her poet's dust."

The White House Inn, now in a dilapidated condition, is another object of curiosity, as the house where Dr. Johnson put up when he visited Edinburgh in 1773, and where he met that "unlucky specimen of Scottish cleanliness" referred to by Boswell: "He asked to have his lemonade made sweeter, upon which the waiter, with his greasy fingers, lifted up a lump of sugar and put it into it. The Doctor, in indignation, threw it out of the window." This reminds one of Daniel Webster's throwing overboard his tooth-brush, greatly to the surprise of a "greenhorn" fellow-passenger, who had requested merely the loan of it—which was granted!

The large Gallery of paintings and extensive Museum here afforded us much pleasure. So, likewise, the view of the Parliament House and Library, St. Giles' Church, and a ramble on Calton Hill. On a Sunday we listened to what we thought a rather dry sermon from the writer of hymns, Horatius Bonar, who is pastor of a small church in the suburbs of the city. He is about sixty, and resembles Martin Van Buren at that age. In the evening we heard the Rev. Dr. Alexander, a more distinguished divine.

In Holyrood Palace, "the ancient residence of Scottish royalty," we were brought again, as we could but feel, very near the unfortunate Queen Mary. We first entered the picture Gallery, "upon the walls of which are suspended De Witt's fanciful portraits of one hundred and six Scottish Kings in a style of art truly barbarous, an interesting portrait of Mary, Queen of Scots, excepted." There are also other portraits of more or less historical interest. We were next shown the rooms of Lord Darnley, in which, among other portraits, are one of the youthful Lord Darnley, and one of his brother. From these rooms is a private stairway leading to the Queen's rooms above. Next we came to the tapestry room, the walls of which are hung with old tapestry;

and in one of the rooms we saw the bedstead of Charles I. The large, old fire-places in some of the rooms are very curious. Queen Mary's apartments were the most interesting. It is said they remain in nearly the same state as when she left them. In her bed-room are her bed and other ancient furniture. "On one side of the room is the door of the secret passage by which the conspirators entered, and adjoining is the cabinet or closet where they found their victim, Rizzio. It is said that he was dragged out from this to the door of the audience chamber, where he was finally dispatched, and the exact spot where the body lay is identified by marks of blood, still visible," and which we saw. Another account states that Lord Darnley, "who himself headed the conspirators, first entered, and casting his arm fondly round the Queen's waist, seated himself beside her at table. Lord Ruthven followed in complete armor, looking pale and ghastly, as one scarcely recovered from long sickness. Others crowded in after them, till the closet was full of armed men. While the Queen demanded the purpose of their coming, Rizzio, who saw that his life was aimed at, got behind her and clasped the folds of her gown, that the respect due to her person might protect him. The assassins threw down the table and seized on the unfortunate object of their vengeance, while Darnley himself took hold of the Queen and forced Rizzio and her asunder. It was their intention, doubtless, to have dragged Rizzio out of Mary's presence, and to have killed him elsewhere; but their fierce impatience hurried them into instant murder. George Douglas, a natural brother of the Earl of Morton, set the example by striking Rizzio with the dagger which he had snatched from Darnley's belt. He received many other blows. They then dragged him through the bedroom and anteroom, and dispatched him at the head of the staircase with no less than fifty-six wounds. The Queen continued to beg his life with prayers and tears; but when she learned that he was dead, she dried her tears and said: 'I will now study revenge.'"

From the Queen's apartments we descended to the Chapel, which was founded in 1128, and is now in beautiful ruins—the walls only remaining. On a tablet in the wall is the following inscription, placed there at the instance of Charles I.:

BASILICAM HANC, SEMI RUTANI,
CAROLUS REX,
OPTIMUS INSTAVRAVIT,
1633.
He shall build ane house for my name, and I will stablish
the throne of His kingdom forever.

In the belfry tower is a marble monument to Lord Belhaven, (1639,) and in one corner of the Abbey "is the royal vault, in which are deposited the remains of David II., James II., James V., and Magdalen, his Queen; Henry, Lord Darnley, and other illustrious persons." Rizzio's grave and the tombs of many others of the Scottish nobility are located in different parts of the Abbey. While examining the inscriptions on these old tombs we were happily surprised at the appearance of a friend from Washington, Mr. J. H. Wilkinson, of the Treasury Department, who, about to return home, kindly offered to report in person to our friends on his arrival.

Rising immediately from Holyrood Palace, which is on the eastern edge of the city, Arthur's Seat, eight hundred and twenty-two feet in height, is conspicuous; and one fine day we walked to its rocky summit, taking our lunch (cakes and sparkling lemonade, purchased there of a Scotchwoman,) and sat on the highest point of the ledge—dangerous of ascent and descent, except to youthful persons like ourselves. It was a day never to be forgotten. Far below us, around the brow of the cliff, is the Queen's Drive. This walk took us to the very spot where Jennie Deans is represented to have met with the ruffian Robertson, and along the foot-path or Salisbury Crags, past the ruins of St. Anthony's Chapel, only small sections of the walls of which remain, and also by St. Anthony's Well, from which we quenched our thirst, and which is thus alluded to in an old song:

> "Now, Arthur's Seat shall be my bed,
> The sheets shall ne'er be pressed by me;
> St. Anton's Well shall be my drink,
> Since my true love's forsaken me."

This Well is very shallow, being only a common spring of good, pure water, gushing up from beneath a large boulder on the hillside. "The path along Salisbury Crags," says Sir Walter Scott, "used to be my favorite evening and morning resort when engaged with a favorite author or new subject of study."

In the Antiquarian Museum, among all sorts of Egyptian antiquities, we saw various instruments of punishment and torture formerly used in Scotland; for instance, the "branks," an iron instrument to fasten on the head "as a correction of incorrigible scolds;" the "thumbikins," used against the Covenanters; and the "maiden," or Scottish guillotine, by which many of the Scottish nobility were beheaded. Here, also, is the repentance stool from old Grayfriars' Church; John Knox's pulpit from that church; the stool which the celebrated Jenny

Geddes hurled at the head of the Dean of St. Giles' when he essayed, on one occasion, to read the Liturgy; a banner of the covenant, used in the battle of Bothwell Brig in 1679; autographs of Queen Mary, James VI., Charles I., Cromwell; and many other relics. It might be tiresome to further particularize.

CHAPTER VIII.

LONDON, JUNE 12.— We left Edinburgh at 3 P. M. on the 8th instant for Melrose, where we stopped over night at the "King's Arms." We arrived in time to visit Melrose and Dryburgh Abbeys before sundown; and in the evening we had the pleasure of viewing Melrose Abbey by "pale moonlight"— certainly a beautiful picture. Dryburgh Abbey is about five miles from Melrose, and in going there we had to leave our carriage near the end of our route and walk the rest of the way, crossing the Tweed on a foot toll bridge. Only some sections of the walls of this Abbey remain standing. In the best preserved part of the building are the tombs of Sir Walter Scott, his wife, his eldest son, and Lockhart, his son-in-law and biographer. The site on the banks of the Tweed is both beautiful and picturesque. Sir Walter's remains were deposited here by his special request, and we have a photograph showing the exact position of these tombs in the ruins. Near by is a colossal statue of Wallace. Melrose Abbey is better preserved than Dryburgh, some portions of it being yet under roofs. Many of the royal families of

Scotland had this for their burial place, and the body of Alexander II. and the heart of Robert Bruce here found their last resting-place. The Monks' Walk is said to have been a favorite resort of Sir Walter Scott.

On the following morning we were driven three miles to Abbottsford, Sir Walter Scott's large mansion, and were shown through the house. It is finely situated on the Tweed. His study, we were assured, remains very nearly as he left it. It is a small room, containing his books of reference in galleries on two sides, his writing-desk, arm-chair, and other furniture. The library is much larger, and is said to contain 20,000 volumes. What most interested us here were the clothes he last wore — a broad-brimmed, white fur hat, plaid pantaloons, striped vest, thick leather shoes, and gaiters. A cast of his head taken after his death also attracted our special attention. In one room, called the armory, are numerous weapons and other curiosities, among which are Rob Roy's musket, bearing the initials R. M. C.; a sword presented by Charles I. to the Marquis of Montrose; a hunting flask of James VI.; Roman spears; two pistols found in Napoleon's carriage after the battle of Waterloo, supposed to have belonged to him; the huge key of the old Tolbooth at Edinburgh; and an axe presented by Washington Irving. In a case are a large number of valuable presents of various kinds from distinguished persons. In the dining-room and library are many handsome portraits and pictures, among them a portrait of Sir Walter's eldest son, represented as a dragoon standing by his horse, and another of Cromwell. In the drawing-room we saw an ebony chair, presented by George IV.

Bidding adieu to Melrose, we took the express train at half past eleven A. M. and reached Leamington, via Carlisle, Lancaster, Crew, Stafford, Rugby, and Kenilworth, by ten P. M. Leamington is quite a summer resort, and is probably the best place to stop for the purpose of visiting Kenilworth and Warwick Castles and Stratford-on-Avon. It is ten miles from here to Shakspeare's birth-place, and we went there the next day, taking Warwick on our way back. We passed one or two hours in Shakspeare's house, which looks just as represented by the pictures we often see of it. It is a very rough structure, coarser inside even than on the exterior. The old kitchen fire-place takes up a great part of one side of the room, which has a stone floor. The rough-plastered walls and ceilings of the rooms are scribbled over with the names of visitors — a fashion of leaving one's card which was prohibited many years ago. The small window-panes are scratched in like manner, and on one of them we read the name "W. Scott," showing that Sir Walter approved of the fashion. In one of the chambers there is a portrait of Shakspeare, said to be authentic. The engraved likenesses we see of him, we should think, were taken from it. One or two of the larger rooms are devoted to a Shakspearian museum, which contains many most interesting relics, of which, among some of the most prominent, are the following: Deed made in 1596, proving that John Shakspeare, the father of the poet, resided in this house; the letter from Richard Quyney to Shakspeare, in 1589, asking for a loan of £30, the only letter addressed to Shakspeare known to exist; Shakspeare's gold signet ring, with the initials W. S. and a true-lover's knot between; his ancient desk from the grammar school;

his jug, from which Garrick sipped wine at the jubilee in 1769; a specimen from an original copy of the "Merry Wives of Windsor;" a sword, said to have belonged to Shakspeare, and a sign of the Falcon Inn, where he is said to have imbibed too freely. From a curiously printed old pamphlet, containing his portrait and one of his plays, we copied the following, attributed to Ben Jonson:

"TO THE READER.
"This figure that thou seest put,
It was for gentle Shakspeare cut;
Wherein the Grauer had a strife
With Nature to outdoo the life:
O, could he have but drawne his wit
As well in brasse, as he hath hit
His face, the print would then surpasse
All that was ever writ in brasse.
But since he cannot, Reader looke
Not on his Picture, but his Booke.   B. I."

Hanging framed in the museum is the following verse, written by Lucien Bonaparte during his visit here many years ago:

"The eye of genius glistens to admire
How memory hails the sound of Shakspeare's lyre;
One tear I'll shed to form a crystal shrine
For all that's grand, immortal, or divine."

From Shakspeare's house we walked to the old church on the banks of the Avon, where he was buried. His grave and that of his wife are in the chancel, and over his is a plain slab bearing these lines cut in old Roman letters:

"Kind Friend, for Jesus sake forbeare
To dig the dust enclosed heare;
Blest be the man yt spares thes stones,
And cvrst be he yt moves my bones."

In the side wall above is a Latin inscription and a

bust of Shakspeare. The sexton showed us an old parchment book, in which we read the record of the birth of William Shakspeare, April 23, 1564; of his baptism, April 26, 1564; and of his death, April 23, 1616. This unpretending building, called the Church of the Holy Trinity, dates back to the eleventh century. We passed, without entering, the Red Horse Hotel, celebrated as the house where Washington Irving put up when he was here.

Warwick Castle, the residence of the Earl of Warwick, is a noble structure, and is kept in good repair. The rooms shown to visitors are filled with a great variety of rare and curious things, including costly inlaid tables, one of which is valued at $50,000; weapons of various descriptions — a gun-barreled revolver made two hundred years before Colt ever thought of such a thing; a valuable collection of paintings, etc. We saw in the porter's lodge some of the most wonderful things which belonged to Guy, the giant Earl of Warwick, (tenth century,) who measured eight feet, eleven inches from head to foot, and whose breast-plate weighs fifty pounds, his shield thirty pounds, and his two-handed sword, five feet, five inches long, twenty pounds. His tilting spear, halberd, chain coat-of-mail, cane, and horse's armor are likewise preserved here; also, his porridge-pot, or punch-bowl, made of bell metal, said to hold one hundred and two gallons. Here, too, are cannon balls which were fired at the Castle by Cromwell. We have a fine photograph of this old Castle as we viewed it from a bridge over the Avon, which runs at the base of the rock on which the Castle is built.

On the 11th we took the train, five miles, to Kenilworth, and walked along the country road, enjoying the scenery, to Kenilworth Castle, about one mile and a half beyond. The ruins of this famous old Castle are scattered over an extent of an eighth of a mile or more, and the only part inhabitable is what is called the Gate House, a building one or two hundred feet square with four towers. Here the keeper resides with his family. The detached portions are every where covered with ivy. Originally there was "a pool, containing one hundred and eleven acres, well stocked with fish," and its waters could be let into the moat, sections of which still exist, around the Castle. The Park, in which this pool or lake was located, but which was drained in the time of Cromwell, contained a large extent of territory with forests well stocked with deer and other game. It was in this Castle that the Earl of Leicester, in 1575, entertained Queen Elizabeth and her Court seventeen days at a cost of $85,000, a pretty large sum in that period.

On the morning of the 12th we left Leamington for London, stopping over one train to visit the Colleges of Oxford, of which there are nineteen in all, called collectively, the University of Oxford. From our carriage our guide informed us of the names of the various Colleges, all the buildings of which look very dingy. In one of them, specially noted on that account, Cromwell kept his horses. In the Bodleian Library we were greatly interested in several very ancient books and manuscripts shown to us. This Library is said to contain 240,000 volumes; and there is also a picture Gallery here, where we saw what is considered one of Van Dyck's oldest and best pictures. In the Museum, among other interesting relics, we saw the lantern carried by Guy Fawkes when he undertook to blow up the British Parliament buildings.

Leaving behind Oxford and its history of a thousand years, at 5 P. M., we are in still more ancient London—a world immediately before us.

CHAPTER IX.

LONDON. JUNE 16.—After enjoying for a few days the elegant hospitalities of an English family whose urgent invitation to make them a visit we found it hard to decline, we are settled down in a private boarding house on Queen's Road, in Bayswater West, near the Royal Oak, and two minutes' walk from Kensington Park. We are likewise within one minute's walk of a station of the Metropolitan Underground Railway, by which we can go to almost any part of the city and return for from four pence to nine pence the single passage; or we can take an omnibus either from Kensington Garden or Royal Oak for about the same price.

Our first day in London being Sunday, we immediately turned our steps to that great center of attraction, Westminster Abbey, where we attended service. On that occasion, and during subsequent visits, we have for hours been deeply absorbed in wandering through this wilderness of tombs, busts, statues, and other monuments of the distinguished dead. We were first drawn to the Poet's Corner, and at once to the slab over Charles Dickens' grave, upon which lay a cross of faded flowers. Above stand the busts of Macaulay, Thackeray, and others. The statues of Shakspeare, Addison, Thomas Campbell, and Thomson, and close by, the statues, busts,

WESTMINSTER ABBEY.

or other monuments of Garrick, Goldsmith, Gay, Southey, Prior, Milton, Chaucer, Dryden, Beaumont, Gray, Spenser, Samuel Johnson, Sheridan, Cowley, Ben Jonson, and many others.

In one of the principal aisles we stood over the new-made grave of Dr. Livingstone, indicated by a marble slab in the floor, bearing his name and date of death; and on this slab some friendly hand had placed a wreath of flowers. In another part of the church is a monumental bust of Sir John Franklin, with appropriate inscriptions—the affectionate tribute of Lady Franklin, recently deceased. We transcribed from this monument the following:

"O ye frost and cold, O ye ice and snow,
  Bless ye the Lord: praise Him and magnify His name forever.
  Not here: the white North has thy bones; and thou, heroic-sailor soul,
  Art passing on thy happier voyage now toward no earthly pole."

On the wall opposite is a monumental slab to Isaac Watts.

The inscription on the base of Addison's statue is as follows:

"Whoever thou art, venerate the memory of Joseph Addison, in whom Christian faith, virtue, and good morals found a continual patron; whose genius was shown in verse, and every exquisite kind of writing; who gave to posterity the best examples of pure language, and the best rules for living well, which remain, and ever will remain sacred; whose weight of argument was tempered with wit, and accurate judgment with politeness, so that he encouraged the good and reformed the improvident, tamed the wicked, and in some degree made them in love with virtue. He was born in the year 1672, and his fortune being increased gradually, arrived at length to public honors. Died in the forty-eighth year of his age, the honor and delight of the British nation."

This epitaph on Addison, written by Thomas Tickle, is inscribed on the marble slab which marks the spot where he was buried:

"Ne'er to these chambers, where the mighty rest,
  Since their foundation, came a nobler guest;
  Nor e'er was to the bowers of bliss conveyed
  A fairer spirit, or more welcome shade.
  Oh, gone forever! take this long adieu,
  And sleep in peace next thy lov'd Montegue."

Next to Addison's is the grave of Charles Montegue, the first Lord Halifax, who lived in the reigns of William III. and George I.

The statue of Shakspeare is very graceful, and the likeness bears a strong resemblance to his portrait in his old house at Stratford-on-Avon. In the left hand is a scroll, on which appear the following lines from "The Tempest:"

> "The cloud-capp'd towers, the gorgeous palaces,
> The solemn temples, the great globe itself,
> Yea, all which it inherit, shall dissolve;
> And, like the base fabric of a vision,
> Leave not a rack behind."

Oliver Goldsmith's likeness is given in profile, under which, on the marble slab in the wall, is a Latin inscription, stating in substance that "he was eminent as a Poet, Philosopher, and Historian; that he scarcely left any species of writing unattempted, and none that he attempted, unimproved; that he was master of the softer passions, and could at pleasure command tears or provoke laughter; but in everything he said or did, good nature was predominant; that he was witty, sublime, spirited, and facetious; in speech pompous; in conversation elegant and graceful; that the love of his associates, fidelity of his friends, and the veneration of his readers had raised this monument to his memory."

John Gay wrote his own epitaph, which we are told is censured by some for its levity. Nevertheless it is on his monument in these lines:

> "Life is a jest, and all things show it:
> I thought so once, but now I know it."

Underneath are the following lines by Alexander Pope:

> "Of manners gentle, of affection mild;
> In wit a man, simplicity a child;
> With native humor temp'ring virtuous rage,
> Form'd to delight at once and lash the age;
> Above temptation in a low estate,
> And uncorrupted e'en among the great;
> A safe companion and an easy friend,

Unblamed through life, lamented in thy end;
These are thy honours; not that here thy bust
Is mix'd with heroes, or with kings thy dust;
But that the worthy and the good shall say,
Striking their pensive bosoms, 'Here lies Gay!'"

He was but forty-five when he died, in 1732.

On the monument of Edmund Spenser is the following:

"Here lies (expecting the coming of our Saviour Christ Jesus) the body of Edmund Spenser, the Prince of Poets in his time, whose divine spirit needs no other witness than the works which he left behind him. He was born in London in 1553, and died in 1598."

The remains of a great many of the sovereigns of England and Scotland are interred here. There is a splendid monument to Mary Stuart, Queen of Scots, erected by her son, James I., soon after he ascended the throne. In 1612 he had her remains privately removed to this church from the Peterborough Cathedral, where they were first buried in 1587. He also caused to be erected here a magnificent monument to his predecessor, Queen Elizabeth. The inscription thereon says that "she was the mother of her country, and the patroness of religion and learning; she was herself skilled in many languages; adorned with every excellence of mind and person, and endowed with princely virtues beyond her sex; that in her reign religion was restored to its primitive purity; peace was established; money restored to its just value; domestic insurrection quelled; France delivered from intestine troubles; the Netherlands supported; the Spanish Armada defeated; Ireland, almost lost by the secret contrivances of Spain, recovered; the revenues of both universities improved by a law of provisions, and, in short, all England enriched; that she was a most prudent governess, forty-five years a virtuous and triumphant Queen, truly religious, and blessed in all her great affairs; and that after a calm and resigned death, in the seventieth year of her age, she left the mortal part to be deposited in this church, which she established upon a new footing. She died March 24, 1602, aged seventy."

Many of the inscriptions, especially those of the royal families, recite important historical facts. For instance, there is an altar erected by Charles II. to the memory of Edward V. and his brother, "who, by their treacherous uncle, Richard III., were murdered in the Tower." The inscription says:

"Here lies the relics of Edward V., King of England, and Richard, Duke of York, who, being confined in the Tower, and there stifled with pillows, were privately and meanly buried, by order of their perfidious uncle, Richard, the usurper. Their bones, long inquired after and wished for, after laying one hundred and ninety-one years in the rubbish of the stairs, (leading to the chapel of the White Tower,) were, on the 17th of July, 1674, by undoubted proofs, discovered, being buried deep in that place. Charles II., pitying their unhappy fate, ordered these unfortunate Princes to be laid among the relics of their predecessors, in the year 1678, and the thirtieth of his reign."

In allusion to this inscription a writer observes: "It is remarkable that Edward was born November 4, 1471, in the sanctuary belonging to this church, whither his mother took refuge during the contest between the houses of York and Lancaster; at eleven years of age, upon the death of his father, 1483, he was proclaimed King; and on the 23d of June, in the same year, was murdered in the manner already related. Richard, his brother, was born May 28, 1474, and married while a child to Anna Mowbray, heiress of Norfolk."

On the monument to George Canning, born April 11, 1770, died August 8, 1827, is the following:

"Endowed with a rare combination of talents, an eminent statesman, an accomplished scholar, an orator surpassed by none, he united the most brilliant and lofty qualities of the mind with the warmest affections of the heart; raised by his own merit, he successfully filled important offices in the State, and finally became first minister of the Crown. In the full enjoyment of his sovereign's favor, and of the confidence of the people, he was prematurely cut off when pursuing a wise and large course of policy, which had for its object the prosperity and greatness of his own country, while it comprehended the welfare and commanded the admiration of Foreign nations."

Longer than by any other, perhaps, we were inclined to linger by the monument of the unfortunate Major John André, so well known, in this country at least, as having been hung as a spy by order of General Washington. On a molded paneled base and plinth, in the wall, is a sarcophagus, surmounted by a half-reclining female figure, her head bowed in grief, and in *bas-relief* on the front are represented on the one hand Washington's headquarters in an open tent, and on the other the British quarters, disclosing in company with officers, what are supposed to represent the mother and sister of André in deep distress, and between the two camps a British officer is represented as bearing a flag of truce to Washington, with a letter from Major André, begging that he might be shot instead of being hung. On the base is the following inscription:

SACRED to the MEMORY
of
MAJOR JOHN ANDRÉ,

who, raised by his merit at an early period of life to the rank of Adjutant-General of the British forces in America, and employed in an important but hazardous enterprise, fell a sacrifice to his zeal for his King and country on the 2d of October, A. D. 1780, aged twenty-nine, universally beloved and esteemed by the army in which he served, and lamented even by his FOES. His gracious sovereign, KING GEORGE THE THIRD, has caused this monument to be erected.

On the plinth is an inscription to the effect that by direction of his Royal Highness the Duke of York, the remains of Major André were removed from Tappan, N. Y., and on the 28th of November, 1821, deposited in a grave near this monument. It is a singular fact that the head of Washington's figure on this monument has been twice taken off; whether from motives of spite or from mere wanton curiosity it is uncertain; but charity might lead us to suppose the latter reason, since the heads also of some of the other figures have been removed—"being so well executed they were too great a temptation for the curious pilferer to withstand." Here is the letter addressed to General Washington by Major André the night previous to his execution, and borne to him under this flag of truce:

"Sir — Buoyed above the terror of death by the consciousness of a life devoted to honourable purposes, and stained with no action which can give me remorse, I trust that the request which I make to your excellency at this serious period, and which is to soften my last moments, will not be rejected; sympathy toward a soldier will surely induce your excellency, and a military tribunal, to adapt the mode of my death to the feelings of a man of honour; let me hope, sir, that if aught in my character impresses you with esteem towards me — if aught in my misfortunes mark me as the victim of policy, and not of resentment, I shall experience the operations of those feelings in your breast, by being informed I am not to die on a gibbet. I have the honor to be, your excellency,

"JOHN ANDRÉ,
"Adjutant of the British forces in America."

It was all in vain; he died on the gallows.

CHAPTER X.

LONDON, July 3. — Our English friends, with whom we have been sojourning as guests, support a handsome team with servants in livery, and have entertained us in regal style. We have had several drives in Kensington and Hyde Parks every pleasant afternoon, where the aristocracy of London vie with one another in their elegance of outfit, and where we had the opportunity of seeing many of them face to face. The principal drive is between Apsley House, the palatial mansion of the Duke of Wellington, and the Albert Monument, a magnificent structure somewhat after the style of the Scott Monument in Edinburgh, lately raised by Queen Victoria in honor of her lamented husband, Prince Albert. Across the street from the Monument is the Royal Albert Hall of Arts, built in circular form, and capable of seating fifteen thousand people. At this point the carriages turn and the great procession moves back and forth on the same carriage-way, lined with thousands of spectators on foot. Continually passing and repassing one another, the occupants of the carriages are enabled to exchange salutations and enjoy a view of the whole inspiring scene. The Queen sometimes drives in the Park, but we have not seen her. The Princess of Wales is often in the procession and bows pleasantly to those who offer their respects.

Parallel with the carriage-way is a horse-course for horseback riding, and this extends, indeed, through the Park and along Rotten Row, another part of Hyde Park, where, at two o'clock in the afternoon, thousands of ladies and gentlemen congregate and promenade for exercise in the open air. On the north bank of a beautiful lake, called the Serpentine, is the Ladies' Mile, another charming drive. From the end of Oxford street, Hyde Park is entered under the marble Arch, a noble structure, which used to stand in front of Buckingham Palace. Opposite the Piccadilly entrance, and near the Apsley House, on an elevated pedestal, is the grand bronze statue of Achilles, inscribed, "By the women of England to Arthur, Duke of Wellington, and his brave companions in arms." The statue was cast from ordnance taken from the enemy during the Peninsular war, and the cost of its erection ($50,000) was entirely defrayed by subscriptions of the fair sex—an example, perhaps, for the women of the United States, if it be that our Washington Monument is ever to be completed.

A ride one day to the Thames embankment took us through many parts of the city. This embankment, which has reclaimed from the muddy Thames fifty acres of land, is a great modern improvement, adding much to the beauty as well as to the health of the metropolis. Another ride six or eight miles to the village of Richmond, by the famous "Star and Garter" Hotel, and through the great Richmond Park, swarming with sheep and deer, was equally enjoyable. On the edge of this Park is the residence of Lord John Russell, nestled among forest trees. On our way we visited Kew Gardens, said to contain one of the most splendid collections of plants in the world. The palm-house, three hundred and sixty feet long by ninety feet wide, is believed to be the largest glass building in existence, except the Crystal Palace at Sydenham, which we have likewise visited, and where we heard concert singing. We may mention that we attended a concert also at Albert Hall, where we heard Mesdames Christine Nilsson and Trebelli Bettoni, Mesdemoiselles Titiens and Varesi, Signor Campinini, and other famous singers. The Hall being pretty well filled, the audience alone was a magnificent sight.

The Mansion House, where we saw the Lord Mayor holding court, is one of the prominent public buildings; and Guildhall, the Hotel de Ville of the city of London, is another which we have visited. In the latter the Lord Mayor and Sheriffs of the city are elected, and here, exalted on lofty pedestals on either side of the west window, are the ancient colossal figures of Gog and Magog, which, being of wood and hollow, used to be carried in the procession on the Mayor's show day. They seem to have been carved to represent giants. We have paid our respects to some of the head officials of the General Post Office, and witnessed some of its wonderful workings. In one room are one thousand clerks of both sexes, whose entire duty it is to attend to the postal telegraph business. Messages are dispatched from here to the various postal stations throughout the city, and received therefrom, by means of pneumatic tubes.

A good part of one day in the Zoological Gardens, where we had the pleasure of meeting Grace Greenwood and her daughter, was pleasantly spent, affording, as it did, an opportunity of seeing all sorts of animals, fowls, birds, etc. Among other interesting sights were some young seals, which surprised us by their almost human intelligence under the training of a funny little Frenchman.

One afternoon we wandered among the tombs and monuments at Kensal Green Cemetery, where we plucked leaves from the grave of Thomas Hood. On one side of the base of his monument, in *bas-relief*, are figures representing a drowned girl being borne "tenderly" in the hands of men; on the other side, the figure of an aged person apparently in distress, and in front that of another man convulsed with laughter. On the top of the square column is a large bust of the poet. Allan Cunningham, John Murray, the eminent publisher, Sydney Smith (Peter Plymley), the Duke of Sussex, Anne Scott, daughter of Sir Walter Scott, and Thackeray, were also buried here.

An hour or two at Madame Tussaud's exhibition of waxworks reminded us of inimitable Artemas Ward and his show of "wax figgers." Taken as a whole it is a ridiculous collection. While Washington and Franklin are tolerably represented, the figures of Lincoln, McClellan, Beecher, and even Dickens, are the merest burlesques. Those of Andrew Johnson and General Grant, grouped with Lincoln and McClellan, might possibly be recognized. The best things here — and these are really good — are a sleeping beauty, with internal machinery causing her chest to rise and fall as if she were breathing; a standing figure of Madame Tussaud, very life-like, with her bonnet on, viewing the Queen and other members of the royal family before her; and lastly, the form and likeness of William Cobbett, the picture of Horace Greeley, sitting as if looking at the show, his broad-brimmed hat and spectacles on, and a snuff-box in his hand. We were assured that this figure has sometimes been taken for real flesh and blood, and that visitors have turned indignantly away from the placid old gentleman because he would not deign to answer their questions or give them a pinch of snuff. With a little more care this exhibition might be made to possess a much greater merit. We sought out one of the proprietors of the concern present and earnestly protested against burlesquing our modern statesmen, warriors and divines in such a shocking manner, when, with a little more pains, they could be correctly represented.

Years might be usefully spent in the study of the British Museum, the granite building of which covers acres. We devoted a rainy day to it. It is open to the public, free, three days in the week. There are the Botanical Museum; the Mammalian, Zoological and Mineral Galleries, the Gallery of Egyptian, Greek and Roman Antiquities, the Sculpture Gallery, in one part of which the curious marbles from Nineveh are exhibited; and then there is the Library of nearly one million printed volumes, and manuscripts and prints without number. Embraced with these is the entire library, seventy thousand volumes, of George III., regarded as very valuable, presented by his successor, George IV. We were highly interested in the room appropriated to autographs, ancient books, etc. We noticed among the autographs those of Washington, Queen Elizabeth, Mary, Queen of Scots, Chaucer, Voltaire, Napoleon, Shakspeare, the Georges and other Kings of England. Here are copies of some of the first books ever printed. "Among the one thousand, six hundred and fifty different editions of the Bible here, is the first issued from the press, called the Mazarine Bible. It is printed on vellum, in the Latin language, by Gutenberg and Faust, in 1455." There is an endless collection of coins of all nations, old jewelry, curious weapons, and almost every other old curiosity under the sun. The Portland Vase is regarded as wonderful, first, because, we believe, its composition is a lost art, and secondly, because, after being broken into one hundred pieces, more or less, it has been restored almost to its original beauty. It is of dark blue glass, adorned with delicate white medallion pictures. The lamented Dr. Horatio Stone, the sculptor, who crossed the ocean with us, advised us to be sure not to overlook it. A fine life-sized bronze statue of Stonewall Jackson is on exhibition here. We understand it is to be sent to Richmond as a present from some of his English admirers. Dean Stanley mentioned to us a singular fact, that while there was in Westminster Abbey an expensive monument—a reclining statue, which we have seen—of the Duke of Montpensier, brother of Louis Philippe, King of France, the only figure of Washington to be seen in any of the memorial halls of London is the small likeness on Major André's monument and a large bust in the basement of the British Museum. We observed this bust, which, if memory serves us, is of plaster, and in an out of the way place. On our visit to the Museum we had the pleasure of seeing the good Queen of Holland,* who, in company with several gentlemen, was also on a visit to this establishment. We should say she is about fifty, tall, with light hair and eyes, and pleasant looking, but not handsome; and our lady companion says she wore a plain dress of dark bluish purpled plaid, and bonnet trimmed with black.

Starting one day for Hampton Court, when we reached Victoria Theater, near Waterloo Bridge, and near where we were to take the cars, we learned that Moody and Sankey were about to hold services in the Theater building, and we stopped to hear them. The house was crowded, the stage being occupied by one hundred or more clergymen, among whom was New-

---

* Died June 2, 1877, aged fifty-nine years.

man Hall, who made a short address after Mr. Moody closed. Since then we have heard Mr. Hall preach one Sunday at St. James' Hall. After an hour's delay we proceeded to Hampton Court, and walked through thirty-two rooms of the palace filled with pictures—eight hundred or more in all—many of them by the old masters,—Titian, Raphael, Van Dyck, and others. There are some wonderful tapestries here. In one room we saw the bed of Queen Anne. This palace was built by Cardinal Wolsey, and presented to Henry VIII., but was subsequently, under the direction of William III., much enlarged. It is of red brick, with stone facings. The garden, adorned with sculptured fountains and beautiful shade trees, is one of the most charming in England. We did not omit to see here the far-famed maze, nor the famous grape-vine, on which there were twelve hundred bunches of green grapes, and which, being one hundred and nine years old, is said to have borne in a single year as many as three thousand bunches. True to his trust, the attendant could not be prevailed on, even for money, to part with a single leaf from its branches. It is trailed under a glass roof.

We have been to the Drury Lane and Haymarket Theaters; neither remarkable for anything we heard or saw there. Indeed, in the latter, where we saw Sothern as Lord Dundreary, we thought the play was decidedly stupid. We have seen him do much better in Washington.

CHAPTER XI.

LONDON, July 8.—It is an event in a man's life to have dined once with the Clothworkers' Company at their magnificent hall in Mincing Lane, London. This is an immensely wealthy society, dating back two hundred years or more; and although it was organized by clothworkers, and under their management for a century, more or less, it is said there is not at present a single clothworker connected with it. The membership is now composed principally, if not entirely, of the aristocratic classes, and everything attending their proceedings is conducted on a grand scale. Their great wealth has been acquired by the rise of real estate, left from time to time to the society by its former members, and they appropriate from it, in acts of benevolence, large sums every year. Its permanent officers are a Master, four Wardens and a Clerk. The Clerk, Owen Roberts, Esq., M. A., is the working officer, who has to attend to all the details. At their state dinners, which are given about once every month, the number of plates set is one hundred and twenty — one table being arranged at the head, and one on either side, lengthwise of the grand hall. The seat of the Master of Ceremonies is at the center of the head table. All the officers wear long robes, and their guests, who are expected to appear in full dress suit, are first received in the saloon or drawing-room, which is elegantly furnished. Dinner is served at nine o'clock, and each member or guest, as the case may be, finds or is conducted to his place at table, where his name appears on a handsome card, bearing the coat of arms of the society. By his plate, also, he finds the bill of fare and an elaborate programme containing the names of the officers of the society and of the artists who are to furnish the musical part of the entertainment. This bill and programme, too, bear the society's coat of arms, whose motto is, "My trust is in God alone," and both are printed in the highest style of "the art divine." All the pieces to be sung, ten in number, are printed in full in the programme, and it should be observed that the musicians have position at the lower end of the hall, facing the Master of Ceremonies, and that it is their province to perform during dinner. Grace is said, with responses, in Latin, "composed by John Reading, A. D. 1681"—all printed in the programme.

As Washington City is famous for its dinner parties and sumptuous state dinners, especially those given by the foreign legations, it may interest some to present a list of the good things served on the occasion of a grand dinner by the Clothworkers' Society, in Mincing Hall, July 7, 1875, thus:

MENU.

Soups.

Turtle   Clear Turtle

Fish.

Souché de Carrelets
Cotelettes de Saumon à la Calcutta   Truite à la Verte
Salmon   Turbot   Whitebait

Entrées.

Vols au Vent à la Financiere
Ris de Veau en Caisses aux Petits Pois
Cailles aux Truffes à la Chesterfield

Removes.

Perigord Pies   Chickens aux Pointes d' Asperge
Warden Pies   Boiled Capons à la Toulouse

Roast Chickens   Hams   Tongues
Haunches Venison
Ducks   Turkey Poults   Goslings

Entremets.

Prawns
Poudins d' Orleans   Clear Jellies
Macedoine aux Fruits   Pine Creams
Marrow Pudding   Meringues de Chantilly
Flans d' Abricots   Maids of Honour

Removes.

Nesselrode Pudding   Iced Souffles
Ramaquins

DESSERT AND ICES

Of course, the choicest brands of wine were also served in profusion.

Dinner over, the first toast, to Her Majesty the Queen, was drunk standing, and then, all joining with the choir, came

THE NATIONAL ANTHEM.

God save our gracious Queen,
Long live our noble Queen,
God save the Queen!
Send her victorious,
Happy and glorious,
Long to reign over us,
God save the Queen!

Thy choicest gifts in store
On her be pleased to pour,
Long may she reign!
May she defend our laws,
And ever give us cause
To sing with heart and voice,
God save the Queen!

The Prince of Wales and other members of the royal family were next toasted, but without rising from the table, they being subjects only, like the rest of the people.

A LONDON DINNER.

Then was sung, by Miss Annie Sinclair,

THE ECHO SONG.

My own true love is far away,
    And I am wandering lonely here
To tend my flocks till close of day,
    While mem'ry wakes the silent tear.
I'm sure his heart is true to me;
    Tho' other lands he's doomed to roam,
His constant prayer I know will be
    To view once more his native home.

Sweet hope is whisp'ring in my heart,
    While time is winging fast away,
That we shall meet no more to part
    When Springtime brings the flowers of May.
Ah! then what happy days in store!
    We'll wreathe with joy the fleeting hours;
No clouds shall darken o'er us more
    To blight the summer flowers.

Next, after other appropriate toasts, came a glee, (four voices,) by Horsley, entitled

"MINE BE A COT."

Mine be a cot beside a hill,
    A beehive's hum shall soothe my ear;
A willowy brook, that turns a mill,
    With many a fall shall linger near;
The swallow oft beneath my thatch
    Shall twitter from her clay-built nest;
Oft shall the pilgrim lift the latch,
    And share my meal a welcome guest.

Around my ivied porch shall spring
    Each fragrant flower that drinks the dew,
And Lucy at her wheel shall sing,
    In russet gown and apron blue.
The village church among the trees,
    Where first our marriage vows were given,
With merry peals shall swell the breeze,
    And point with taper spire to heav'n.

Still other toasts intervening, the songs, all good, were continued to the close, and this (also by four voices) was the last —

"GOOD NIGHT."

Bim, bim, hear us singing,
  Now sounds the midnight hour!
Hark! how the chimes are ringing:
Voices your way be winging
  High to our lady's bower,
  Charm her with magic power:
While we our watch are keeping,
  May she in slumber light,
Calm and secure be sleeping:
  So let us say, "Good night."

Bim, bim, chimes are ringing!
  Ye zephyrs lend your aid!
What we afar are singing,
Still to her ear be bringing:
  Breathe o'er this gentle maid,
  Where she in rest is laid!
While we our watch are keeping,
  May she in slumbers light,
Calm and secure be sleeping:
  So let us say, "Good night."

The company left the table about midnight, the last act in the evening's entertainment, except smoking, being the passage of the "Loving Cup." This ceremony is thus described by F. W. Fairholt, F. S. A.:

"THE LOVING CUP" is a splendid feature of the Hall-feasts of the City and Inns of Court. The cup is of silver or silver-gilt, and is filled with spiced wine, immemorially termed "Sack." Immediately after the dinner and grace, the Master and Wardens drink to their visitors a hearty welcome; the cup is then passed round the table, and each guest, after he has drunk, applies his napkin to the mouth of the cup before he passes it to his neighbor. The more formal practice is for "the person who pledges with the Loving Cup to stand up and bow to his neighbor, who, also standing, removes the cover with his right hand, and holds it while the other drinks; a custom said to have originated in the precaution to keep the right or 'dagger hand' employed, that the person who drinks may be assured of no treachery, like that practised by Elfrida on the unsuspecting King Edward the Martyr, at Corfe Castle, who was slain while drinking. This was why the Loving Cup possessed a cover."

CHAPTER XII.

LONDON, JULY 10.— We have passed portions of several days in the South Kensington Museum, which is about twenty minutes' walk through Kensington and Hyde Parks from our boarding house — admission free three days in the week. This Museum, founded in 1852, is to us the most interesting of anything of the kind in the city. The antiquarian might find more to command attention in the British Museum, because it is there where are deposited all the strange old things that have been brought to light from under and above ground since the days of Adam; but to passing travelers like ourselves there is vastly more of stirring interest in the Kensington collection. One long room in the basement is given to ancient state vehicles, including a sedan chair, which are well worth seeing. Models of the great monuments, and of other wonders of the world are brought and to be brought here; and by and by one need not go beyond London to see copies or *fac-similes* of almost every object of art, of which we read, in all parts of the world. Here is a reproduction in plaster, full size, but in two sections, of the Trajan column in Rome; and the same also of the "Apprentice's Pillar" in Roslin Castle. Full-sized models of celebrated gates and other Eastern monuments are likewise presented, as well as a large collection of sculptures, porcelain, jewels, arms, armor, paintings, carvings in ivory, wood and stone, unique furniture, tapestries, and thousands of other things impossible to enumerate. Extravagant prices have been paid for some of these articles. There is a French candlestick of date 1550, in Henri deux earthenware, which cost $3,750, and in the same case four other articles of the same ware, the whole costing $9,100. Many of the paintings and large quantities of the most expensive jewelry here are the private property of the nobility, who have loaned the same for the gratification of the public. Like other valuable collections of pictures, etc., in the Museum, many of these doubtless will eventually become the property of the institution as donations outright. The collection of paintings, called the Sheepshanks Collection, comprises two hundred and thirty-four oil paintings, and the Vernon Collection one hundred and sixty-two, besides seven cartoons of Raphael, brought from Hampton Court. In the former are masterpieces by Landseer, Wilkie, Leslie, and Rosa Bonheur; and among the latter, choice works by Gainsborough, Eastlake, and other celebrated artists. The cartoons by Raphael were executed in 1514, by order of Leo X., as patterns for tapestries in the Sistine Chapel of the Vatican. They represent the Death of Ananias; Peter and John at the Beautiful Gate; Christ's Charge to Peter; Healing the Lame Man; Paul and Barnabas at Lystra; Elymas, the sorcerer, struck blind; Paul preaching at Athens; and the Miraculous Draught of Fishes. There is an Art School and Library connected with the institution.

The National Picture Gallery, free to visitors Tuesdays, Wednesdays, and Saturdays, and to artists on Thursdays and Fridays also, is another point of attraction. It is situated on the north side of Trafalgar Square. Here we had the pleasure of meeting Mr. Miller, one of our most talented Washington artists. Besides the large number of paintings permanently located here, others by the various artists of the metropolis and from the interior are from time to time placed here on exhibition and for sale. This Gallery is said to contain pictures not only by the best English artists, but also by some of the greatest painters of the Italian, Spanish, Dutch, French, and Flemish schools. Among the latter may be mentioned Raphael's Catherine of Alexandria, which cost $25,000, and his Pope Julius II.; Correggio's Holy Family, Ecce Homo, and Mercury Instructing Cupid, for which $50,000 was paid; The Rape of the Sabines, and Judgment of Paris, by Rubens; Visions of a Knight, and The Holy Family, by Murillo; Christ Disputing in the Temple, by Leonardo da Vinci; and The Family of Darius, by Paul Veronese. In the hall stands the celebrated Waterloo Vase, composed of materials taken during the Peninsular war from a French ship, which was conveying them to Paris to be converted into a monument to Napoleon.

In the East India Museum we saw a large collection of dresses, weapons, ancient and modern, idols, agricultural and other instruments, specimens of the natural productions of the East Indies, and, indeed, of almost everything else to be seen in that country. One day at the South Kensington Museum, among the visitors, we were pleased to meet twenty East Indiamen, dressed in their native costumes. They were from Bombay, probably in a merchant vessel, but were called Alaskians. Some of them wore immense turbans, and their shoes were pointed at the toes. It did us good to see them enjoy the sights.

Trafalgar Square, ten minutes' walk from Westminster Abbey and the Parliament buildings, is one of the great central points of London. It is a large open space, where a considerable number of streets converge. Here stands a magnificent monument to Nelson, a column one hundred and seventy-seven feet in height, surmounted by his statue. On the four sides of the base, in bronze *bas-relief*, are represented the Death of Nelson; the Battle of the Nile; the Battle of St. Vincent; and the Battle of Copenhagen. At each of the four corners of the base is an immense granite figure of a lion, *couchant*, the work of Sir Edward Landseer. There is also in this Square a fine equestrian statue of George IV., and bronze statues of Sir Charles Napier and General Havelock.

Charing Cross is another famous point, and to feel ourselves quite at home here in Piccadilly and Fleet streets, in the Strand, Trafalgar Square, and at many other points, with familiar names, in London, is a new and pleasant experience. To the south of Charing Cross are Whitehall and Parliament streets; and to the west Cockspur street and Piccadilly. At the head of Parliament street is a bronze equestrian statue of Charles I. The name of Charing Cross is supposed to have been derived from the village of Charing, "though tradition has it that the place was so called after Eleanor, the *chère reine* (dear Queen) of Edward I.," who caused to be erected here a handsome cross to her memory. This cross "stood a monument of royal love for more than three hundred and fifty years, and was at last, in June and July, 1647, pulled down by order of the Long Parliament, and its stones used to pave the street before Whitehall!" Subsequently this was the scene of the executions of many of the regicides. Here, on the 21st of June, 1837, Victoria was proclaimed Queen.

We went on a free day to see the Tower of London, when we encountered at the entrance gate such a crowd, generally not of the most genteel appearance, that we were glad to retire from their company. We thought it quite proper in a burly policeman to caution us to keep an eye on our watch-chains. We found it every way better to pay our shilling admission fee, as we did on a subsequent day, when, with a small company, guided by a warder in the picturesque costume of a yeoman of the time of Henry VIII., we had a good view of such parts of this old fortress as are shown to visitors. It consists of various ranges of buildings and several streets, comprising within its walls an extent of upward of twelve acres. In the various armories are kept arms sufficient to equip over one hundred thousand men. Trophies of celebrated victories, every kind of ancient weapons, instruments of torture, and thousands of other curiosities find a place here. In the Horse Armory are figures of the Kings of England, on horseback, chiefly dressed in the ancient armor. Swords, pikes, spears, pistols, and other war instruments are arranged on the walls in many curious devices. Queen Elizabeth is represented as standing by the side of her horse, arrayed in the same dress and armor she wore at Tilbury in 1588, when she made her memorable speech to the assembled army. We were in the Bloody Tower, where Richard III. had his two nephews put to death; in the Boyer Tower, where the Duke of Clarence is said to have been drowned in a butt of Malmsey; in the Brick Tower, where Lady Jane Grey was confined; in the Beauchamp Tower, where Anne Boleyn was imprisoned; and in the White Tower, where Sir Walter Raleigh was beheaded, and where we saw the fatal block and axe in the execution room. We entered his prison lodgings, a cell ten feet long and eight feet wide, formed in the thickness of the wall, and receiving no light except from the doorway. It was here within this Tower that, tradition says, Sir Walter Raleigh wrote his history of the world. The crown jewels, which are immensely valuable, are kept carefully guarded in a small room of the Tower and within an iron grating. Among these is the crown made for the coronation of Queen Victoria, at a cost of $600,000; St. Edward's crown, made of gold and embellished with diamonds, rubies, emeralds, pearls and sapphires; the Prince of Wales' crown; the Queen's diadem; St. Edward's staff; the Ancient Queen's crown; the royal scepter; the Queen's scepter; the ivory scepter made for Marie d' Este, James II.'s Queen; the rod of equity, the curtana, or pointless sword of mercy, two swords of justice, a baptismal font, a beautiful service of sacramental plate, the coronation bracelets and spurs, and the anointing vessel and spoon, all used at the coronation; and last, but not all, a golden salt-cellar of most beautiful workmanship. These gems were all pointed out and their use fully explained to us by a special attendant.

On the afternoon of the 30th of June we rode three quarters of an hour by rail to Windsor Castle. The Queen being there we were admitted only to the Round Tower, the Chapel, and the "Mews," or Queen's stables. In the Mews we saw seventy beautiful horses, many of them with pet names, and a great many carriages. In one building are the carriages in use by the Queen and Prince Albert during his lifetime; but since his death she has not allowed them to be used, and they will probably pass into the catalogue of royal relics intact. In the vault of St. George's Chapel are the remains of many of the sovereigns of England and of other members of the royal family. The marble monument here to the Princess Charlotte, wife of Leopold I., is touchingly beautiful. There is a fine monument, also, to the Duke of Kent, and one in *bas-relief* to Prince Albert, whose remains were deposited in a mausoleum a short distance from the Castle. The Prince of Wales was christened and married in St. George's Chapel. The following hymn, composed by his father, was sung at the wedding, Jenny Lind Goldschmidt assisting the choir:

> "This day, with joyful heart and voice,
>   To Heaven be raised a nation's prayer:
> Almighty Father, deign to grant
>   Thy blessing to the wedded pair.
>
> "So shall no clouds of sorrow dim
>   The sunshine of their earthly days;
> But happiness in endless round
>   Shall still encompass all their ways."

The sexton, who opened the doors to us, said he was present at the baptism and marriage of the Prince.

The view from the tower, where a communicative soldier is stationed to point out all places of interest, is very fine. Not more than half a mile off, on the other side of the Thames, lie the village of Eton and Eton College in plain sight. We could see the college boys playing on the green. At the right we could see the house of William Penn and the little church and monuments in the graveyard where Gray wrote his immortal Elegy. Near by is Runnymede, where King John signed the *Magna Charta*. Extending westwardly from the Castle is the Long Walk, three miles, bordered by forest trees. From the tower we looked down upon a garden of flowers in full bloom. A walk around the terrace of the Castle was very pleasant, and had there been time we should have been glad to take a stroll through the Park, which comprises about three thousand eight hundred acres. The village of Windsor is an interesting old place.

CHAPTER XIII.

LONDON, JULY 12.— We have been to the top of St. Paul's and conversed in the Whispering Gallery across or around the inner circle of its spacious dome. We have also attended service here, when we heard a good sermon by Rev. Dr. Wright, on the efficacy of prayer. The music was magnificent. There are two large organs, facing each other at the end of the choir or chancel, and near the pulpit, over which is suspended a sounding-board from the rim of the dome. One organist plays on both organs at once, by means either of pedals extending from one to the other under the floor, or by electricity. The grandeur of the surroundings added much to the effect, sitting there, as we did, under the beautiful dome, with statesmen, scholars, and warriors, all in sculptured marble, and, as we imagined, looking down upon us and listening to words of wisdom and to music whose echoes softly expired in the distant recesses of aisle, tower, and transept in strains of heavenly melody. Like Westminster Abbey, St. Paul's is a place of tombs and monuments to the distinguished dead. In the crypt lie the remains of Nelson and Wellington, side by side, and of Sir Christopher Wren, the architect, who designed and superintended the erection of this magnificent structure, which was completed from its foundation in thirty-five years. The remains of Sir Joshua Reynolds, Benjamin West, Sir Thomas Lawrence, and James Barry were also buried here, and among the principal monuments are those of Bishop Heber, John Howard, Sir John Moore, Nelson, Wellington, Sir Joshua Reynolds, Lord Cornwallis, Sir Ralph Abercrombie, and Dr. Johnson. Many of the officers and soldiers of the army, as well as sailors, painters, and poets are commemorated by monuments more or less elaborate. We were especially interested in one inscription, which we copied from the base of two life-size marble statues, standing side by side in officers' uniform, as follows:

"Major General Sir Edward Pakenham and Major General Samuel Gibbs, who fell gloriously on the 8th of January, 1815, while leading the troops to an attack on the enemy's works in front of New Orleans."

The tomb of Sir Christopher Wren bears the following inscription in Latin:

"Beneath lies Christopher Wren, the architect of this church and city, who lived more than ninety years, not for himself alone, but for the public. Reader, do you seek his monument? Look around!"

St. Paul's stands in an elevated position at the end of Ludgate Hill, in the city of London proper. It is in the form of a Latin cross, five hundred and fourteen feet in length and two hundred and eighty-seven wide. It is built of Portland stone, and is said to have cost $4,000,000. The dome is supported by eight immense piers, each of them forty feet at the base. There are three domes, in fact; an outer one of wood, covered with lead, and an inner, with a brick one between. Its great bell, which strikes the hour, and is heard from a long distance, is never tolled except on the death of some one of the royal family. The view from the dome is superb.

In the forenoon of the 4th of July, which was Sunday, we went to Temple Church near Temple Bar. This church is more than six hundred years old, and used to be the church of the Knights Templar, as it is now of the Barristers. It contains many monumental effigies and sculptured portraits of its ancient owners. Oliver Goldsmith was buried here. Close by are the Temple Gardens, celebrated by Shakspeare as the scene of the plucking of the red and white roses — the badges of the Houses of York and Lancaster. Temple Bar is so called from its being the boundary line between London and Westminster, which used to be marked by a bar, posts, and chains. These were superseded by a gate, which was taken down after the great fire, and on that as well as on the present gate, erected in 1670, the heads of rebels and traitors used to be exposed. This custom was continued as late as 1772. "The curious custom of closing the gates and not admitting royalty into the city until permission had been demanded of the Mayor standing on the city side, was last observed when the Queen opened the Royal Exchange in 1844."

In the afternoon of the 4th we listened to a glorious discourse by Dean Stanley, in Westminster Abbey. The church was packed with attentive listeners as far as his voice could be heard. He took for his text the 21st and 22d verses of the fifth chapter of St. Matthew: "Ye have heard that it was said by them of old time, Thou shalt not kill; and whosoever shall kill shall be in danger of the judgment. But I say unto you, That whosoever is angry with his brother without a cause shall be in danger of the judgment: and whosoever shall say to his brother, *Raca*, shall be in danger of the council: but whosoever shall say, Thou fool, shall be in danger of hell fire." He spoke of the evil of hard words, both between individuals and nations; and in the concluding portion of his sermon he referred to the relations between Great Britain and the United States, comparing the past with the present, in a manner most gratifying certainly to every American present. "What American," he asked, "is there who is not proud of that English ancestry which he then [in the time of the Revolution] spurned behind him? What Englishman is there who is now not proud of the once dreaded name of Washington?" and he quoted this stanza:

> "No distance breaks the tie of blood:
> Brothers are brothers evermore;
> Nor wrong, nor wrath of deadliest mood,
> That magic may o'erpower."

So much pleased were we with this discourse, that on the following day we ventured to address a note of thanks to the Dean, and request a copy of it for publication at home. Taking this note to the Abbey, we were directed to his adjoining residence, and delivered it to his doorkeeper, who shortly returned with an invitation from the Dean for us to walk up stairs, and we were conducted to a room which appeared to be used both for a sitting and dining room. In a few moments the Dean came in with his sermon in his hand and extended to us a cordial greeting. He is, we should judge, not much over sixty, slightly built, rather below medium size, and frail looking. His manners are wholly free from anything approaching ostentation, and his countenance beams with kindness and benevolence. He loaned us his sermon without hesitation, and we have copied and sent a large portion of it for publication in the *Christian at Work*, New York. In the course of a pleasant conversation he called attention to a large number of portraits suspended around the room, observing that they were those of nearly all of his predecessors. We took leave, much pleased with our call. On a subsequent day, when we called to return his sermon and get him to decipher some words we could not make out—much of it was written in a sort of short hand—he received us as though we had been old acquaintances, and gave us two of his autographs. We have his photograph, also bearing his autograph, in our collection.

At the solicitation of the publisher, we took to London a bound volume of the *Christian at Work*, New York, for the Rev. Mr. Spurgeon, who had expressed a desire for it because it contained several articles he had written for it. On our arrival we addressed a note to him, asking where we should leave the volume, and expressing a desire to hear him preach. In answer he sent us two tickets, and said he would be pleased to have us bring the book to his Tabernacle on a succeeding Sunday, when he should be present to conduct the services. Accordingly, when the day arrived, we ventured to invite an English lady friend to accompany us, believing that by using the big volume for one ticket, three of us would be able to pass the guard at the gate. Strangers are admitted only on tickets of admission. We were correct in our calculation, being all admitted without hesitation, and immediately conducted to good seats on the main floor. The clerk was then sent for the book, which we had left with the gatekeeper, and took it with our card to Mr. Spurgeon's study, returning with an invitation for us to call at his room after service. The main floor of the Tabernacle is provided with three hundred and fifty-one pews, the first gallery with one hundred and forty, and the second with one hundred and seven. These galleries, which are very wide, extend entirely around the interior, and at one end there is a spacious raised platform instead of a pulpit. Under this is a low and more spacious platform, which was occupied by inmates from a blind asylum and other people. The room is lighted by a small dome or lantern from above, as well as from the side windows. It is well adapted for hearing; and there are seats for five thousand persons, or space for six thousand five hundred sitting and standing. It was crowded the day we were there. The leading singer sits, with many others, on the pulpit platform, and occupies a position at the front during the singing. There is no musical instrument, and the congregation, all standing, generally assist in singing. Mr. Spurgeon read the first hymn, and afterward repeated the whole or part of each verse as the singers took it up, he joining with them.

During the singing of the following two hymns, while the congregation stood, he kept his seat, joining occasionally in the music. Without any attempt at eloquence, he gave us a plain, practical discourse occupying about one hour, commanding rapt attention throughout. His strength evidently lies in his powerful physique and voice, and in the earnestness with which he enforces his views, founded in piety and deep conviction. As soon as the services were over, we all three went to his study, and, although many were waiting to see him, were first admitted. He received us in a jovial manner, as though he had long known us, remarking upon our royal cognomen, and inquiring, with much apparent interest, after his friends in New York. He was much pleased to receive the volume, saying he desired to preserve copies of his own writings. He wished us every happiness in our journey, and his bearing toward us was in all respects most cordial. He is broad-shouldered, stout, with a full round face, and under fifty, if he is over forty years of age.

CHAPTER XIV.

LONDON, July 15.—Through the politeness of our minister to the Court of St. James, General Schenck, who gave us a card of introduction to Hon. Mr. Anderson, M. P. from Scotland, we have been several times into the House of Commons and House of Lords while those bodies were in session. Mr. Anderson waited upon us with great kindness each time we called on him, and on his pass we were readily admitted to the galleries. Once we had seats in the Diplomatic Gallery of the House of Lords on General Schenck's official admission tickets, which were not supposed to be transferable — thus, by inference, at least, having had the honor of representing the United States before that august body. From our short experience we might judge that the position is an easy one to fill. The gallery set apart for the Diplomatic Corps and other officials is but one or two seats deep, and extends on both sides of the hall. Among the few members we heard speak in the House of Lords was Lord Stanhope. The proceedings were of little interest to us. In the House of Commons, where the members sit with their hats on, we were better entertained. Once or twice the ladies of our party (some English friends were with us) were given seats in the ladies' gallery, set apart for the ladies of the nobility, where they are shielded from the gaze of the members by a lattice work; or, more properly speaking, perhaps, where they are thus prevented, either by frowns or fascinating smiles, from bringing to bear any undue influence upon the members below. We were sorry not to see Gladstone; but we saw Disraeli, Mr. Ward Hunt, head of the Admiralty, and Mr. Bright, several times, and heard the two former speak. We also saw Professor Fawcett, the blind member, whose wife, a charming lady, we one day called on with our English friends; and some other noted members were likewise pointed out to us. On one occasion the question before the House was whether there should be a naval school established at Dartmouth, the government side being in the affirmative. Many members spoke, and the debate was both lively and spicy. When the vote came to be taken, a division was called for, tellers

were appointed, and every member except one left
the room—those in the affirmative going out at one
door at the end of the hall, and those in the negative
at another on the opposite side. A stranger at our
elbow informed us that the single member remaining
was from Ireland, and that he was allowed to keep
his seat for the reason that he came to the House
as he came into the world, without either arms or
legs. We do not know on which side he voted;
but one thing is certain, though he might be the
most inveterate Fenian, he could never be guilty
of taking up arms against his government. In the
vote thus taken the government was sustained by
ten majority only.

One afternoon Mr. Anderson took us all through
the Parliament buildings, into the libraries, committee-rooms, chapel, (there is a small chapel here with
a baptismal font in one corner,) crypt, and out into a
fine open space, accessible only to members, directly
on the banks of the Thames, where they can go for
a quiet siesta, or for exercise, without the danger of
being disturbed. He showed us in the crypt the
exact spot where Guy Fawkes placed the gunpowder
to blow up the Parliament buildings in 1604—the
grand object of which horrible plot was "to prepare
the way for the restoration of the Roman Catholics."
This bold conspiracy, notwithstanding it was "commenced by its daring contrivers with every possible
precaution that seemed necessary to secure success,"
failed through timely discovery. The present House
of Parliament, or New Palace of Westminster, stands
on the site of the old Houses of Parliament, which
were destroyed by fire in 1834. It fronts nine hundred feet on the river, and covers eight acres of
ground. It is a noble structure, but it would look a

great deal handsomer were it on an eminence. It stands low, communicating with Westminster Hall, which is sometimes flooded at high tides by the waters of the Thames. The exterior is of hard magnesian limestone, from Yorkshire. Its cost was $8,000,000.

Westminster Hall, founded originally by William Rufus in 1097, "was rebuilt in its present form by Richard II., who, in 1399, kept his Christmas here with great magnificence, the number of his guests amounting to ten thousand each day." The main room, which is on the lower floor, is immense, and this is the principal entrance to the Houses of Parliament. It "appears to have been designed for royal banquets and entertainments, and the coronation feasts have been held here for ages. Courts of justice were, however, held here in very early times, in which the sovereign himself was accustomed to preside; and the ancient stone *bench*, whereon the monarch sat, is said to be yet in existence beneath the pavement in the upper end. Hence the *Curia Domini Regis*, or Court of King's Bench, which is one of the four Supreme Courts now regularly held beneath this roof—the other Courts being Chancery, Common Pleas, and Exchequer." These Courts are now held in comparatively small rooms, opening from the main hall, in which the barristers in their black gowns and powdered horse-hair wigs, looking very funny, are every day seen promenading with one another or with their clients. We often looked into these Court-rooms, where the judges, also in wigs and red robes, were seated on high benches, considerably above the bar. "In cases of Parliamentary impeachment the spacious area of the hall itself is fitted up as a Court, as it was for the trial of William

Wallace, Sir Thomas More, the Protector Somerset, Thomas, Earl of Stratford, Minister of Charles I., and also that of his equally ill-fated sovereign. Here, likewise, in modern times, were tried Hastings, for misconduct in India; Lord Byron, Lord Ferrers, Lord Melville, in 1806, for misappropriation of the public money. The last coronation dinner held there was that of George IV."

Directly across the street from the House of Parliament and Westminster Hall is Westminster Abbey, all on the west side of the Thames, which at this point runs due north, while further down it runs nearly due east, so that the London Tower, on the same side of the river, stands on its northern banks. Viewing the Thames from the dome of St. Paul's, it has the appearance of a huge serpent pursuing its tortuous course through the city. The magnificent Westminster Bridge spans the river immediately at the north end of the Parliament House. Five minutes' walk from here, by Westminster Abbey, on Victoria street, is the office of the United States legation. General Schenck and daughters reside near Kensington Gardens, in the western part of the city. He told us he frequently walks to or from his office through Kensington and Hyde Parks. They hold a weekly reception, and we have done ourselves the honor of paying our respects to them, when we were happy to meet at their house Mrs. Henry Howard, the accomplished daughter of George W. Riggs, Esquire, on her way to the Hague, where her husband, so long and favorably known as one of the secretaries of the British legation in Washington, has been promoted to a higher position. General Schenck, being in ill health that day, was not present at the reception; therefore his daughters, who appear to be very popular with our English cousins, were obliged alone to do the honors of the occasion.

In one or two of our excursions through the city we have had a good view of Newgate, the principal prison, so well known, in London. This is where all criminals sentenced to death for crimes committed in the county of Middlesex suffer the last penalty of the law. "The antiquity of this building is prodigious if viewed in connection with what it was meant to continue or restore; for on this spot stood a Roman fort. If considered in its present capacity as a prison, it is still very ancient. During nearly seven hundred and fifty years have the guilty or unfortunate been here incarcerated. An underground passage leads from the cells to the dock in the Old Bailey Sessions House;" and there is a prison van, which just fits this aperture, thus preventing the escape of prisoners during removal.

In our wanderings one day we went as far as Bonhill-field Burying-ground, in Bonhill Row, Finsbury. It appeared to be away to one side of the city; and our guide said it used to be one of the great fields appertaining to Finsbury Farm, Bonhill-field, Wallow-field, and the High-field, where the three windmills stood. It was used as a pest-field during the great plague of 1665, when nearly one hundred thousand of the population of London fell victims to that terrible disease. Soon after it was converted into a cemetery for the Dissenters, and so it has been continued ever since. John Bunyan was buried here, in the vault of his friend Strudwick, a grocer, in whose house he died August 31, 1688. There is a fine monument to him here with figures illustrative of the "Pilgrim's Progress." The mother of John and Charles Wesley was also buried here, and so was De Foe. The inscription on her tomb states that she was the mother of nineteen children. From near the tombs of all these noted persons we plucked leaves to send home. On the opposite side of the street to the cemetery we saw the house in which John Wesley died, and his tomb is just in the rear thereof.

We can go nowhere in London without seeing more or less to interest. One day, abandoning all thought of care, we walked all the way from Cheapside along Newgate street, Holborn viaduct, High Holborn, Oxford street, and Edgeware and Bishop's road, to our own lodgings in Queen's road, half the length of the city. Hearing only English spoken, we might have forgotten and thought ourselves in New York; for some portions of the business streets seemed like Broadway. Cheapside is the great center of the retail trade, and perhaps the most active and crowded part of London. It is said to have derived its name from having been the market of the Ward of Chepe. "It was the northern boundary of Roman London, all beyond being marsh and bog." In 1631 it was called the "Beauty of London." It is full of historical recollections. It was here that Edward I. erected one of the nine Crosses raised in memory of Eleanor, his Queen. It stood for over three hundred years on the spot where her body rested, on the way from Lincoln to Westminster, but was finally "demolished on the 2d of May, 1643, in the mayoralty of the regicide Isaac Pennington, to the noise of trumpets, the tramp of horses, and the cries of the multitude." It was here that Wat Tyler caused Richard Irons and others to be beheaded in 1381; and in 1450 Jack Cade caused Lord Say to be put to death here in the same manner.

Having purchased Cook's tickets to Geneva, via Holland, Belgium, Germany, and Austria, taking the principal cities in Switzerland and Chamouni in our route, we must bid good-bye to London for the present.

CHAPTER XV.

AMSTERDAM, JULY 18.—Here we are in Holland, stopping at the Amsted Hotel, the leading public house in Amsterdam, and said to be the best in Holland. We left London in a pouring rain, at seven P. M., on the 16th, took the steamer from Harwich about nine, and reached Rotterdam next morning at half-past nine, after a most wretched night of sea-sickness, so far as the writer was concerned. His fair companion having been so fortunate as to secure a lounge, passed the night quite comfortably. No such luck for him! Every berth in the gentlemen's cabin was engaged, and the best that could be done for him was a mattress on the cabin floor across the stern of the boat, a hard pillow about two inches thick, one blanket, and a wash-bowl as a *compagnon de lit*. This arrangement, however, had this advantage—it avoided the necessity of undressing. But such a bed, and such an irregular rocking, pitching, and twisting! All night long the boat was dancing a crazy jig, and you might as well have tried to dodge chain-lightning as attempted to accommodate yourself to its erratic motions. Travelers between England and the Continent may well bid the day good speed when they may make the passage by rail through a submarine tunnel. We made only a short stop in Rotterdam, but long enough to see that it is a large city; and we had a good view of it as we approached it by the river Meuse, whose green banks, after such a night, were beautiful to behold. The city is threaded by canals, with draw and stationary bridges, and much of the communication is by ferryboats. In the market-place there is a bronze statue of Erasmus, and the house in which he was born, in 1467, is still preserved.

From Rotterdam we proceeded to the Hague, the capital of Holland, and a charmingly neat and clean city, also abounding in canals. The streets and sidewalks are well paved and shaded by long rows of trees, and extending into the city stands a large forest, kept entirely clear of all underbrush. A drive of one or two miles through this forest took us to the "Queen's House in the Woods." The grounds around it are beautifully laid out, and adorned by flower gardens, fountains, and statuary. In appearance the exterior of the Palace is unpretending, but its rooms and furniture are remarkably fine. The ball-room is very spacious, and is full of paintings, many of which illustrate the life of Frederick, the first King of the Netherlands. Family portraits adorn the billiard-room. There is a Chinese and likewise a Japanese room, each provided with furniture from those countries respectively. The former has furniture upholstered with white embroidered silk, and the latter with light green silk, elaborately worked, all gifts to the Queen from those countries. We understand that the Queen's family consists of herself, husband, and two sons. The King occupies his Palace in the city, paying only occasional visits to the Queen; Harper's Handbook says "once a year," but that seems unreasonable. We passed but did not enter the King's Palace. We have visited the old and new House of Lords and House of Commons, having to pay fees to three attendants before we could get in; as we were obliged to pay, also, one guilder (one franc each) admission fee to the House in the Woods. The chief attraction was in the National Museum, (admission free,) formerly the Palace of Prince Maurice, where there is a large collection of paintings, mostly by Dutch and Flemish artists. We saw here the famous picture of the "Young Bull," by Paul Potter. It is stated that Napoleon seized this picture and had it hung up in the Louvre in Paris, notwithstanding the Dutch government offered him $100,000 to leave it undisturbed. It represents a young bull with white and brown spots, a cow reclining on the greensward before him, a horned ram, with a sheep and lamb, lying at his head, and an old cowherd leaning against a large tree, under the shade of which and an adjoining tree all (life size) seem to be resting in quiet contemplation. Another noted picture is "Venus Asleep," by Poussin. We turned away, without reluctance, from a large painting by Rembrandt, representing the dissection of a dead man by a professor and his pupils. It is considered a great work of art. There is here also a Royal Cabinet of Curiosities, comprising costumes of the Chinese and Japanese, a large collection of Japanese ware, weapons, coats-of-mail, and thousands of other things of more or less interest.

Amsterdam is an hour and a half by rail from the Hague. Here, too, there is a Royal Palace, regarded as the most magnificent building in the city. We

AMSTERDAM.

went into the bell-tower and stopped to hear the chime of bells there. From this point we had a good view of the city and surrounding country. The whole city rests on piles, and it is divided by deep canals into no less than ninety islands, which are connected by hundreds of bridges. Descending from the tower, we were shown through the various rooms of the palace, one of which, called the marble room, is unusually superb, and in all of which are many fine paintings, the most striking of which, perhaps, is a large one representing the blowing up of his ship by Van Speyk rather than surrender to the Belgian forces. In the Museum, likewise, we saw some five hundred pictures, with some of which we were much pleased. Those of the Dutch and Flemish schools predominate. One large painting by Rembrandt represents the "Night Patrol;" and a still larger one, considered the masterpiece of Van der Heist, "represents a banquet of the *Garde Bourgeoise*, which took place June 18, 1648, in the grand Salle de St. Loris Docle in the Single at Amsterdam, to celebrate the conclusion of the peace of Munster." There are twenty-five figures, said to be all portraits, in this picture. Rembrandt's "Five Masters of the Draper's Company" is also regarded as one of his greatest works.

From the Museum, wishing to take a carriage to the Zoological Gardens, we were not a little amused as well as puzzled to find that we were utterly unable to make any of the hackmen understand what we wanted. We did not understand a word of Dutch, and those "foreigners," as Mark Twain might call them, were equally ignorant both of English and French, which we tried upon them in vain. At length an omnibus driver, who understood a few words of French, came to our relief, and, showing a handful of Dutch coin, we managed, through our interpreter, to get one of the hackmen to understand what he was to receive to carry us to the Zoological Gardens and thence to our hotel. He took us to the Gardens, where the gate-keeper, who speaks French as well as Dutch, instructed him, at our request, to be ready at a given hour to convey us the rest of the way. When that time arrived he was nowhere to be found, and a perfect bedlam was raised around our heads by a dozen other hackmen who wished to get a job. Finally, disgusted with all Dutch hackmen, we started on foot, and soon came to a street car which brought us to our hotel, where we expected our hackman would call for his money. Strange to say, however, he did not make his appearance; but, as we were to leave that afternoon and desired to be on the safe side, we handed the stipulated sum to the cashier of the hotel, to be given to the hackman should he call; and this notwithstanding the latter fulfilled a part only of his contract. The probability is that he knowingly left us in the lurch because he secured a more lucrative job, and that the hotel clerk appropriated our small change to his own use. Before visiting *Deutschland* again we intend to take a few lessons in *Deutsch*.

There are many elegant dwelling houses in these cities, and one peculiarity of nearly all of the dwellings is that small mirrors are hung extended outside of the windows, the one reflecting up and the other down the street, so that the inmates may see what passes outside without being themselves seen. All the women in the streets are very neat in appearance, and either wear funny looking caps pinned on by fantastic looking pins, or go with their heads bare; and they wear, also, long aprons. Some of the laboring classes of both sexes wear pointed wooden shoes. Netherlands is an appropriate name for Holland, since its whole territory, we imagine, is flat, low land. As far as we have been able to see the face of the country, it is a web of dykes and canals, navigated by boats and canoes. Lots, not containing more than one acre of ground, on which stand the farm-house and other buildings, are entirely surrounded by water; and the country is everywhere dotted with windmills.

ANTWERP, JULY 20.—For compartment companions from Amsterdam last evening we had three young Scotch gentlemen on their way to Switzerland, and a part of the way two interesting young school girls, who, understanding only Dutch and Flemish, contributed much to our amusement, while they were equally amused by our strange language and efforts to make ourselves understood by them. In company with our new Scotch acquaintances we have had a very enjoyable day in Antwerp, which is a much more interesting city than we expected to see. Here are three or four of the most beautiful and richly adorned churches in Europe; and this is the native place of Antoine Van Dyck, whose paintings, with those of Rubens and others, contribute so much to their adornment. Here, in the principal Cathedral, is the great masterpiece of Rubens, "The Descent from the Cross," and what is regarded as his next best work, "The Elevation to the Cross;" also, his "Resurrection of the Saviour," and "Assumption of the Virgin." In the Church of St. James, too, there are many of his paintings, among them his "Holy Family;" and in the Church of St. Augustine his great picture of "The Marriage of St. Catherine."

In the latter church "The Ecstacy of St. Augustine," by Van Dyck, attracts marked attention. On the outside of St. Paul's Church there is what purports to be a representation of Calvary — statuary figures representing Christ on the Cross, Mary Magdalene, and others in attendance; beneath, Christ lying in the sepulchre, a sort of grotto; and at the side, Purgatory, behind an iron grating, exhibiting numerous unfortunate sinners, apparently suffering the "tortures of the damned." We ventured to suggest that they had suffered long enough, and that St. Paul's would be improved by the removal of the whole frightful picture. There is a very large collection of paintings in the Museum, including one of Van Dyck's greatest works, "The Crucifixion," Rubens' "Dead Christ," and his "Crucifixion of Christ between two Thieves;" "Boors Smoking," by Teniers, also a native of Antwerp, and other noted works by celebrated artists. Among the artists copying pictures here, we met one evidently very accomplished, a gentleman without arms, who held his brush by the toes of his right foot. His name, which he wrote with a pencil in our catalogue, is Charles Felu. He was engaged in and had nearly finished copying a portrait of "Our Saviour," regarded as a very superior work of art; and strange as it may seem, the copy appeared equal in every respect to the original. We here sat in a chair which Rubens kept as his favorite seat. We rode along Rubens street past the house, a handsome edifice, in which Rubens lived and died, and over the front of which there is a bust of the great painter. In the square, in front of the Cathedral, there is a fine bronze statue of him.

CHAPTER XVI.

FRANKFORT, July 26.—In one hour from Antwerp we reached Brussels on the evening of the 20th of July, and remained there about three days. Brussels is pleasantly situated on the river Senne, although some of the streets running back from the river are rather too steep. It stands mostly on the acclivity and top of a hill. It has a magnificent park, two grand boulevards, and many fine squares. On the 21st there was a royal parade, and religious services were held at the Cathedral of St. Gudule, it being the anniversary of the late King's death. There was a great crowd and considerable military display. With some difficulty we obtained admission to the church, where we hired chairs to stand upon, in order to see over the heads of the populace. There were present the King and Queen, judges of the court, officers of the army, all the foreign ministers, and other officials, all in their uniform or regalia, save the American consul, who represented the United States on that occasion, our minister, Mr. Jones, having recently resigned and left for home. The judges wore long robes, faced with scarlet silk. Most of the officials had taken their seats before the arrival of the King and Queen, on whose appearance they all rose, and the King and Queen bowed pleasantly right and left to them as they passed to their seats at the right of the altar. We had a good view of all these dignitaries. The King is a tall, fine looking man, between forty and fifty, we should judge, and the Queen, a very pretty lady, is somewhat younger. At the close of the ceremonies they passed out first, bowing as when they came in. There was a grand flourish of trumpets both inside of the church and in the streets. We have a photograph of the pulpit of this church, and, like the one in St. James' at Antwerp, of which also we obtained a good photograph, it is remarkable for the beautiful carving, which must have cost no small sum. "The pulpit of St. Gudule is formed of wonderfully carved groups of figures, representing the expulsion of Adam and Eve from Paradise. The figures are the size of life. Above the pulpit, which is supported by the tree of knowledge, stands the Virgin, holding the infant Jesus in her arms, who is endeavoring to thrust the cross into the serpent's head." In fact, the churches, some of them, in both these cities abound in wonderful carvings, mostly of wood, but some in ivory — all remarkably perfect. In the old square in the lower part of the city, where the Hôtel de Ville is situated, the architecture of four several centuries is represented. Brussels is regarded as perhaps the best place for laces; therefore we made it an object to visit several lace stores and manufactories of lace in different parts of the city. All the people here whom we met spoke French, thus enabling us to transact business with them much easier than we could do in Holland, where Hollandaise and Flemish are the languages generally spoken among the common people. Besides several of the churches, all interesting as containing magnificent altars and many fine paintings, we visited the National Gallery of Fine Arts, and a gallery of very beautiful modern paintings and statuary near the King's Palace. The former is divided into three departments; "the first contains the paintings of the great Flemish masters, from Van Eyck to Rubens, and their numerous pupils; the second contains a splendid Library of two hundred thousand volumes and twenty thousand manuscripts; many of the latter were collected at a very early period by the Dukes of Burgundy, and are of great value; the third, the Museum of Natural History, which is in the lower story, and surpasses in extent and value every other in the kingdom." In the gallery of modern paintings are many of Verboeckhoven's works, remarkable for their true resemblance to nature, his sheep and cattle being perfect. We have been also to the famous Wertz Gallery, where there are some very curious pictures, better designated, perhaps, as monstrosities. There is one horrible picture here, representing a person come to life in his entombed coffin. Among the natural pictures we were particularly struck with one of an old concierge sitting asleep by a window, his newspaper open before him. Beneath was a picture of two beautiful maidens — one leaning over the window-sill, showing both bare arms and bust, and the other showing head, shoulder, and one side of bust. Near the floor a fine picture of a dog, with white nose and paws, lying asleep in his kennel by his lunch bowl. Another, the picture of a maiden leaning out of a window on her right arm, and showing most of her bosom, in her right hand a flower and in the left a bouquet, and pressing back the green window curtain. Looking over her shoulder is the beautiful face of another maiden. All these figures stand out from the canvas in a wonderful manner.

On the 22d there was a grand military review by the King; and from the number of regiments present we infer that the whole military force of Belgium was called out on that occasion. Preferring to visit the Gallery and other places of interest, we did not seek positions on the field, but we saw great bodies of troops marching through the streets, affording a good opportunity to judge of their appearance. What struck us as most remarkable was the small size of the men. Compared with some of our own regiments we used to see in Washington during the late war, they were little more than pigmies; nevertheless, they doubtless understand well how to handle the musket and saber. Beyond the military the crowd was immense. On the evening of the 21st we witnessed splendid fireworks at the foot of the Park. Our pleasant Scotch friends took leave of us in Brussels, where we at the same time made the acquaintance of Mr. Usher, United States Marshal, from Massachusetts, with whom we made a trial to find our Minister, not then knowing that he had gone home.

We left Brussels at two o'clock P. M., and arrived at Cologne at ten P. M. on the 23d. We have never anywhere seen more productive fields than we saw on this route, particularly between Brussels and Liege. They are loaded with grain, now being cut and stacked, rank potatoes, beets, clover, etc. On this part of the route the face of the country is quite level, and the order in which trees are growing in the fields and on both sides of the highways, together with the abundant crops, gives the observer a landscape view on which it would seem the eye could never tire.

At Cologne the greatest interest centers in the Cathedral, which, although commenced in 1248, is not yet completed. It is most remarkable for its great dimensions and magnificent Gothic architecture. As a Gallery of Art it is far behind two or three of the churches we visited in Antwerp; but it contains some fine paintings by Rubens, who was a native of this city, and other artists. Numerous wonderful relics are shown here, for pay—among them the bones of the three wise men of the East, who came to Bethlehem to present their offerings to the infant Saviour; one of St. Matthew's bones; and the skulls of the Magi, crowned with diamonds. In the Church of St. Ursula, likewise, there are other relics equally wonderful, including "the chains with which St. Peter was bound, and one of the clay vessels used by the Saviour at the marriage in Cana." The skeleton of St. Ursula herself, surrounded by the skulls of some of her followers, is also exhibited in a coffin; and in the Cathedral there is a large painting of her with her eleven thousand virgins, who, tradition says, made a pilgrimage with her on foot from Basle to Rome, where they were received with great honors by the Holy Father. She was the daughter of the King of Brittany; and on their return, we have it from the same authority, that, because they refused to break their vows of chastity, they were all put to death by the Huns.

There are at least three bridges across the Rhine at Cologne—one being built on boats; one of iron, three arched spans; and the third a square-built, massive structure of iron and stone, with two separate carriage-ways. We walked over the latter, from which we had a good view of the river as well as of the city, through the business part of which we also chose to make our way on foot and look, at pleasure, at whatever attracted our attention, not forgetting to buy a couple of bottles of Cologne at the very headquarters of that celebrated article.

At the moment of starting from Cologne up the

Rhine, at nine o'clock on the morning of the 25th, Mr. Trask, from Portland, Maine, who was traveling with his wife, introduced himself and wife to us, and we all became companions for the day, which, though a little raw, was passed very pleasantly. The varied scenery which came under our view as we glided along afforded us much pleasure. Cities and villages, castles and ruins of castles, sweet cottages and elegant mansions, with their adornings, terrace above terrace, sometimes to the number of thirty or more, along the rugged banks, covered with grape-vines — fields of waving grain — together presented a picture both novel and beautiful.

> "Above the frequent feudal towers
> Through green leaves lift their walls of gray,
> And many a rock which steeply lowers,
> And noble arch in proud decay,
> Look o'er this vale of vintage bowers."

We were the most interested, perhaps, in the many castles on either side, the names of which we learned as we passed them. A few miles above Bonn, on the opposite side of the river, is the celebrated Drachenfels, the highest of a group of seven mountains, on the summit of which stands an old castle, said to have been once the fortress and watch-tower of the robbers of the Rhine.

> "The castled crag of Drachenfels
> Frowns o'er the wide and winding Rhine,
> Whose breast of waters broadly swells
> Between the banks which bear the vine."

At or near Falkensberg stands the old Cathedral of St. Clements and the restored Castle of Rheinstein, the summer residence of Prince Frederick of Prussia. At the base of this Castle is a sweet little chapel, and both are nestled in a forest of shade trees upon the side of the precipice, on a peak of which, near by, is an elegant summer house, resembling a Swiss cottage. On one of her visits to Prussia, Queen Victoria was entertained here. At Coblentz the river is spanned by boats, forming a bridge from that city to the strong fortification of Ehrenbreitstein on a high point opposite. It is said that this fortification, perhaps the strongest in Germany, is capable of accommodating one hundred thousand men, and that provisions for eight thousand for ten years could be stored in its magazines. At Coblentz there is a royal residence sometimes occupied by the Emperor of Germany. Opposite the Castle of Ehrenfels is the celebrated "Mouse Tower," associated with the tradition graphically related in rhyme by Southey. The story goes that the summer and autumn had been so wet that in winter the corn continued to grow and lay rotting on the ground; yet, rather than gather it,

> "Every day the starving poor
> Crowded around Bishop Hatto's door,
> For he had a plentiful last year's store."

At length, having become tired of their begging, he appointed a day for them all to come to his great barn, promising to furnish them there with a winter's supply of food.

> "Rejoiced at such tidings, good to hear,
> The poor folk flocked from far and near;
> The great barn was full as it could hold
> Of women and children and young and old.

> "And when he saw it could hold no more,
> Bishop Hatto he made fast the door;
> And while for mercy on Christ they call,
> He set fire to the barn and burnt them all.

>"'I' faith it is an excellent bonfire!' quoth he,
> 'And the country is greatly obliged to me
> For ridding it, in these times forlorn,
> Of rats that only consume the corn.'"

The result was that the Bishop never slept again. The next morning he found the rats had eaten his portrait out of its frame on the wall, consumed all the corn in his granaries, and that an army of ten thousand of them was on its way to attack him. Filled with consternation, he hastened across the river and shut himself up in this tower; but the rats followed, and, breaking into the tower, soon devoured him.

>"They gnawed the flesh from every limb,
> For they were sent to do judgment on him."

A short distance above the "Mouse Tower" is "Bingen on the Rhine;" a place also made famous by song. We will not attempt to relate the story of the dying soldier whose home was "on the vine-clad hills of Bingen—fair Bingen on the Rhine." "He who runs may read." Most of the way, thus far, the shores on either side are more or less mountainous; but as we approach Johannisberg, celebrated for its fine wines, and as the residence of the late Prince Metternich, the country grows more level, and so continues as far at least as Mayence, where, late in the evening, we took the cars and arrived at our hotel in Frankfort about half-past eleven.

CHAPTER XVII.

NUREMBERG, July 28.—Before leaving London we provided ourselves with a few £10 circular notes, which we found very convenient, and, being drawn to our order, they were quite safe. On some parts of the continent they bring a small premium. Going to the bank in Frankfort on the morning of the 26th to get one of these changed, and observing in the same building the sign of the United States consul, we stopped to pay our respects to him, and were kindly received. Mr. Webster, the consul, had just returned from Homburg, and informed us that return tickets to that celebrated watering-place were sold for fifty cents each—the cars running several times a day. He proposed that we should make a trip there, and that he should meet us on our return late in the afternoon. To this we readily agreed. Meantime, however, we took a turn through the city to see some of the monuments, and Dannecker's noted statue of "Ariadne"—a nude female figure seated on a tiger. This statue, pictures of which are often seen, is regarded as a remarkable work of art. It is a novel way of showing off the beauties of the human form. It matters little what name is given to these statues. This is called "Ariadne." Some are called "Eve," some "Venus," some "The Greek Slave," others "Proserpine," "Clytie," and so on. Near the villa in which this statue of "Ariadne" is exhibited is a massive monument, erected by the King of Prussia to the memory of the Hessians who fell in defense of Frankfort. The base is of granite, surmounted by a military device, cast from cannon taken from the French. In the city are the triple Gutenberg monuments, and fine bronze statue monuments also of Goethe and Schiller. Schiller's represents him crowned with laurel and holding a book in his hand. We spent a good part of the day delightfully at Homburg, which must not be, as it sometimes is, confounded with Hamburg, the great commercial city on the Elbe. Until within a few years, Homburg, like Wiesbaden and Baden-Baden, not to mention other similar watering-places, was a great resort for gamblers, and for summer recreation of everybody else who might desire a charming location where they could enjoy free of charge the mineral waters of the springs, the daily music of a large band, and the luxurious drawing and gambling rooms of the Kursaal. It is a paradise of a place. The springs, the waters of which are like those of Saratoga, are situated in a grove, some fifteen minutes' walk from the Kursaal, which is on the main street of the village. Connected with the Kursaal, which is still kept open and provided with a reading-room where newspapers from all quarters may be perused, there is a first-class restaurant, beautiful garden, music pavilion, etc. On the north side, fronting the garden, through which are walks leading toward the springs, there is a spacious veranda, where visitors may sit and sip their coffee, wine, or beer, and listen to the music of the band. In one part of the building there is a theater room, and another part is devoted to baths, medicinal or not, at one's pleasure. Since gambling has been prohibited here, visitors, if they come to stop a few days or more, are taxed a reasonable sum toward defraying the expenses of the band and keeping everything in order. We were happy to meet here Mrs. Senator Sprague, who, with one of her children and maid, had come over from Nauheim, where they are stopping, to spend the day. On our return to Frankfort, Mr. Webster met us at the station, and took us in his carriage to the Palmer Gardens, a new and most charming place on the border of the city, where there is a Kursaal, not unlike that at Homburg, and where the band discoursed sweet music during the evening. There are here, also, an extensive hot-house of plants, flowers, etc., and an artificial lake for boating and skating. On the following day Mr. Webster again joined us and showed us other principal places and objects of interest in the city. The Römer, or Town Hall, is a singular-looking old building, in which the ancient Emperors of Germany flourished, and where we saw full-length portraits of forty-six of them. Like many of the houses in the old part of the city, the building stands gable-end to the street and has very steep roofs, with windows of very small-sized glass. The different roofs connect at the eaves. In the Jewish quarter we saw the house in which the elder Rothschilds, three generations back, were born, and which the family would never allow to be taken down, notwithstanding some of the adjoining houses of the same character fell a few years ago, and, as we were informed, killed some of the inmates. This and several others of the old houses near it, look as though they were ready to fall. They bear curious inscriptions and devices over the doors, and are in all respects unique. Luther's house, which we also saw, has a much more respectable appearance; and so has the house in which Goethe was born, August 17, 1749—the date of his birth inscribed in German over the door, where his father's coat of arms, three lyres, is still preserved.

Our next stopping place was Nuremberg, six hours by rail from Frankfort, on the afternoon of the 27th. This is off the usual route of European travelers; but we do not regret the diversion. Nuremberg is a very old city, of some eight hundred thousand inhabitants. It is situated on both sides of the river Pegnitz, which is crossed by six or eight bridges. The old wall and dry moat fifty feet wide, and the turrets on the wall still remain. We entered the city over a bridge spanning the deep moat, and through one of the old gateways. The houses, built in every imaginable shape, on narrow, tortuous streets, and all their surroundings, give the place a very ancient and odd appearance. The next morning after our arrival we called on our consul, Colonel James M. Wilson, from St. Louis, who spent the day with us in going about the city, and invited us to tea, when we made the acquaintance also of his accomplished wife, and of the vice-consul and sisters. We went first to the old Inquisition Chamber, which is under ground; or, rather, there are several rooms connecting with each other, some of which we saw only by the light of a tallow candle, carried by our female guide. The walls of the first room are covered with instruments of torture. Here is what was called the "Spanish Cloak," being a barrel with one head out, and the other perforated to fit the neck of the victim, whose head was encircled by a wire cage. Thus enrobed, drunkards, and others guilty of such minor offences, were condemned to walk the streets. The "Torture Chair," seat, arms, and back is filled with iron spikes, and the victim was strapped to it and weights attached to his hands and feet. If this was not sufficient, a spiked cylinder was rolled over his body. Here, likewise, are thumb-screws, thumb-hammers, instruments for cutting off, little by little, the ears, nose, tongue, and fingers, and for pulling out the tongue; also ladles for applying melted pitch or lead. A kind of spring tongs, with long handles, was used to catch persons to be arrested. This instrument, on being pressed against the back of the neck, would open and encircle it by a "Spanish Collar" of iron spikes, and then spring back, holding the victim as in the jaws of a steel trap. Other instruments were for cutting off the head; and these, with the beheading block, are also to be seen. Still lower underground are other rooms, or vaults, provided with other frightful instruments of torture. One is called the "Stretcher," by which the victim was slowly torn limb from limb by means of a windlass, his feet being fastened to iron rings in the floor, and his arms to a yoke under a hole in the ceiling, through which the windlass was worked. Another, called the "Spanish Mule," is a high board, sharpened at the upper edge, and the victim, seated thereon, had heavy stones attached to his suspended feet. "The Cradle" is a half cylinder, with pointed spikes for mattress and pillow. Colonel Wilson informed us that as late as 1803 a woman was rocked to death in this cradle. Her husband being accused of theft, both were put to the rack to make them confess. He survived the proof of his innocence, but soon after died also from his cruel treatment. The circumstance had the good effect to cause the people to rise against such horrible punishments, and the law was abolished. The most barbarous instrument of all remains to be described—"Die eiserne Jungfrau," being an iron case about eight feet high, with the form and features, when closed, of a woman.

It is provided with doors like a wardrobe, on the inside of which are twenty-three iron spikes, from six to eight inches long—one for each eye, and twenty-one to pierce the body of the victim. Being placed inside, the doors were closed upon him and pressed home by means of a lever from the opposite wall of the narrow vault. This, of course, was certain death; but that there might be no mistake, the body was dropped through a trap door underneath, and, falling upon a set of knives worked by machinery, was cut in pieces! We secured photographs of this "Iron Maiden," showing both her exterior and interior features.

From viewing the statue and house of Albert Dürer, and the house of Hans Sachs, we drove a mile or two out of town to see Dürer's tomb in the old cemetery. It is a plain stone, about one foot thick, resting on a low molded base, with a raised headpiece for the inscription. As Longfellow, in his poem on Nuremberg, beautifully says:

> "*Emigravit* is the inscription on the tombstone where he lies;
> Dead he is not, but departed — for the artist never dies."

Hans Sachs, the cobbler poet, was also buried here. Many of the tombstones were very singular. One had upon it a bronze casting of a man's skull, jaw and thigh bones, with a nail through the skull, to indicate that the person buried here was killed by a nail driven into his head by his loving wife. But the oddest sight, perhaps, was at the house in the cemetery where the dead are laid out, as if asleep in bed, with the handle of a bell-wire in one hand, that they may ring a bell should they come to life. Their bodies are conveyed there immediately after death, and allowed to remain several days before burial.

We looked through the glass windows and doors at seven corpses lying there at the time. On the way to the cemetery, cut in an old stone wall skirting one side of the road, are seven representations of figures, the principal of which is that of Christ bearing the cross—the last description showing that he had fainted and fallen under it. They are very odd-looking.

We went into the Church of St. Lawrence, a Gothic building erected in 1274-1477. The western front, with a majestic chief portal, is adorned with splendid sculptures of events in the life of Christ. On the north is the magnificent "Bridal Door." In the interior, in addition to many splendid pictures, the beautiful star-window over the organ, and other painted windows of beautiful design, there is the "Sakramentshaeus' Cherr," the superb work of Adam Krafft—a shrine reaching from the floor nearly to the roof, the base of which consists of three kneeling figures—the master workman and his two assistants—supporting the whole structure on their shoulders. Of this Longfellow writes:

"In the church of sainted Lawrence stands a pix of sculpture rare,
Like the foamy sheaf of fountains, rising through the painted air."

There are several superbly carved altars in this church; and the pulpit, also, is very remarkable.

The Church of St. Sebald is equally interesting. It dates back to the tenth century. Both of these churches, each having two towers, were wrested from the Roman Catholics by the Protestants in the Reformation, and are still held by them. The main door on the south side of St. Sebald's has a representation in *bas-relief* of "The Last Judgment," a work, we should think, of years; and the "Bride's

Door," on the north, is richly ornamented by figures showing the Wise and Foolish Virgins. The greatest treasure of this church is the world-renowned bronze "Shrine of St. Sebald," by Vischer—1508-1519. The admirable statues of the Twelve Apostles stand at the side of pillars, which support the canopy; above them the Prophets, masterpieces of art and workmanship. At the base of the eight pillars: Nimrod, Samson, Perseus, Hercules; and the virtues: Strength, Temperance, Charity, and Justice:

"In the church of sainted Sebald, sleeps enshrined his holy dust,
And in bronze the Twelve Apostles guard from age to age their trust."

Behind the high altar are three figures in *bas-relief* representing Judas' Kiss, the Mount of Olives, and the Lord's Supper. The stained windows are splendid. In this church there is a taper, in a small suspended vessel of oil, which has been kept burning for two or three hundred years, and the order is that it shall never be extinguished. A person, in recognition of some merciful deliverance, left by will a sum of money, the interest of which goes to defray the expense of this perpetual offering.

We visited a fine Gallery of paintings, among which are many by Albert Dürer—one the portrait of an old Burgomaster, is considered remarkable. "King Midas as Judge, the Passions assailing him;" "The Triumphal Entry of Maximillian;" and the "Band of the Town Musicians," all by Dürer, are also regarded as masterpieces. In allusion to him, Longfellow observes:

"Fairer seems the ancient city, and the sunshine seems more fair,
That he once has trod its pavement, that he once has breathed its air!"

The Castle here, founded by Emperor Conrad II. in the tenth century, is another point of some attraction, as having been the favorite residence of nearly all of the old German Emperors. It contains some fine pictures, by Dürer and other artists. In different squares there are four beautiful fountains, and several monumental statues, including one of Melancthon. In fact, we could not go the length of a square anywhere in the city that we did not find more or less to excite our curiosity. It is altogether one of the most quaint and interesting old places we have visited.

"Quaint old town of toil and traffic, quaint old town of art and song,
Memories haunt thy pointed gables like the rooks that round them throng."

CHAPTER XVIII.

BERLIN, August 1.—We left Nuremberg at seven on the morning of the 30th ultimo, and going to Ratisbon,—or Regensberg, as it is called on some of the maps,—we hired a coachman to drive us six miles to the Walhalla, or Temple of Fame, a magnificent white marble edifice, erected by the late King of Bavaria, in the northern end of which, opposite the main entrance, is a niche destined to receive his statue. It is situated on a hill several hundred feet in height, overlooking the Danube and surrounding country for a long distance. Its length is two hundred and eighteen feet, its breadth two hundred and two feet, and it is surrounded by fifty-two fluted Doric columns, like the Parthenon at Athens and the Church of the Madeleine in Paris. The main saloon is one hundred and sixty feet long, forty-eight wide, and sixty feet high. It is intended as a great memorial hall, and to contain, among other works of art, the busts and statues of the most distinguished men of Bavaria. Being comparatively new, the number is not yet large; but among about one hundred busts are those of Albert Dürer, Martin Luther, Schiller, Goethe, Mozart, Wallenstein, and Charlemagne; and there are also six angelic white marble statues of "Victory," by Rauch. We say angelic, because they are full-length figures, life-size, of beautiful females, with wings. They are differently posed, but all except one hold one or two wreaths, and this one holds a laurel branch in her right hand. They are all exquisitely beautiful, and we readily recall them to sight as well as mind by photographs of them in our collection. There is, we think, a carriage road to or quite near to the Temple on one side; but, as being the shorter way, we were left to walk a quarter of a mile to it in a foot-path up the steep hill, covered to the top by a fine forest. Were this magnificent Temple not so far out of the course of ordinary travel, it would undoubtedly be universally visited and admired. Returning by coach to the village or city of Ratisbon, we again took the train and reached Eger at eight P. M., where we stayed over night.

It was a long ride from Eger to Leipsic, our next stopping place (it took from half past eight in the morning till half past four in the afternoon) but we were fortunate in having for a traveling companion Mr. E. J. Sobeck, of Luditz, Bohemia, who, although unable to speak his own Bohemian tongue, could speak German, English, French, Spanish, and Italian. At present his principal business is that of an extensive hop merchant, shipping enormous quantities of that article to all quarters of the world.

He is also an architect and a professional musician, but has not practised the latter profession for many years. He told us that in 1836 he traveled through most of the United States as a member of a Bohemian band, playing on the clarionet. He said they performed in Washington, and spoke of the pleasure he enjoyed in a call on President Jackson, whom they saluted with a serenade. From Baltimore to Pittsburg they rode in a mail stage. Subsequently he was the leader of a band in the service of the Queen of Spain; and when Jenny Lind was in her glory he traveled and performed for a time with her. He is a man of commanding appearance, fine address, and evidently well educated; in fact, our true ideal for a Senator. Everything on the route was interesting to us. The buildings are odd looking, the costumes of the peasantry queer, especially of the women, who work with the men in the fields; and the manner in which oxen are harnessed, with a yoke passing directly below their horns, thus drawing from the head instead of the breast, added to the novelty. Cows are also made to work in the same manner. The crops seem abundant. At the stations, where very short stops were made, beer was brought for sale at the car windows. It is offered in thin pint glasses the shape of wine casks, and sold very cheap, glass and all—the glass to be thrown away after its contents are drunk. We have, however, preserved one of them, and may find it useful.

Our approach to Leipsic carried us directly through the field where the principal part of the great battle of Leipsic was fought, on the 16th, 17th, and 18th of October, 1813, between the army of Napoleon on the one side, and the allied armies of Prussia, Russia,

and Austria on the other, resulting in the defeat of
Napoleon, who occupied the city at the commencement of the battle. His force was said to have
numbered one hundred and seventy thousand men
against three hundred thousand of the allied army,
whose loss was only fifty thousand, while his was
eighty thousand. Sir Walter Scott, in his "Life of
Napoleon," gives a description of the town and a
vivid account of the battle. He says: "The venerable town of Leipsic forms an irregular square, surrounded by an ancient Gothic wall, with a terrace
planted with trees. Four gates — on the north those
of Halle and Ranstadt, on the east the gate of Grimma, and on the south that called St. Peter's gate—
lead from the town to the suburbs, which are of
great extent, secured by walls and barriers. Upon
the west side of the town, two rivers, the Pleisse
and the Elster, wash its walls, and flowing through
meadows divide themselves into several branches
connected by marshy islands." On this side, thus
protected, Napoleon was enabled, or permitted, lest
his troops if headed off at every point might become
desperate, to keep open a line of retreat toward the
Rhine. It is supposed that he did not expect any
serious attack on the northern side; therefore his
preparations were chiefly made on the southern side
of the city; but on the second day the Prussian
General, Blucher, made a violent attack, and obtained great advantages on the north side. The
next day was occupied, without any serious conflict,
by both armies in preparation for the final struggle
of the 18th, which resulted in Napoleon's defeat and
most disastrous retreat. In retreating, nearly his
whole army was obliged to pass through the city;
and, although commenced on the night of the 18th,

it was morning before all succeeded in making their escape. They were then fiercely pursued by the victorious allies, joined by the Saxon and Baden troops, who, at the moment of his defeat, had abandoned Napoleon; and the fight was continued hand to hand through the city. Added to this, the only bridge to serve as an exit for the whole French army having been mined by Napoleon's orders, to be blown up as soon as his army should be safely over, was, through some mischance, thus prematurely destroyed, and a large number of the French, unable to escape, were taken prisoners.

It was with no slight interest that we looked upon the scene of this great battle, during which Napoleon had his headquarters at the Rathhaus, or Town Hall; and it was in this Hall that the commander of the allied army, Marshal Schwarzenberg, afterward died. We visited the market-place, from which we were soon, however, driven by an awful smell of what they called cheese; went to the University, through the principal business streets, park, etc. Not caring to stop here longer, we left on a slow train at one in the afternoon, and reached Berlin, the capital of the German Empire, at half-past six, on the 31st of July.

CHAPTER XIX.

BERLIN, August 4.—Our first day in Berlin, August 1, was Sunday, and in company with Hon. H. N. Conger, of New Jersey, United States Consul at Prague, and his wife, we went to the house where it was expected religious services in English would take place, but none were held, there being no minister, and we turned our steps toward the King's Palace, to which we were admitted on payment of one mark, about twenty-five cents, each, and were shown through the principal rooms. This magnificent edifice, called the Old Palace, has an interior inclined plane walk, wide enough for a carriage-way, paved with brick, to the third story. Whether the old sovereigns used to ride over this road or not, we did not learn; but we found it easy of ascent. The seven or eight rooms shown to us were sumptuously furnished, and the Royal Chapel contains many fine works of art. The throne room is very large, and is gorgeously decorated. Another splendid room contains statues of the Brandenburg Electors and various allegorical figures. Before entering these rooms, as in the Temple of Walhalla, we were all obliged to put on over our shoes large felt slippers, which could be kept on only by sliding along without raising the feet. The floors of polished wood are as smooth as glass, and this precaution is observed to prevent injury. There is a story to the effect that this Palace was formerly haunted by a ghost in the shape of a lady in white who made her appearance only when some member of the royal family·was about to depart from this life. At the gate of the Palace are two bronze horses with grooms.

On entering Berlin we were at once attracted to its magnificent boulevard, called Unter den Linden strasse, which runs from one end of the city to the other. The Royal Palace and many other splendid mansions, as well as shops, are situated on this street, at the head of which, where it enters a forest of grand old trees, is the Brandenburg gate, surmounted by a magnificent triumphal arch erected in 1789. On top of this arch is the car of victory, which Napoleon took to Paris, and returned after the battle of Waterloo. Just beyond this gate, in the edge of the grove, stands the new monument to commemorate the victory of the Germans over the French in their late war. It is very grand and beautiful. Its base is of polished stone, like the Scotch marble, with bronze entablatures on the four sides, representing in *bas-relief* a battle, the surrender, return home of the army, and their welcome reception. The likenesses of the Emperor William, Bismarck, and Von Moltke are readily recognized. Others, doubtless, are equally good. Next above these entablatures is a gallery surrounded by marble pillars, and next a tall column of granite or sandstone, embraced by three rows of cannon cut in the stone, pointing upward, and connected by wreaths, all in gold leaf. The whole is surmounted by a splendid statue of Victory, also in gold leaf, with a wreath in her right hand and a scepter in her left.

In the middle of Unter den Linden street is the colossal equestrian statue of Frederick the Great— one of the grandest monuments, no doubt, in Europe. The pedestal is of granite, twenty-five feet in height, on the four sides of which are bronze groups, life-size, of thirty-one of the leading generals and statesmen of the Seven Years' War. Over these, on each corner of the pedestal, are figures of Justice, Prudence, Fortitude, and Temperance; "between these are *bas-reliefs* representing different periods in the life of Frederick: the Muse teaching him history; Mercury giving him a sword; walking in the gardens of his Palace, surrounded by his favorite companions, greyhounds; playing on his flute; in the weaver's hut, and drawing the plan of a battle after his defeat at Rollin. On the front tablet is the following inscription: 'To Frederick the Great. Frederick William III., 1840, completed by Frederick William IV., 1851.' The equestrian statue is seventeen feet high, and most perfect in all its proportions; a mantle hangs from the monarch's shoulders, his stick hanging from his wrist; all is most perfect and true to life."

We have visited the Museum, at the entrance of which stands a fine bronze statue of the Amazon, and an enormous vase of polished granite sixty-six feet high. The city abounds in statues, the fronts of several of the mansions on Unter den Linden street being surmounted by them. The exterior front of the Museum is ornamented by frescoes, representing allegorically the creation of the world. The interior consists of three departments—the Antiquarian on the first floor, the Sculptures on the second, and the Picture Gallery on the third. The number of interesting things here is endless, and we cannot attempt any lengthy description. Among the noted pictures is Raphael's "Madonna Ancajani," representing the Virgin and child in the stable; a series of twélve paintings, by Van Eyck, called "The Worship of the Spotless Lamb;" "Io and the Cloud," and "Leda and the Swan," by Correggio; "Resurrection of Lazarus," by Rubens; and "St.

Anthony Embracing the Infant Saviour," by Murillo. We were particularly interested in many of the relics to be seen here, including Napoleon's hat and his decorations as Emperor, which, in haste to escape, he left in his carriage at Waterloo; also the walking cane, flute, and the uniform of Frederick the Great, which he wore on the day of his death, and a cast of his face after death; likewise the tobacco pipes and other articles which belonged to his father.

The principal shops here are unusually fine; and many of these are under or in an extensive arcade abounding in almost everything to attract the eye and invite the expenditure of money.

One evening, in the heart of the city, we went to a gorgeous beer garden, an open space capable of holding ten thousand people, surrounded by buildings with shade trees, and lighted by seventy thousand gas jets in every form of beauty almost that ingenuity could invent. It presented a perfect fairy scene; and there were two fine bands, one in a balcony on either side in the center, and they played alternately. Visitors could be seated or promenade at their pleasure.

An excursion of a few miles to Charlottenburg was very enjoyable. Here is a plain Palace built by Frederick I.; but what we went specially to see were the monuments of Frederick William III. and his Queen, Louise, so celebrated for her beauty, and a photograph of whose full length portrait is now before us. Their tomb and marble monumental statues are in a small Doric temple. The statues are separate, each in a reclining position, as upon a bed or lounge, and raised on a beautifully carved and paneled marble base. The works are considered

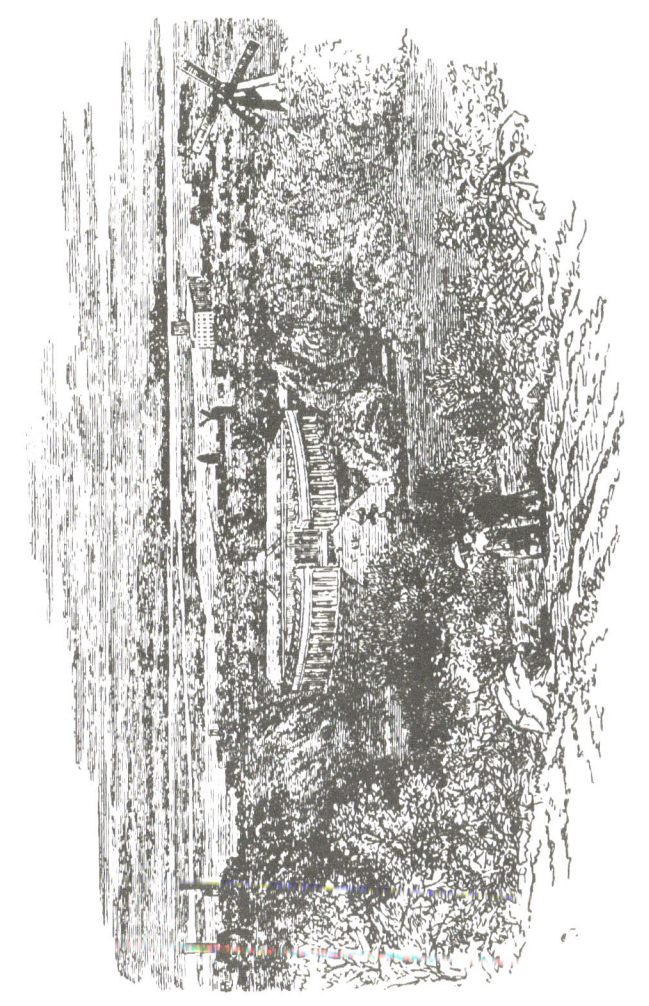

SANS SOUCI.

the masterpieces of Rauch, the sculptor previously mentioned in these sketches. The temple is located in one of the sweetest of groves.

On the 3d of August, in company with the Rev. Henry M. Field and niece, now on their tour around the world, and of his nephew, Lieutenant Field, on leave of absence from the United States steamship Franklin, we passed the day most agreeably at Potsdam, eighteen miles by rail from Berlin. There are here five royal residences, called, respectively, the Royal Palace, the New Palace, the Marble Palace, Babelsburg, and Sans Souci — all of which we visited. As some of these Palaces are two or three miles apart, we hired a coachman for the day. They are all situated in a beautiful park or garden, adorned with fountains and statuary. In the old Palace, or in Sans Souci, we saw some of the furniture used by Frederick the Great, including stuffed chairs, in some of which he used to have his dogs sit with him at table; and on the covering of one in which he died are spots stained by his blood, from having been bled in his last hours. The rooms containing this furniture are said to be nearly in the condition in which he left them. The apartments which Voltaire used to occupy when on his long visits to the King were also shown to us. The New Palace, erected by Frederick the Great after the Seven Years' War, is very costly and grand, and contains many fine paintings and other rare works of art. One great hall, called the Grotto, is a marvel of art and beauty. It is spacious, and lined throughout with shells and precious stones artistically arranged. For instance, flowers are represented by shells, amethyst. sapphire, amber, crystal, onyx, agate, coal, quartz. copper, silver, and gold, in their original state, etc.

The large chandeliers are entirely of white crystal. The fairies could not desire a more enchanting grotto. Sans Souci is approached by a succession of terraces, covered with vines and ornamental trees. There is a succession of low buildings with a colonnade, from which a fine view is obtained of the garden and adjacent palaces. Frederick the Great died here, where we saw the old clock, which he used himself to wind up, and which was stopped at the moment of his death, twenty minutes past two. Near by stands the famous historical windmill, which Frederick the Great desired to purchase, that he might pull it down and extend his gardens in that direction. The miller refusing to sell, the King brought suit against him and was defeated. He afterward erected the present windmill "as a monument of Prussian justice." In the vicinity of Sans Souci, also, there is a beautiful villa, called the Charlottenhof, built in Pompeian style, with a bath, fountains, statues, and bronzes, taken from the ruins of Pompeii. Here we entered two small rooms which Baron Von Humboldt occupied when residing with the King. His writing desk, chair, toilet stand, with comb, hair-brush, and small mirror, and other furniture, are seen as he left them

In the Garrison Church, an unpretending house of worship here, we stood by, and saw by the light of a candle, the metallic coffin of Frederick the Great. It is in a plain vault, to which we were conducted by the female custodian entrusted with the key to his tomb.

After an hour for lunch and rest, we went to the Babelsburg Palace, the most charming of all, where the Emperor and Empress now reside. In Germany it is customary to sleep singly, and, like us travelers, the Emperor has his single bedstead, and a very plain one indeed — a common low wooden article, such as you may buy anywhere in the shops. The walls of one small room are covered with a large number of horns and stuffed heads of wild animals, all slain by him in his earlier years. We were shown his walking stick, a rough twig with part of the bark peeled off, which he cut when a lad, and which he still uses in his garden walks. We felt like doing a little Yankee whittling on it; but presuming he prefers it as it is, we did not offer our services.

Of all the palaces we have yet seen, could we have our choice for a residence we should choose this. Taken with all its surroundings, its beautiful apartments furnished with everything in the way of art that heart could desire, the enchanting view of river, fountains, gardens of flowers, or other charming sight, no matter in which direction the eye is turned, it comes the nearest to what we might fancy Paradise to be of any place within our knowledge. Our advice is, if you go to Berlin do not fail to see Potsdam.

CHAPTER XX.

DRESDEN, August 16.—We came here from Berlin on the afternoon of the 4th instant, and were driven directly to a private boarding-house previously kindly recommended to us by Lorenzo Brentano, Esquire, United States consul, where we have been made comfortable and quite at home during our stay. The house is kept by the wife of a Hungarian officer, now absent on duty, to be gone two years. She is a lady of refinement, and has two beautiful children, a girl and boy. Dresden is pleasantly situated on both sides of the Elbe, the part called the "Old Town" being on the right and the "New Town" on the left bank of the river. The old stone bridge connecting the two towns is a magificent structure one thousand four hundred feet in length and thirty-six in width. "On the center pier a bronze crucifix has been erected to commemorate the destruction of the fourth pier from the side of the Alstadt by Marshal Davoust, to facilitate his retreat in 1814, and its restoration the same year by the Emperor of Russia." There is also a railroad, carriage and foot bridge half a mile further down.

We have spent a good deal of our time in the picture Galleries, which are among the finest in the world. Admission is free four days in the week. These Galleries, the Armory, and the Museum of Natural History are all contained in a building called the Zwinger, which "was originally intended as the vestibule of a new palace, which Augustus II. intended to erect in the early part of the eighteenth century, but was never carried further. It is a fine group of buildings surrounded by an inclosure planted with orange trees, and forming an elegant promenade, much frequented by the citizens." Only an artist may hope to give any satisfactory description of the pictures in these Galleries, the more noted of which have been often described. Here is Raphael's "Madonna di San Sisto," with its angelic faces, a separate room being devoted to its exhibition. It is being constantly copied and engravings and photographs of it are common. Holbein's "Madonna" is likewise exhibited in a separate room set apart for it. Some of Correggio's most celebrated pictures are seen here,—"The Virgin and the Infant Christ in the Manger;" "The Virgin and Child with Saint George;" "The Virgin and Child with Saint Francis;" and his "Recumbent Magdalen." Other noted pictures are the "Reclining Magdalen," by Bartoli; "Tribute Money," by Titian; "St. Cecilia," by Carlo Dolce; "Adoration of the Wise Men," "Marriage in Cana," and "Finding of Moses," by Paul Veronese; "Judgment of Paris," and "Garden of Love," by Rubens; "The Entombment," by Rembrandt; Van Dyck's portrait of "Old Parr," at one hundred and fifty-one years; "Bacchus and Child," by Guido; "The Vestal Virgin," by Angelica Kauffman; and "The Chocolate Girl." This last is a full-length portrait of a beautiful waiting maid, carrying a cup of coffee on a small waiter. Attracted by her great beauty, an Austrian nobleman made her his wife, and so she became famous as "La Belle Chocolatière."

The Military Museum is a store of interesting relics and curiosities. Here are all sorts of weapons, from the early ages to the present time. The trappings of the war horses are richly set with precious stones and gold and silver decorations, while the armor of their riders is fashioned to protect the human form in the fiercest contest with the spear or sword. We saw here the robes worn by Augustus the Strong at his coronation as King of Poland; also the horse-shoe which he broke by the pressure of his hand, his cuirass, weighing one hundred pounds, and his iron cap, twenty-five pounds. "He is said to have lifted a trumpeter in full armor, and held him aloft in the palm of his hand; to have twisted the iron bannister of a stair into a rope; to have made love to a coy beauty by presenting in one hand a bag of gold and breaking a horse-shoe with the other." We were not less interested in seeing the cocked hats of Peter the Great and Frederick the Great; also, Napoleon's boots, which he wore at the battle of Dresden, and the shoes he wore at his coronation. Goethe's note-book was also shown to us.

The Museum of Natural History afforded an hour's agreeable entertainment. The wonder of Dresden, however, is the "Green Vaults." These are in the basement, or on the ground floor of the Schloss, or Royal Palace. An admission fee of two thalers ($1.50) is charged for one to six persons. This is the treasury of the Saxon royal family, and is said to contain the most renowned collection of precious things on the continent of Europe. "It occupies eight rooms of the western wing of the Royal Palace, and comprises not only the jewels and the silver vessels of the royal family, but also a great many specimens of the finest works of art from the end of the sixteenth to the beginning of the eighteenth century." The name "Green Vaults" is supposed to have come from the green hangings which originally adorned the rooms. This rich collection of treasures was begun in the reign of Duke George the Bearded (1539;) but "the Elector Augustus, who reigned between the years 1553 and 1586, was the first who deposited in these vaults a large collection of various rare and valuable productions of art, which he partly inherited, purchased, or received as presents from other princely persons." What these sovereigns began their successors completed; "but it was not till the reign of Augustus the Strong, whose taste for the fine arts was cultivated and refined by travel and study, that this collection was raised to its present state of excellence." The first room is devoted to bronzes, the larger portion being statues, groups, and models of different sizes, and works of art, for the most part copies of ancient sculptures. The most remarkable of these is a crucifix, by John of Bologna. The expression given to the dying Saviour is very striking. Here is a small statue of Charles II. of England, known by the name of "St. George and the Dragon." It was worked out of a solid piece of iron by a blacksmith of Nuremberg, who lived in the sixteenth century. Next is a group representing "Hercules Crushing the Giant Antæus," supported by his mother, the earth. "A Nymph Bathing" is a pretty thing, and so is "Venus with the Mirror." Scores of other interesting objects elicit our attention as we pass around the room and enter the Cabinet of Ivories, which are very wonderful in construction. The art of carving is here carried to the highest point of ingenuity and excellence. Almost everything is represented from a goblet to a battle scene and allegorical groups of every nature. Here is a model of a Dutch Frigate, by James Zeller (1620.) On the sails the arms of Saxony and Brandenburg are carved in relief, and on the frigate the names of the Saxon Electors till the time of George I. The cordage is of gold wire. The pedestal represents Neptune seated in a shell, drawn by two sea horses, while behind him sits a Triton blowing a conch. One group of one hundred and forty-one figures in one solid piece of ivory, represents "The Fall of the Angels." It is the work of a Neapolitan Monk of the seventeenth century, and was presented by a Princess of Sicily to the Saxon Court. The third room is called the Chimney Room, from its having a superb enameled fire-place, which was arranged by the Court Jeweler in the reign of Frederick Augustus the Just (1782.) This fire-place is highly ornamented with *relievos* of precious stones set in mosaic. Here, also, are tables exquisitely inlaid with jasper, agate, chalcedony, cornelian, lapis lazuli, and other choice stones, made to represent flowers, fruits, leaves, birds, animals, etc. We see, too, an endless variety of paintings in enamel, embracing portraits of distinguished characters, "The Judgment of Solomon," "The Repast of the Olympian Gods," "The Crucifixion," as well as others. There is a collection of ambers of remarkable beauty. One large piece is carved to represent "The Three Graces;" and among the smaller objects are some pitchers of elegant form and workmanship. Cups, vases, and sugar-boxes are formed of ostrich eggs, set in silver gilt, and there is no end of other curious objects. The fourth, or Silver Room, is filled with all kinds of articles of silver and gold, including goblets, plates, jewel-boxes, clocks, rare coins, etc. We made special note of a Danish drinking cup in form of a horn, on which are admirably engraved, in nine rings, small mythological figures and crowns in gold enamel, adorned with rubies. It is of date 1650. The next room is called the Hall of Precious Things. It contains, among other objects, a large collection of cameos and other gems in rock crystal, and a large number of costly vessels, also cut out of stones of the second class. One is a rock crystal goblet once belonging to Martin Luther. We were particularly pleased with an ebony cabinet in the form of a Turkish palace, adorned with a great number of large and small plates of pure rock crystal. But the most striking object, perhaps, in this room is an immense pearl, as large as a hen's egg, arranged with smaller pearls, to represent the Court Dwarf of the King of Spain. In the sixth room, called the Corner Closet, are numerous other curiosities of almost every description. Here is seen the celebrated golden egg, a most surprising and ingenious work, intended for a scent box. "When opened on the bottom, a reservoir for perfumes is disclosed; when opened on top, at first is seen the yolk of an egg in gold and enamel; under this is a chicken of the same material, and inside this is a seal in the form of a Polish crown, richly adorned with small diamonds, pearls, and cornelian, on which is engraved a French device with the inscription, *Constant malgré l' Orage.* This crown also opens and discloses a diamond ring, under the largest stone of which is painted a burning heart and the motto, *Constance et Fidelité.*" In the Wood or Armory Room is a large collection of carvings in wood. The eighth is the Jewel Room, containing jewels valued at $15,000,000, including the Crown Jewels. Many of these are described in the catalogue, to which we are mainly indebted for the few descriptions here given. In one case we saw two rings which belonged to Martin Luther. On one of them is a small compass, on which is painted a skull of a dead body with a Latin inscription; the other is set with a small cornelian stone, on which are engraved a rose and a cross, the emblems adopted by Luther, and intended to signify that "a man's heart is in perfect peace when resting on the cross." It is said to have been worn by John George I. to the day of his death. In the same compartment is a gold ring with a stone bearing an eye; this ring belonged to Melancthon. Two other rings with small watches belonged respectively to Kings Frederick Augustus I. and Anthony. One glass shrine contains several fine canes, adorned with jewels; another, a magnificent collection of swords of state used by the Saxon Electors in the sixteenth century. The hilts of most of the swords are made of gold and enamel, adorned with precious stones. Some of the hilts are of rock crystal. There are many precious arms from the East, such as Turkish, Japanese, and Burmese swords and poignards, adorned in the highest manner; and among them we saw a splendid Polish saber, which belonged to John Sobieski. The mention of one other curiosity may suffice; this is the "Court of the Great Mogul," by Dinglinger. It represents the birthday of the Emperor of India in Delhi. In the center of a large silver slab, on a throne approached by steps, sits the Great Mogul. Around and before him are one hundred and thirty-two small figures done in gold and enamel in every variety of attitude. Here are represented deputations from the different Provinces of his Empire, who approach with their respective trains, doing homage and offering presents of horses, elephants and camels, splendidly decorated palankeens, vases, clocks, and services, all richly adorned with precious stones and executed in gold and enamel. Around the Emperor are his ministers and guards and three ambassadors in a kneeling posture on the steps. In the foreground is a balance which has reference to the ceremony of weighing the Great Mogul every year on this day and fixing the amount of tribute which each Province had to pay accordingly for the current year. Other designs represent thank and victory offerings. To accomplish this work, it is said to have taken Dinglinger, his brothers and sons, (not enumerated,) and fourteen other workmen, eight years, from 1701 to 1708, laboring incessantly. It was then brought to Augustus the Strong, who bought it for fifty-eight thousand four hundred and eighty-five thalers, (about $44,000.)

Something of the social life of the Germans may be seen at their beer gardens, where they resort for rest and recreation, and where one is always sure to hear fine music. Here all care for the time being seems to be dismissed, and in the presence of such tranquillity, even the nervous and hurrying American is constrained to pause and learn a useful lesson in animal economy. At some of these gatherings at the "Grosser Garten" we saw many German officers, whose fine physique and soldierly bearing excited our admiration. Indeed, whenever we met the military of Germany we were particularly impressed by the splendid appearance of both officers and men, who were generally large, muscular, and looking every inch the trained soldier. Supposing the Belgian, whom we have seen, to be a fair specimen of the French soldier, one need not wonder at the late triumph of Germany over France.

There are in Dresden many magnificent streets

128   SKETCHES OF TRAVEL.

with fine dwellings and shops, but Prager strasse is the principal street for shopping. Here is the place to purchase damask table linen and enameled porcelain of every description. The traveler who stops to see the beautiful enameled brooches and other kindred things here should go prepared to carry some of them away, for there are nowhere in Europe more charming or desirable objects to purchase.

CHAPTER XXI.

VIENNA, AUGUST 20.—After a pleasant sojourn of about two weeks in Dresden we left that city at 12:40 on the 16th of August, and arrived at Vienna near 8 o'clock next morning. The scenery along the river Elbe, between Dresden and Tschethin, a part of the country called Saxon Switzerland, is exceedingly bold and beautiful. Mounts Königstein and Lilienstein rise at some points to the height of twelve hundred feet in perpendicular columns, against which some of the inhabitants of the valley have built their houses, using those mountains for the rear walls thereof. These and many other houses on the way are quite odd in appearance, having in their roofs windows in the shape of eyes. Indeed, it is impossible to describe all the odd things that meet our sight, whether in country or city. All through Germany and Austria the costumes of the peasantry are more or less singular, and, as we have before remarked, it is a sight to behold the women, brown and stalwart, at work in the fields, reaping, mowing, gathering the crops, and doing men's work generally, even to shoveling dirt and propelling the wheelbarrow in labor on railroads and other highways. We have seen them sawing and splitting fire-wood, and carrying it, and also coal, in huge baskets, from the streets up one or more flights of stairs—loads that one would think too heavy for the strongest man. In one instance we observed a man and woman, supposed to be husband and wife, sawing and splitting wood together. The saw was rigged with a handle at each end, and it was a wonder to see how quickly they would put it through a large stick of hard wood. There was no wrangling here about "woman's rights,"—the woman being in every sense the equal of her husband. The women also attend the cattle, sheep, and geese in the fields, where there are no division fences. Of geese we have seen as many as two hundred in a single flock. It is laughable to see the railroad officials, all of whom are in uniform, as the train passes the smaller stations without stopping. At some of these, women as well as men are on guard, and as soon as the train nears the station, they may be seen standing erect and "dressed" as on parade, with hand to cap or hat by way of salute to the train guards, sometimes with one arm extended and pointing the way the train is going, as much as to say, "The road is clear; go ahead." We may be no safer on railroads here than in our own country; but somehow we get to feel that we are, owing perhaps to the much larger number of officers actively connected with the roads, both at the stations and on the trains, all of whom appear to understand their business thoroughly and to have an eye to the safety of passengers.

We reached Lissa about sundown, at which place we changed conductors; but time was allowed there for refreshments, and as our conductor was a gentleman wearing the uniform of an officer, and had been very polite to us, we invited him to join us in a glass of lager. This familiarity, as we afterward learned from an intelligent Bohemian lady, an English officer's wife whom we met there, was regarded as rather too democratic for this country, although she heartily approved of it. We ourselves, however, were innocent as General Grant would have been of anything out of place in this little act of courtesy, and we are free to say that we had no cause to regret it; for, through the good offices of that lady, or of the lager, or, more likely, of both combined, our conductor said a good word for us to his brother officer on the connecting train, and we had a whole compartment to ourselves all the way to Vienna, thus enabling us to secure as comfortable a night's rest as though we had been on a Pullman sleeping car.

We need not say that Vienna is an exceedingly beautiful and attractive city; and of course we started at once to see the prominent objects of interest in town and vicinity. What was the old city is only some three miles in circumference, and where its walls or fortifications once stood is now a fine boulevard. Its streets are comparatively narrow, and it has altogether an ancient appearance, while the new, exterior portion is airy, with wide streets and more elegant buildings. The new additions have increased the size of the city to twelve miles in circumference. We went first to the Imperial Painting Gallery, in the Upper Belvidere. It is in a fine palace, situated in a commanding position, with a spacious flower garden in front. There is a very large number of paintings in the different rooms, nearly all of the celebrated old masters being represented. We took note of several with which we were particularly pleased, among them the celebrated "Ecce Homo," by Titian; "The Annunciation," by Paul Veronese; "Diana and Callisto with the Nymphs," by Titian; "The Saviour at the House of Simon the Leper, with Mary Magdalene at his Feet;" and "St. Andrew Refusing the Emperor Theodosius admission into the Church of Milan," by Rubens. Next we proceeded to the Armor Historical Gallery in the Lower Belvidere, where there is an extensive collection of armor of every description and a Museum of countless other things, including a variety of ancient musical instruments, jewelry, Eastern costumes, etc. An hour or two was passed here agreeably.

Schönbrunn, the summer residence of the Emperor, is situated a short distance from the city. It is a magnificent palace, and the grounds around it are exceedingly beautifnl, being laid out into flower gardens and groves of shade trees, trimmed along the gravel walks to present perpendicular walls of green foliage, and adorned with sculpture and costly fountains. After being shown through the palace, which is furnished with everything to please the eye, we strolled through the grounds or rested in quiet contemplation, admiring their loveliness, and thinking of dear friends far away. In one of the rooms of the palace we saw a portrait of the unfortunate Maximilian, painted when he was a lad twelve or fourteen years of age, and a marble bust of him as an adult. How sad the reflections excited by these likenesses! Induced by Napoleon III. to assume the scepter of power in a foreign land; Emperor in name only, for a brief period; betrayed, condemned to death, and shot; his poor, devoted wife distracted, overwhelmed with grief, a hopeless maniac! It was melancholy also to remember that it was in this palace that the young Napoleon II., Duke of Reichstadt, died. In the vaults of the Church of Capuchins we looked upon his coffin, which is of copper, bearing a raised cross. Near by are the coffin of his grandfather, Emperor Francis I., and those of Joseph I., (this is of silver,) Joseph II., Maria Theresa, and some eighty others of the royal family. The latest is that of an uncle of the present Emperor. He died only a few months before our visit.

The Cathedral of St. Stephen is the largest and most graceful perhaps in the city. Its spire, said to be one of the tallest in the world, is very beautiful. From near its top a view may be had of the Danube on the margin of the city, and of the great battle-fields of Wagram, Lobau, and Esling. Our guide-book states that the crypt of this church has been the burying place of the royal family for centuries, but for the last two hundred years only the bowels of the dead have been interred here, their bodies having been deposited in the Church of the Capuchins, and their hearts in the Church of the Augustines, which is another of the handsomest churches in the city. This last is specially noted for Canova's celebrated monument to the Archduchess Christine. "It consists of a pyramid of marble thirty feet high, in the center of which is an opening representing the entrance to the vault. This is reached by two broad marble steps, which are the base of the pyramid. Ascending the steps is a figure representing Virtue bearing an urn, which contains the ashes of the deceased. By her side are two little girls carrying torches; behind them is a figure of Benevolence supporting an old man bowed down by age and grief. A little child accompanies him, the very picture of innocence and sorrow. On the other side is an admirably drawn figure of a mourning genius, and at his feet crouches a melancholy lion. Over the entrance to the vault is a medallion of the Archduchess, held up by Happiness, while a genius is presenting her with a palm, indicative of success." We have a photograph of this monument. We visited both St. Stephen's and the Church of the Augustines, as well as that of the Capuchins.

Prader strasse is a grand boulevard, both for riding and walking; and the Volksgarten is also a place of great resort, especially in the evening, when Strauss' band plays. There are also other public gardens in other parts of the city. In the People's Garden, where we passed one evening, there are two fine equestrian statues of Austrian Emperors.

Our last day's sight-seeing in Vienna, or rather in its vicinity, was planned by our United States minister, Hon. Godlove S. Orth, and admirably conducted by him, who, with his wife, met us at Mödling, not far from their country residence, twelve or fifteen miles from the city, and went with us several miles further on to Laxenburg, another summer residence of the Emperor; thence to the fortress of the Empress Maria Theresa, called the Castle of Francenburg. The Palace of Laxenburg is comparatively modest for a royal residence, and the Emperor residing there at the time of our visit, it was not open to strangers. We were, however, admitted into all parts of the little castle, which was erected by Maria Theresa, in imitation of a feudal castle, and is a complete museum of antiquities. It stands in the center of an artificial lake, which adds greatly to the beauty of the surrounding landscape, all within the grounds of the Palace. In one of the rooms there is a *fac-simile* of a chamber of torture, with its instruments, and in a small dungeon below, a full-sized figure of a man, representing a prisoner in a sitting posture; and as we stood gazing at him, we were startled by the sudden rising of his right arm and movement of his body as though alive. We soon saw that this was produced by a secret spring, touched by our guide unobserved by us; but the trick was well calculated to frighten one for the moment.

From Laxenburg we returned with Mr. and Mrs. Orth to Mödling, where their carriage was waiting to convey us all to their house in the mountains. Here we spent the remainder of the day, taking dinner with the family, consisting of the parents and their son and daughter, both nearly of age. They occupy a rented house, formerly occupied as a monastery, delightfully situated upon the side of a sharp hill, from which a charming view of mountain and valley is obtained. We are indebted to their kindness and courtesy for a full measure of enjoyment. On our way back to the railroad station we stopped to see the ruins of the old Castle of Lichtenstein, and reached our lodgings at Hotel Tauber early in the evening.

CHAPTER XXII.

MUNICH, August 22.—We were so much delighted with Vienna that we were reluctant to leave, and it is not a matter of surprise that so many of our patriots are willing to take up their residence there as Ministers of the United States. We were eight hours in reaching Salzburg, our next stopping place on the 20th of August, the hottest day we have felt in Europe, and one of the few in which summer clothing such as we wear at home would have been acceptable. The scenery along the route a part of the way was very beautiful. Salzburg, it may be remembered, is the place where the Emperors of France and Austria had a friendly meeting in the summer of 1867. It is situated on the swift river Salza, a considerable part of the town being built against the side of a steep mountain. There is a most romantic old castle here, now used principally as a barrack. It was built in the eleventh century, and long occupied as the residence and stronghold of some of the nobility. It stands on a high bluff, or ridge of rocks, overlooking the city. This ledge was tunneled in 1767 by the Archbishop Sigismund. We were driven through this tunnel out a short distance into the country, and also through the principal parts of the town, passing Mozart's house and monument. The streets are very narrow, and the houses quaint looking. The costumes of the people are peculiar. The women wear short gowns and petticoats with red or yellow aprons and black silk bandeaux.

A carriage ride of twenty miles, much of it on the banks of the Salza, which is filled by the melting of the snow plainly visible on the mountains, while the valleys through which we passed to Lake Königs were smiling with the harvests and fruits of the season, was novel and romantic indeed. It took us among a strange people, the Tyrolese, where the Austrian money with which we started was at a discount, and where we were rowed by two strong women, with one man at the helm, for several miles on this lake, winding around between mountains seven thousand feet high on either side, and looking at some points as though about to fall upon us. We stopped at St. Bartholomew, a hunting seat of the King of Bavaria, where there is a public house and a small chapel. Notwithstanding the great height of the mountains bordering this lake, which are covered generally with low evergreen trees, and although in no place is the lake more than about half a mile in width, the water is said to be, as it looked, very deep. So high, steep, and near together are the mountains that the reverberations from a small gun of the caliber of a horse-pistol were nearly as loud as the report of a cannon. We returned to the place of starting on the lake, the time occupied in each direction being three-quarters of an hour. On the way back to town some of our party had a still more novel experience in visiting the Hallein salt mines. On arriving there some fifteen or twenty travelers, of whom the writer was one, made preparations to enter. The ladies were required to put on caps and trowsers, the latter being large enough to admit their skirts, minus crinoline, while the gentlemen were furnished with frocks, overalls, and felt hats — both sexes being rigged out, also, each with a leather apron tied on behind, and each provided with a dull oil lamp or tallow candle to light them on their way up an inclined plane through a narrow tunnel, a mile, more or less, into the side of a high hill or mountain. As one may well imagine, we presented a laughable appearance, and our most intimate acquaintances would have been unable to recognize us in this queer uniform. One thing, indeed, which puzzled us not a little was to divine the object of putting our aprons on behind instead of in front; but on this point we were not long kept in the dark, albeit, we soon found ourselves in a very dark place. This cone-shaped tunnel, in which car-rails were laid, was of just sufficient width and height to admit of our walking comfortably in single file; but at distances of fifteen or twenty rods apart were recesses deep enough for standing room when the cars were passing, and, by stooping slightly, persons could pass each other in the narrowest part of the way. On the ground, along one side of the tunnel, runs an iron pipe, through which salt water is drawn from a lake in the interior, toward which, led by our guide, lamps and candles in hand, we were walking to the number of eight or ten (the rest of the company having preceded us) when we heard a rumbling sound, which we supposed to be of falling water, or from the working of machinery in the mines. Instantly, however, we were undeceived by a cry from the German guide, interpreted by one of our party, that a car was coming and that we must get out of the way, the guide at the same time turning and rushing by us as though frightened half out of his wits, thus increasing our alarm, while we all also turned and ran with the utmost speed we could command in this dark hole, and just succeeded in reaching one of those recesses above described when a car, a sort of wooden horse, loaded with passengers, flew past us! What the result might have been had we failed in this run for life no one knows; but in all probability some or all of us would have been seriously if not fatally wounded. In a few minutes another and then another car shot by, while we were debating whether we should proceed or return. Finally, one stout Dutchman and his wife, quite in a rage, not unjustly, turned back; but being assured that there was now no danger to apprehend, the rest of us again took up our line of march. It can hardly be doubted, however, that it was a foolhardy undertaking, since, besides the risk of broken bones from the rail cars, we might all have been engulfed by the closing up of the tunnel, which was walled or lined over the top and sides only a short distance from its mouth. The rest of the way it was left precisely as excavated through the salt earth, which appeared to be of about the solidity of hard pin-gravel. No matter, we had enlisted for the campaign, therefore we pushed on, and soon reached a point where our leather aprons were brought into use. First, however, we think we came to the lake, which, surrounded by a row of dull lamps, appeared to be an acre or so in extent, and entering a boat we were rowed across it. It looked black and tasted very salty. Everything here looked black, except the dim lamplight, which served only to make darkness visible. We will not say that we thought we were in the infernal regions, but we will admit that a sort of shudder came over us lest, as out of a deep sleep, we might be in some such place! From this landing we now prepared to descend into a vast pit, seventy feet deep from the top over our heads—the distance from where we stood to the bottom being forty or fifty feet. A large, smooth piece of timber, with a rope for a guard, extended at about the inclination of an ordinary staircase—if anything, a little steeper—to the bottom, and this was to serve as our carriage-way. Each gentleman now being furnished with a thick leather hand-shoe to protect his right hand in grasping the rope, our guide seated himself astride this beam and slid down a few feet, bracing himself to allow us to follow suit. This, with lamps in our left hands, we did at once—the ladies (our special companion not among them) being sandwiched between and holding to the shoulders of the gentleman who clasped the rope. The word was given, and off we shot into the darkness below. Our guide managed in some way to check our fall so that no bones were fractured; but, although this may be a very good way to prove the utility of leather aprons, especially when worn behind, we are not prepared to recommend the performance, either for healthy exercise or amusement. Extending from the bottom of this pit there is a shaft in which the miners descend five hundred feet further into the bowels of the earth; but having no desire to explore regions so far *inland*, we did not ask to enter. After collecting some specimens of rock salt, which lay here in heaps, ascending by a steep flight of stairs, we all mounted astride a wooden horse, sandwiched as before, and by our own momentum were carried swiftly down the rail into daylight, perfectly content with our first experience of salt mines and inclined planes.

It was half-past nine in the evening when we reached our hotel in Salzburg; and the interest of our ride was heightened by signal fires kindled high up on the sides or tops of several mountains far apart (in commemoration, we understood, of some event,) and other demonstrations—in one place, for instance, a beautiful floral arch, under which we had the honor of passing, having been erected over the highway.

A ride of five hours by rail on the following day took us to Munich, this beautiful capital of Bavaria, of which and its many interesting objects it will be our pleasure in our own good time to write.

CHAPTER XXIII.

MUNICH, August 31.—Some parts of this city may be said to be emphatically on the river, for—

> "The torrent flow
> Of Isar, rolling rapidly"

under many of its houses, shops, and manufacturing establishments, furnishes excellent motive power. The principal part of the city, however, lies on the northwest side. It is said to be nearly seventeen hundred feet above the level of the sea; and being not far from the mountains, it should, and doubtless does, command a pure and healthy atmosphere in all seasons of the year. Our stay here has been very pleasant, the more so from being in home-like quarters at a private boarding-house kept by a very competent lady, Fräulein Dahlweiner, who received very prominent notice a year or two ago through a Book of Travels by Helen Hunt. Although no doubt kindly intended by the authoress, the manner in which she is made to figure in the book is very distasteful to her, as she did not hesitate to signify to us in lending us the book to read.

The first day after our arrival was Sunday, when there was a grand military review by the King, Louis II., of Bavaria. Extending for a mile or more from the western boundary of the city is a level plain covering many acres, and admirably situated for such a display. The troops,— infantry, artillery, and cavalry, — with splendid bands, assembled at the further side, which was bordered by a hill, lined with spectators. The greater crowd of spectators, however, was on the south side, near the city, where we were content to take our stand, especially as no carriage was to be had, and we walked over a mile to this point. After maneuvering for some time in the distance, the troops came down in grand array, with colors flying, now with stirring music of drum and fife, next with that of a full brass band, of which there were several, and then would come the shrill sound of the trooper's horn, conveying some order readily comprehended and obeyed. The King and his staff, all mounted on splendid steeds, and in gorgeous uniforms, took position nearly in front of us, thus affording us a satisfactory sight as the various regiments passed in review. The King is a large, fine-looking man, with a full, round face, and light complexion. Near the close, the Queen, an elegant-looking lady, in company with two or three other ladies in a carriage, made her appearance on the field, when they were saluted by the King and his staff and loudly cheered by the crowd. The King was also vociferously cheered by the citizens, who were out in such numbers that few could have stayed at home. In the afternoon we atoned somewhat for our wickedness of the forenoon by attending service at the English Episcopal church, whose temporary pastor from England was a boarder at our house.

We have visited here two or three of the finest cathedrals we have anywhere seen, in one of which is a large crucifix suspended from the center of the roof; and in some or all of them are private altars set around the sides, very richly ornamented, and abounding in choice pictures, statues, statuettes, etc. It was an odd sight here to see priests in their robes marching in a solemn manner through the streets, headed by attendants, also in caps and long gowns, bearing a crucifix and lanterns elevated before them.

There is a great deal of interest to be seen here, and we have been quite industrious in going to one or more places every day. The Museum must be one of the most extensive and interesting in Europe. Almost every old thing that could be thought of may be seen there, including all kinds of ancient armor, furniture, jewelry, coins, and statuary. The Glyptothek (Sculpture Building) is a fine edifice, plain outside, but highly finished and beautiful within. It has a number of galleries, and is filled with sculpture—some of the statues and busts being remarkably fine. The old Pinakothek is the gallery of old paintings, which rank no doubt with those of the best galleries in other cities. We have been many times to this gallery, and could spend weeks in it agreeably in looking at the pictures, numbering, it is said, nearly thirteen hundred. A great many of the paintings are by Rubens, while there are some by Murillo, Dürer, Van Dyck, Guido, Carlo Dolce, Correggio, and many other artists of the old school. Murillo's four celebrated pictures of Italian beggar children are here, and we have obtained photographs of them. One room contains several thousand original designs by Michael Angelo, Rubens, Correggio, Dürer, Rembrandt, and others of the old masters. The new Pinakothek, like the old, is a magnificent structure, and contains fifty-two rooms filled with modern paintings and other works of art. The portrait of Lola Montez, which formerly hung in the Gallery of Beauties in the Royal Palace, is now in a room here devoted mainly to paintings on porcelain, which are remarkable for their beauty. We may remark in passing that we have seen the neat frame house which Lola Montez occupied when she was on such familiar terms with the late King. Happy as we are to gaze upon the celebrated works of the old masters, we are free to say that we enjoy the modern paintings we see here quite as well if not better. Whether on canvas, glass, or porcelain, it would seem impossible to excel these modern pictures. We have seen nowhere anything more perfect or more exquisitely beautiful. Most especially do we admire many of the landscape paintings and descriptions of rural life. Here was one of a little girl, which we imagined might be a picture of a dearly beloved one away across the water. She is represented as sitting down in the grass of a meadow, with straw hat on and red umbrella over her head, plucking buttercups and daisies. Her face was beautiful, and she appeared happy as a lark. The pictures of the Swiss and Tyrolese scenery, embracing lake, mountain, hill, and valley, are superb. In one room, peculiarly constructed as regards the light, there are twelve or fifteen very large paintings, reaching from the ceiling nearly to the floor, and filling the room — all descriptive of Eastern cities and country landscape. Their mellow, yellowish light casts over one a feeling of listless drowsiness; and thus surrounded, it would not be strange were we for the moment to believe ourselves actual travelers in those distant lands.

We went one day to the Art Exhibition Gallery, where there is a large collection of paintings for sale —all modern, and mostly, it is presumed, by German artists. The one we should prefer—the price of it being about $400—represents Beethoven at a piano, with four of his friends listening enraptured by his music. It is a perfect gem.

The Royal Palace, too, is filled with pictures, in one room of which we saw fourteen large historical paintings arranged after the manner of those in the rotunda of our Capitol. There are two rooms, called Halls of the Beauties, devoted exclusively to portraits of beautiful women. In company with us on our visit to this Palace were the English pastor already mentioned and another English gentleman who had spent thirty years as a teacher of English in Munich. The pastor facetiously called him our "guide, professor, and friend," and he was entitled to be so considered, for he was very efficient as a guide; as a professor, he had taught several of the royal ladies, whose portraits were before us; and he was very friendly in his bearing toward us all. He gave us the names of many of these beauties, some of whom are still living, and all, we believe, are of modern times. The floors of some of the rooms are of polished marble. In one is an ancient ivory chandelier, made by one of the Electors of Maximilian I.; in another, costly tapestry, filling five large panels, besides a piece composing a magnificent bedspread to the bed here occupied by Napoleon in 1809. In the gold embroidery, which cost eight hundred thousand florins, forty persons were constantly employed fifteen years. In the Throne Room are twelve large gilt bronze statues, costing five hundred ducats each. (A ducat is about two dollars and twenty-eight cents, and a florin forty cents.) In the Antiquarium is a large collection of Egyptian, Roman, Greek, and German antiquities, all more or less interesting. The Treasury Room is loaded with precious jewels, valuable stones, and other costly articles. The Chapel is highly adorned and contains many valuable articles appropriate to the place. We might speak of the many celebrated paintings seen here, but our recollection of them is too imperfect to admit of our doing justice to them. In the Court is a curious grotto of shells, with busts of females, made or covered with small shells, presenting the appearance, at a little distance, of persons recovered from small pox. Under the arch of the entrance-way is a stone weighing three hundred and sixty-four pounds, and in the wall three spikes — one at the height of twelve feet, one at nine and a half, and the third a little lower. Duke Christopher, son of Albert III., is said to have hurled this stone to a great distance; and, showing his agility in leaping, the upper spike marks the point where his heel struck in leaping from the ground. The heel of Prince Conrad touched at the place of the second, and Prince Philippe's at the third nail.

We have been shown through the Royal Foundry, where we saw models of the statues of Washington, Jefferson, Marshall, Clay, Benton, Everett, Lincoln, and other Americans, and also of the bronze doors leading from the rotunda of our Capitol. We likewise saw portions of the bronze statue of Seward now being cast for the city of New York.

RUHMESHALLE.

One evening we went with our pastor and professor to a lager beer brewery, where one helps himself to a mug holding between one and two quarts, and gets it filled with beer from the tank. There were ladies along, and they were rather averse to partaking of the delicious beverage in so rustic a manner out of the common mug; but truth (so precious to some travelers that they are very sparing of it) compels us to record that the mug, or jug, as it is called here, was returned empty.

We spent a few hours delightfully one evening at the theater, where we heard and saw performed Wagner's opera of "Tannhäuser." The curtain rose at six and the play was over by ten o'clock.

One beautiful afternoon we were driven beyond the city a mile or more to see the famous statue of Bavaria and Ruhmeshalle (Hall of Fame.) This fine hall, situated on high ground, "consists of a large Doric portico of Bavarian marble, forming three sides of a quadrangle and an open side, in the center of which rises Schwanthaler's colossal statue of Bavaria, about one hundred feet high, including the pedestal. There are forty-eight columns, with busts of eminent Bavarians. In the tympana are female statues, representing Bavaria, the Palatinate, Swabia, and Franconia, and in the frieze are upward of ninety metopes adorned with figures of victory and with reliefs symbolical of the arts and occupations of civilized society." The statue, as it is well known, represents a female standing by the side of a lion, also of colossal size, in a sitting posture. It is ascended by a flight of forty-nine steps in the interior. Eight persons at one time may be comfortably seated within this lady's head; and it is said that as many as twenty-nine men and two boys were crowded within it, at one and the same time, on the day the statue was raised. There are many other monuments, not as conspicuous, but equally attractive, here, as ornaments of the various public squares and principal streets, which are spacious and beautiful. There is the Charles Gate and Gate of Victory, the latter, especially, a most imposing structure, "built after the model of Constantine's Triumphal Arch at Rome." It is crowned by a colossal statue of Bavaria in a triumphal chariot, harnessed with four lions. Finer still is the Propylæum, "a triumphal arch in the old Doric style, with *bas-reliefs*, commemorating the modern Greek War of Independence and King Otho." The equestrian statues of Louis I. and Maximilian II., both of colossal size, are specially grand. There are also monuments here to Goethe, Schiller, and other distinguished Germans. Altogether, we are charmed with Munich.

CHAPTER XXIV.

ZURICH, September 8.—We left our boarding-house in Munich at half-past six on the morning of the 1st instant. It rained hard when we started, but the clouds soon disappeared, and the afternoon was very pleasant. At Lindau, where we changed from the cars to the steamboat on Lake Constance, there is a fine harbor formed by substantial circular walls, quite ornamental, leaving an opening only sufficient for the passage of vessels. Upon the abutment of the wall at one side of this opening stands a light-house, and on the other, sitting on a high pedestal, is a colossal lion, looking seaward. The effect is both striking and beautiful. Near the steamboat landing there is a monument to Maximilian II. The lake is thirty-five miles long and eight miles wide. The Rhine passes through it, as the channel of the Rhone goes the whole length of Lake Leman. The shores are lined with small villages and country villas, presenting a charming picture. Our sail on the lake to Romanshorn was delightful. Here we took the cars for Zurich, arriving at half-past four, after a most agreeable passage. Remembering that this was the day of a golden wedding of some of our relatives in the old Pine Tree State, we celebrated it in a suitable manner in our snug compartment on the train, after leaving Romanshorn. Our kind landlady in Munich, Fräulein Dahlweiner, had provided us with a nice lunch, consisting of ham sandwiches, cold chicken, bread, pears, peaches, and grapes, and availing ourselves of a short stop at a small station, we got our lager glass filled with *vin ordinaire*, so that we were enabled to do full honors to the occasion — drinking the health of the happy couple, "and all their family."

Between Munich and Lindau the scenery is not remarkable; but from Romanshorn to Zurich it is picturesque and beautiful. The land along the road is all highly cultivated, and men and women were busily engaged gathering the crops and preparing the ground for winter grain. On our arrival at Zurich we were driven to the Hôtel Bauer au Lac; but not having telegraphed, the best accommodations that could be offered us were two single bedrooms on the fifth floor, in the attic, which we accepted for the night, with the promise of a good room next day. This settled, we hastened to the consul's office for our letters, which we were most happy to receive from home, and then, seating ourselves on the margin of the lake in front of our hotel, we devoured them with a keen appetite, at the same time enjoying the beauties of the lake. On the following morning we called again at the office of our consul, S. H. M. Byers, Esquire, from Iowa, and were soon acquainted with each other. He had left his office when we called last evening. On his invitation we went, by steamboat, with him to his villa, five miles up the lake, and took dinner with the family, consisting of himself, wife, and two children, both born in Switzerland. They had as guests, also, Mr. Young, United States consul at Manheim, and his wife by a second marriage, an interesting German lady. The place rented by Mr. Byers was formerly occupied as a monastery, and goes under the name of "Wangensback." It forms part of a vineyard eight hundred years old. The sides of the house are covered with grape-vines loaded with grapes, which are protected from the birds by gauze network. In the surrounding fields the vines are not trained over trellisses, but on poles, six or eight feet long, driven into the ground; and from a little distance the vineyards look like New England corn-fields. There are few or no fences to guard them; but the law provides a severe penalty for the theft of even a single bunch of grapes. The residence chosen by Mr. Byers and his accomplished wife is just such a one as a poet would naturally choose; and he devotes all his leisure time to literary pursuits. He has held his office about six years, during which he has taken much pains to collect information about Switzerland, and has embodied it in a small volume just published. He first became known, we believe, as a writer by his song of "Sherman's March to the Sea," which the General has inserted in the second volume of his "Memoirs." It was written while a prisoner in Columbia, South Carolina, where, and in Libby Prison, he was confined some sixteen months. It shows how trifling a circumstance, comparatively, sometimes changes the current of a man's life. His song having been brought, incidentally, to General Sherman's notice, he at once sent for and attached him to his staff, he having then just escaped from the Columbia prison, where "there was an excellent glee club among the prisoners, who used to sing it well, with an audience often of rebel ladies." It consists of five stanzas and a chorus, commencing:

>Our camp-fires shone bright on the mountain
>   That frowned on the river below,
>As we stood by our guns in the morning,
>   And eagerly watched for the foe;
>When a rider came out of the darkness
>   That hung over mountain and tree,
>And shouted, "Boys, up and be ready!
>   For Sherman will march to the sea!"

The war over, he was in a favorable position for preferment, with influential friends to present his claims, and very soon he received the important appointment he now holds. Well, after dinner, at a seasonable hour, he returned to town with us and kindly assisted in our being established at the Pension Neptun, a delightful boarding house on the margin of the city and lake. Here we had little to do except to rest. Zurich is eligibly situated at the foot of the lake, extending for some distance along either side both of the lake and of the river

Limmet, its northern outlet. Many of the streets are wide; in the elevated parts there are fine promenades, presenting charming views of the lake and snow-clad mountains beyond, and there are numerous elegant residences, as well as large manufactories, public buildings, and churches. The University and Polytechnic Buildings are very prominent, as are also the Town Library and the great Cathedral. It was in this Cathedral, built in the eleventh or twelfth century, that Zuinglius began the Reformation. It is very plain and nearly destitute of ornaments in the interior. The Church of St. Peter, where Lavater used to hold forth, is a very common looking structure. This learned philosopher and divine, it may be remembered, died from a shot fired by a French soldier in the battle of Zurich, 1779.

In the old Arsenal many interesting relics are exhibited, among them what purport to be the battle-axe, sword, casque, and coat-of-mail of Zuinglius, and William Tell's bow which he used in shooting the apple from his son's head. The greatest curiosities we saw here are in the Museum, being relics of the inhabitants who lived away back in the age of barbarism, and, as a means of protection against their enemies, built their dwellings on piles in the lake. These relics have from time to time been found in the lake, and have been carefully preserved. Among them are rude earthen cooking utensils, hammers, arrows, and hatchets of stone, awkward looking fish-hooks, finger rings, and other articles.

The street sights are odd. Here are dogs harnessed into carts, pulling like good fellows, with their masters or mistresses, who assist in drawing heavy loads;

women carrying upon their heads large tubs filled with wine and beer bottles. The dress of the common people is different from any we have seen elsewhere — every Canton in Switzerland has its peculiar costume, differing one from the other; and here is a truck so long that it requires a man with a rudder in the rear end to guide it through the streets. Another noticeable thing is the absence of soldiers, with the sight of whom we had become so familiar, particularly in Germany and Austria.

We have spent a part of two days in a trip to Ragatz, three hours by rail from Zurich, where we were most happy to meet an esteemed acquaintance and friend, Rudolph Schleiden, LL. D., formerly for many years the minister from Bremen to the United States. Indeed, we went there purposely to see him, as, in response to a dispatch from us, he telegraphed: "I am here, and most happy to learn that I may expect you." He stood ready at the door of the Quellenhoff to receive us, as we alighted from our carriage. Of course, we talked over old affairs, particularly in reference to the Bremen Postal Convention of 1853, with which he and the writer had much to do. Both were advocates of low postage, and immediately agreed on a project, which was confirmed by the proper authorities, reducing the letter rate between the United States and Bremen from twenty to ten cents — twenty cents being then the lowest rate from the United States to any part of Europe, and this applied only to the city of Bremen. The next lowest rates were twenty-four cents to Great Britain and thirty cents to Germany. Now five cents takes a letter to any part of Europe. For several years after his departure from the United States, Dr. Schleiden served as a member of the

Prussian Parliament. His residence is at Freibourg, Baden.

Dinner over, Dr. Schleiden called a carriage and we rode two miles or more into the gorge of Tamina, an opening in the mountain where the walls, two hundred and fifty feet in height, come so near together at the top that in some places one may step across from one side to the other. For much of the way there is space only for the carriage road at the side and above the rapid stream which is one of the principal tributaries of the Rhine. At the end of the carriage-way is an old monastery, now used for a hospital and bathing house. From here we walked about three hundred yards further up the gorge to a hot spring, which we reached by turning into a dark tunnel, dug through the solid rock, at right angles from the stream, a distance of five or six rods. We drank of the water, which is as hot as one usually likes to take his tea. We did not detect any taste of sulphur or other mineral; therefore, we conclude that if the water is heated from the regions of his Satanic majesty, some means have been devised to avoid the smell of brimstone. This water is carried in wooden pipes, securely encased in masonry, to one or more of the hotels in the village, where it is used for bathing—hundreds of invalids resorting thither every year to try its healing qualities. It reaches the baths, two or three miles distant, with only two degrees less of heat than it possesses when it comes out of the mountain.

The scenery around Ragatz and for much of the way between there and Zurich is grand beyond description. The road takes us along the full length of the narrow Lake of Wallenstadt twelve miles, and between high rugged mountains. The valley through which we passed is loaded with its grain, corn, and fruits of various kinds; and the people appeared to be in the enjoyment of almost perfect happiness, so far removed are they from the busy, bustling world.

CHAPTER XXV.

LUCERNE, SEPTEMBER 13.—We were so pleasantly situated in Zurich that we would gladly have tarried there longer; but we must get over the mountains to Chamouni before cold weather, and there is little time to spare. A ride of one hour and a half by railroad brought us to Lucerne, where we find ourselves at another excellent boarding house, located, with reference to the lake, similarly to our house in Zurich. We passed through Zug and one or two other villages, and the scenery all the way is very beautiful. Lucerne is situated at the northeastern end of the lake of that name, and is separated by the river Reuss, which is spanned by three bridges, two of which are curiosities in their way. They are covered, and on the ceiling of one of them "are numerous pictures representing episodes in the lives of St. Leger and St. Maurice, patron saints of the city." The other "is ornamented with thirty-six pictures representing the Dance of Death." By the side of the latter, in the middle of the river, there is an ancient and picturesque tower, in which the archives of the city are kept. The old wall of the city on the land side, surmounted by numerous watch-towers, still stands, extending around from shore to shore, and from this wall, which is mostly on high ground, a charming view of the city, lake, and mountains is obtained. On the left is Mount Righi and on the right Mount Pilatus. There is a railroad from Vitznau on the lake to the top of the Righi; but we felt safe in the village and concluded not to go there. While weighing the matter a poor German girl fell from a point near the summit and was killed. No one saw her fall, but it was supposed that she lost her balance in reaching for flowers. This circumstance may have turned the scale against our going, but we knew we must climb high mountains before reaching the valley of Chamouni, and from these we hope to get extended views, equal, at least, to any from the Righi.

The principal object of attraction here is "Thorwaldsen's Lion," of colossal size, cut in high relief out of the side of a sandstone ledge. He was a native of Denmark, and at that time (1821) engaged in his profession at Rome, whence he sent the model, and the work was executed by Ahorn, of Constance. The figure of the Lion is twenty-eight feet long and eighteen feet high. He "holds the fleur-de-lis in his paws, which he endeavors to protect with his last breath, his life-blood oozing from a wound made by a spear which still remains in his side." This monument, as appears by a Latin inscription under the figure, is dedicated to the officers (twenty-six) and soldiers (seven hundred and sixty) of the Swiss Guards who died in Paris in 1792 defending the royal cause. It is in every respect unique. It has for its foundation and support the solid ledge, which rises thirty feet, more or less, perpendicularly, overhung with evergreen vines, and at the base is a pool of spring water within a railing. Near by is what they call the Glacier Gardens, where immense basins have been worn in the ledge by the action of heavy bowlders moved by the falling waters.

The most attractive shops here are those of wood and ivory carvings, which, as everybody knows, are very wonderful. They show great ingenuity and industry.

An excursion by steamboat to Fluelen, the southern end of the lake, and back occupied one day full of enjoyment. Lucerne, regarded as the most beauful in Switzerland, is also called the Lake of the Four Cantons; and it extends around between the mountains for many miles, presenting, with its arms —to Kussnacht northerly and southerly to Alpnacht—somewhat the shape of a cross. The boat stops at many landings, and the traveler may, if he choose, rest at any one of them and take a subsequent boat on his return ticket. We landed first at Fluelen, the end of the route, whence carriages run to Altorf, two miles, where there is a rough statue of William Tell, said to be on the spot where he stood when he shot the apple from his son's head, and the exact distance his son stood from him is there marked down. On the eastern shore of the lake, near Fluelen, is a small shrine, built in 1388, called Tell's Chapel. It stands at the point where he sprang ashore from a boat, in which he was being conveyed as a prisoner, and made his escape. It is called "The Mecca of Switzerland," as on every Sunday after Easter "a procession of boats, richly decorated, proceeds slowly to this chapel, where, after mass is celebrated, a patriotic sermon is preached to the worshiping pilgrims." A few miles further north, near the opposite bank, is a high perpendicular rock, bearing in gilded letters an inscription in commemoration of Frederick Schiller as the poet of William Tell. This rock rises abruptly out of the water in shape of a huge trunk of a tree, its sides being perpendicular for many feet, tapering to the form of a sugar loaf. From a distance it has the look of a giant sentinel. Not far from this is a sloping ledge, covered with verdure and chestnut trees, which our guide-book speaks of as the "Rutli of Schiller," and as the point where, according to tradition, Walter Furst, Werner Stauffacher, and Arnold de Melchthal, on the night of the 7th of November, 1307, accompanied by thirty men from the three cantons of Uri, Schwytz, and Unterwald, met for the purpose of taking a solemn oath at the break of day to deliver their country from the tyranny of their Austrian oppressors.

We landed at Brunnen, a small village on the east side of the lake, and walking a mile or more along the Axenstein turnpike, we sought a shady nook in the forest, where we ate with a keen relish a nice lunch, with an abundance of sweet grapes for dessert, which our landlady had kindly provided for us. This magnificent turnpike has been built, at immense expense, many miles along the rocky margin of the lake, in some places the mountain being tunneled for it, and at others excavated from the lake side, a rough pillar being left here and there to support the overhanging mass. A sea wall, with handsome granite coping, runs along the outer side. The architecture is that of Nature and Art combined, and the effect, especially from the lake, is grand indeed. Leaning upon the skirting wall of this smooth highway, we feast our eyes, too, on scenery most superbly grand and beautiful, as we survey the lake, dotted with charming villas upon its sloping banks, and "Alps on Alps" in the back ground as far as the eye can reach. In our rear, on the Axenstein Mountain, not easy of access, is a large hotel, which can be seen from the lake. We thought of walking to it, but there was insufficient time before the last steamer for Lucerne, and we, therefore, contented ourselves with resting in the woods and loitering along the turnpike till the boat arrived to take us back. While thus resting, we heard strange sounds in the mountains, which we imagined might be either from snow avalanches or an earthquake. There was something terrible, first in the deep, smothered report, and then in the distant, louder reverberations from mountain to mountain. The mystery, however, was soon solved by a Swiss gentleman whom we met on our way to the village. He said the sound was caused by blasting in some mountain which was being tunneled for a railroad. We proceeded to the steamboat landing, and were speedily conveyed to within a short walk of our temporary home at Pension Kaufmann. The next day was Sunday, and in the forenoon we went into an old church where there were Roman Catholic services, and heard the music. Many poor people, kneeling before plaster images of the Virgin and of the crucifix, were engaged in their devotions, and we looked on and listened in silence. If we could not believe in their religion, we could but respect their apparent sincerity.

Attached to our boarding house is a garden, in which we sat one day in the shade and read aloud Byron's "Prisoner of Chillon" in anticipation of soon seeing the famous Castle of Chillon on Lake Leman. Our room overlooks the lake, and there being now a good moon, we enjoy a fine view of both night and day. In the evening we have counted nearly a dozen row boats gliding to and fro upon the lake, their happy occupants giving utterance to their buoyant spirits in lively conversation, laughter, and song. Comfortable seats are provided along the street by the lake — a favorite resort for all.

CHAPTER XXVI.

THUN, SEPTEMBER 20. — At ten o'clock on the morning of the 14th instant, in company with Mr. Thomas Evans, a prominent business man, and his daughter, from Washington, we started in a steamboat from Lucerne and proceeded to Alpnach, where we took four inside seats, previously engaged, in the main body of a diligence for Brienz, over the Brunig Pass. The diligence, drawn by four horses, is constructed for carrying at least nine passengers, including one on the driver's seat. The *coupé* accommodates two, and there is a high seat behind which also holds two. On this trip there were two diligences filled with travelers, besides a private carriage carrying two; so we went by *twos* all round. The road was very dusty, and, as one of our ladies remarked, when we alighted for a three franc dinner ready for us at Sarnen, we looked like millers. This fine dust somewhat marred the pleasure of the trip; but as our stage was generally ahead, our party suffered less in this regard than those behind. On the whole, it was an exciting ride — sometimes on the borders of lakes; sometimes on roads like that of Axenstein, cut through and in the sides of mountains; then again we were on the summit of a mountain looking away down into flourishing, inhabited valleys, every available spot of which was under cultivation. So high were we that the rivers running through the valleys and cascades on the opposite mountain sides looked like silver threads in the sunlight. Now and then we passed a rustic dwelling, its projecting gable end to the south, snuggled in against a side hill or ledge to protect it from the cold blasts of winter. A considerable part of the way is through forests of spruce, pine, and hard wood, cords of which lie piled here and there by the roadside, and looking as though it had experienced rough usage, as it no doubt had, in being pitched down the steep mountains, scraping the bark off and bruising its cut ends like a beetle. It was near sundown when we reached Brienz, a village of some two thousand inhabitants, at the head of the lake by that name, and here we went immediately upon a small steamboat, which, in fifteen or twenty minutes, took us across to Giesbach, where we stopped over night to see the Giesbach Falls illuminated. Here is a succession of cataracts formed by a large body of water, tumbling and frolicking over rocky beds down a mountain several thousand feet high into the lake. Leaving our baggage, except what we carried in a shawl-strap, at the steamboat landing, we made our zig-zag way on foot up the side of the mountain one thousand feet to a magnificent hotel, situated on a plateau just large enough to afford suitable room for it, with its "dependence," until recently the main hotel there, and an adjacent garden. From the new hotel to the "dependence" there is a covered way. From the balcony of the hotel the falls, which have been bridged at several points for beauty of effect, are in plain sight; but the stream much of the way is concealed by the woods. Between eight and nine o'clock lantern lights are seen moving through the forest up the mountain and stopping near the different cataracts. Men have been sent with their chemical preparations for Bengal, or some other kind of lights, and expectation is now on tip-toe for the signal of illumination. We have not long to wait. A rocket is let off, and instantly a bright light appears, first at the upper falls, then at the next, and so on until all are in a blaze of various brilliant colors. The rustic bridges looked like amber, then like iron at white heat, and then like molten gold, as the colors were changed. The illumination lasted four or five minutes only; but it is a charming sight no traveler should miss. The charge to meet the expense is one franc to each guest.

At half past eleven next morning we returned to the landing and awaited the arrival of the steamboat for Interlachen, meantime being entertained by four wandering women singers, whose music was quite unique. Whether native or Tyrolese we could not tell; but their singing was both odd and funny. In about an hour and a half later we were in Interlachen, comfortably lodged at Pension Reber, recommended to us by our landlady at Lucerne. Our room, with a balcony, looks out upon the Jungfrau, covered by snow all seasons of the year, and on either side, in full view, are other mountains of immense height nearer the village. Interlachen is situated between the Lakes of Thun and Brienz, some seventeen hundred feet above the level of the sea. It is surrounded by high mountains, and while there is little of interest here in the way of art, it is blessed with all the charms of nature. The walks in the vicinity are delightful; there is one handsome promenade in the village shaded by walnut trees, and the grounds around the Kursaal, where there is music by a band three times a day, are very pleasant. Invalids go to the Kursaal, or to an institution connected therewith, for goat's whey, prepared under medical supervision; there is here also a grape cure establishment. Goat's whey is dispensed at half past six every morning during the summer at five francs a week for each person. To meet the expenses of the Kursaal, all visitors to Interlachen are charged in their board bill a fee of half a franc for one day, one franc for two or three days, and two francs a week, no matter whether they visit the Kursaal or not. However, nearly everybody goes there to hear the music, and nobody, we imagine, objects to contributing his mite toward the general entertainment.

Sight-seeing is comparatively easy in Switzerland, provided one does not care to climb too many mountains. It does not fatigue like cathedrals, museums, and galleries of paintings. The grand scenery of nature and the pure air we breathe here seem to satisfy. The villages are quiet, the living generally excellent—what delicious bread, butter, and honey are served!—and everything invites to peaceful rest. One, too, must be insensible indeed not to have his devotional feelings excited in a high degree as he beholds here the wonderful works of the Creator:

> "Mark the sable woods
> That shade sublime yon mountain's nodding brow;
> With what religious awe the solemn scene
> Commands your steps! As if the reverend form

Of Minos and of Numa should forsake
The Elysian seats, and down the embowering glade
Move to your pausing eye."

We left Interlachen in the forenoon of the 18th, and arrived at Thun in about two and a half hours, stopping at Pension Itten. We made the passage by railroad a short distance only to Neuhaus, thence the rest of the way by steamboat on Lake Thun. On the railroad they have open cars of two stories — the better to take in the surrounding scenery. From the lake the scenery is especially fine. The Jungfrau, Matterhorn, Monch, and other high mountains, whose names we did not learn, loom up in the distance, some covered with snow, while others are dark and frowning; and the banks of the lake smile with their beautiful villas and gardens. The village of Thun, containing about four thousand inhabitants, has, for the most part, a very ancient look, and we see here many odd-looking people, not a few of whom are stunted and suffering from that frightful malady, the goiter. Their dress is more or less singular. Here is a peasant woman returning in front of us from church on Sunday. She has on a short black petticoat, tight black velvet jacket, white muslin sleeves, starched stiffly, reaching to the elbow, long black mits, extending also to the elbow, with a silver necklace, attached to which are silver chains falling to and fastened at the waist in front. The river Aar runs through the town, along one side of which still stands a high wall built centuries ago; and there is on the hill overlooking the main village, and reached by long flights of stairs, an old cathedral, which looks as though it might have been built in the days of Moses the Prophet. Near by is the old Castle of Keyburg. We saw scarcely a decent looking store in the place. On the main street, which is narrow and dirty, there are rows of shops, one above the other, with side walks, as in the old town of Chester, England. Here and there are steps to go from one story to the other. In some parts there are two and in others three tiers of these little shops. The finest dwelling houses are outside of the village, as is also the principal hotel, the Bellevue. Mons. Rougemont, a wealthy gentleman of Paris, has a magnificent palace — a modern castle — on the margin of the lake, with extensive grounds beautifully laid out and kept in perfect order. Before leaving home Consul General Hitz advised us by all means to stop at least one day in Thun, and knowing now, after two days' sojourn here, what a delightful place it is for rest and recuperation, we are sure we should have been very much *out of tune* had we neglected to follow his kind advice.

CHAPTER XXVII.

FREIBURG, September 21.— We left Thun at noon yesterday, and reached Berne, the capital of Switzerland, in about one hour by rail. The river Aar almost encircles the city, which is mainly situated on high ground. On the south side there is a platform or terrace, handsomely laid out in walks, provided with seats and planted with shade trees. From here we have a magnificent view of the Bernese Oberland — a long range of snow mountains — and the intervening landscape. On the side of this platform toward the river there is a wall one hundred and eight feet high, between which and the river is what is called the Old Town. It makes one dizzy to look down upon the roofs of the houses flanking the river. "Near this giddy verge a marble slab records the following extraordinary escape: In 1654, Theobald Weinzapfli, a student of the place, unable to manage a restive horse which he rode; or having, according to the proverb, 'a spur in the head as well as in the heel,' was precipitated into the Lower Town. Strange to say, he escaped with only a broken arm and leg, and survived the accident thirty years as a preacher." To the horse, of course, the leap was fatal.

In the evening we attended an organ concert in the Cathedral, the most prominent structure in the city, and noted specially for some remarkable sculpture at the outside of the main entrance, representing "The Last Judgment." The interior of the church, which dates back to the sixteenth century, has few ornaments. There are monuments to Zahringen, the founder, and to Steinger, the chief magistrate, and the organ is regarded as among the best. We listened to the performance upon the organ in a dim lamplight. We have heard as good, if not better, organ playing in Washington. In front of the Cathedral stands a bronze equestrian statue of Rod d' Erlach. The horse has his left foreleg raised as if about to start into a gallop, while his rider holds a flag staff, with the flag furled, in his right hand, the foot of the staff resting on the stirrup. The base of the statue is of white marble surrounded by an iron railing, at the corners of which are four bronze bears in a sitting posture. The bear is a prominent figure in Berne wherever you go, being conspicuous in the armorial bearings or coats-of-arms of the Canton. At the entrance of the Morat Gate are two huge bears in stone, and in a den — or rather two dens, or pits, with a division wall between them — near the river several live bears are constantly kept at the public expense. In the center of one of these dens is erected the stem of a tree with its branches, on which, from time to time, they dispel dull care in frolicsome exercise. We went to see them. Their dens are encased with granite blocks, and are sunk from ten to fifteen feet below the street, so that spectators may have a good view of them over the wall, raised three or four feet high on the street side. They appeared very friendly, and did not wait for an introduction before begging us for bread and fruit, which is the only food the public is allowed to give them. They would sit upright, stand on their hind legs, reaching as far toward us as possible, and make various other signs indicating their wishes as plainly as though they had spoken the words. . In the year 1861, an English captain, on a spree, undertook to walk around on the broad wall of their inclosure, and fell into it. A waiter at our hotel told us that a rope was lowered to him, which he seized and held until he was raised part of the way up before the noise attracted the attention of the bears in their adjoining lodge; but from some cause he fell again to the bottom, and was instantly torn in pieces by them. A fellow-traveler, from Connecticut, gave us an amusing account of his experience in getting to see these wild beasts. He had but an hour before he must take the train, and he started on foot for the bear dens, trusting to his Yankee shrewdness to find the way, although he could not speak a word either of German or French. Meeting a citizen he accosted him with the inquiry, "Where are the bears?" The citizen shook his head; he was as ignorant of English as the stranger was of the French language. Still, the latter could not comprehend why so simple an inquiry could not be answered, and he reiterated in a louder and more impressive tone, "Where are the bears—the bears?" The citizen looked alarmed. "Was the stranger crazy?" he thought. By this time our friend took in the situation, and bethought himself to try another language; so he set to growling as near like a bear as he could. The citizen, instantly relieved, exclaimed in French, "*Oh! oui, oui! les ours, les ours!*" (Yes, yes! the bears, the bears!) and at once conducted him to the desired locality.

In reference to the superstitious estimation in which bears are held by the people of Berne, Dr. Beattie remarks: "At what period, or from what circumstance, they were first emblazoned on the patriotic standard, is a question that has been variously interpreted. Some trace its origin to René, Duke of Lorraine; others think that it arose from the circumstance of a certain Glado May bringing home with him from the battle of Novara, in 1510, two young bears as a trophy of victory."

There is a fine Museum here containing specimens in Zoölogy, Ornithology, Mineralogy, etc. An interesting object is the stuffed skin of the noted dog Barry, which had been the means of saving the lives of several travelers on the St. Bernard Pass. He looks as natural as life. At one of the fountains in the city, called the Ogre's Fountain, is "a grotesque figure, said to resemble Saturn, devouring children, while in his pockets and girdle others are sticking out for future consumption." The old clock tower is another object of curiosity. When the clock is about to strike the hour, a figure of a rooster, perched high up on the side of the tower, flaps his wings and crows. Then the figure of an old man moves its head and yawns; and next a company of bears, standing on their hind legs in military array, march around in front of the tower. At every hour of striking in the day time we imagine these maneuvers are observed by a greater or less number of interested spectators.

The Federal Palace, or Capitol of Switzerland, is a fine stone structure, corresponding in style and architecture with the republican character of the government. Everything about it looks substantial, and what there is of art here in the way of ornament is choice and refined, embracing an interesting collection of paintings, engravings and statuary.

A large proportion of the shops here are entered from low arcades, extending for whole blocks, rendering them dark and, we should think, rather disagreeable, although at the outer edge of the arcades goods are also displayed for sale, and in pleasant weather various kinds of light work, such as shoemaking, sewing, etc., are carried on there. Through the middle of the principal streets there is a narrow canal, filled with a rapid current of water, which serves to carry off the sweepings of the street into the river.

A singular sight was that of a dozen convicts, more or less, of both sexes, in their prison costumes, harnessed to horse-carts loaded with farming tools, which they were dragging through the streets as if returning from work in the fields to their prison quarters for the night. Another odd thing we have seen nowhere else was a huge tread-wheel, fifteen or twenty feet in diameter, which from four to six men, their hands on the shoulders of one another, were revolving by walking on the inner side of the rim, by which power heavy blocks of stone were being raised in the erection of a building. The wonder is that convicts were not put to this work, for it is evidently "hard labor."

The women appear to do most of the marketing, and it is a novel sight to see them come in with their merchandise, fruit, vegetables, and what not—some with horse and cart, some with dogs to help them draw their loads, and others carrying their burden upon their heads. It is surprising to see how much these dogs will draw, and how well they seem to understand their business.

Freiburg, one hour and a half by rail from Berne, was our next stopping place, on the 21st of September. On our arrival at noon, in company with Mr. Thomas Evans and daughter, previously mentioned, from Washington, we took an open carriage and were driven around town and out over one suspension bridge a mile or two into the country, and back over another suspension bridge, both of which are among the most noted in the world. The first was finished in 1838, under the supervision of Monsieur Chaley, a French engineer, and up to a recent period, if not to the present time, it had the longest single span of any bridge extant, being nine hundred and five feet between the porticoes or suspension piers. Its height above the river Sarine, which runs through the city, is one hundred and seventy-four feet. The breadth of the roadway is forty-one feet. Soon after this bridge was opened its strength was tested "by causing a train of fifteen pieces of heavy artillery, drawn by fifty horses, and attended by three hundred persons, to pass along it at the same time." Not the slightest indication of yielding could be detected in any part of the structure. It is mentioned as a pleasing circumstance that the whole of this work was completed without serious accident to a single person engaged in its construction. We have no data showing the length or height of the bridge last built; but it cannot differ much from the first. We felt when riding over them as we imagine we might feel in a balloon. We have photographs presenting a good view of them, as well as of the city, which is one of the most picturesque imaginable. The bridges span not only the river, which is not very large, but the valley in and upon the sides of which the city, with its ancient walls and watch-towers, is situated. The streets, of course, are generally quite steep, and they abound in ornamental fountains. Many of the buildings have an antique and grotesque appearance, and one might travel the world over to find a place where more novel enjoyment could be crowded into an excursion, such as we have made, of two hours.

> "Here beauty and primeval nature dwell;
> Evergreen forests — fountains ever clear —
> Haunts of the fabled muse — how shall I tell
> The transport ye inspire in stranger's ear?"

We timed our ride so as to get back to the great organ concert (much better than the one we heard in Berne) in the Cathedral, which was founded in 1283. The tower of this Cathedral is three hundred and fifty-six feet high, and it is said to have the finest ring of bells of any church in Switzerland. At the principal porch are *bas-reliefs* representing "The Last Judgment." The old Duke Zahringen, who founded this city, as well as the city of Berne, seemed to have a fancy for this kind of pictures. It is to be hoped, however, that when he "put off this mortal coil" he did not go the way the most of his fellow-beings are represented by these frightful pictures to have departed. If he did, he must have found himself in the condition of the man who, not long since, is reported, while in communication with his wife through a spiritual medium, to have implored her to send him his coolest summer suit. The following is a description of this church ornament: "In the center we see St. Nicholas; above him the Saviour; to the right an angel weighing humanity in a balance; below, St. Peter introducing the just into Paradise; to the right a demon with a pig's head is dragging in chains a group of criminals; on his back he carries a basket filled with malefactors, which he is preparing to precipitate into a grand cauldron; in one corner is hell, represented by a monster filled up to overflowing with the condemned; above, Satan on his throne."

It is remarked as a singular fact that in the higher part of this city the inhabitants speak the French, and in the lower part the German language. The French are said to show a much greater partiality or aptitude for trade than their neighbors, the Germans. One of the sights here is a large linden tree, planted in 1476, in commemoration of the battle of Morat. Here, also is the University of Freiburg, a celebrated seat of learning.

CHAPTER XXVIII.

"The Switzer's Land! where grandeur is encamped
   Impregnably in mountain tints of snow;
Realms that by human foot-print ne'er were stamped,
   Where the eagle wheels and glacial ramparts glow!
Seek, Nature's worshiper, those landscapes!—go
   Where all her fiercest, fairest charms are joined!
Go to the land where Tell drew Freedom's bow;
   And in the patriot's country thou shalt find
A semblance 'twixt the scene and his immortal mind."

THUS Campbell sang: and Rousseau, in approaching Switzerland by the Jura, exclaimed in ecstasy: "Ce paysage unique, le plus beau dont l'œil humain fut jamais frappé! Séjour charmant auquel je n'avais rien trouvé d'égal dans le tour du monde! —l'aspect d'un peuple heureux et libre!" Dr. Beattie expresses nearly the same sentiment: "Whoever," says he, "has traveled much, and compared the various attractions presented to him in the course of his peregrinations, will generally be found to admit that if there be any country which merits more attention than the rest, *that* country is Switzerland." So far as our own experience extends, we accord fully with these sentiments. One here seems raised, as it were, above the bustling, anxious world to an elevation nearer to the heavenly spheres—to a height from whence one obtains a clearer view in looking "from Nature up to Nature's God."

Our stay in Freiburg was short—a few hours only between trains—on the 21st of September, when we proceeded to Lausanne, two and a half hours by train, reaching there about seven, P. M. All along we were enchanted by the scenery. Speeding on, suddenly, as we emerged from a tunnel, we caught our first view of Lake Leman, which, almost at our feet, broke in all its beauty on our vision, while its hithermost border was smiling with grape vines and apple, pear, and plum trees loaded with fruit.

> "Clear, placid Leman! thy contrasted lake,
> With the wide world I dwelt in, is a thing
> Which warns me with its stillness, to forsake
> Earth's troubled waters for a purer spring."

On the 22d, in carriage and on foot, we visited the most interesting parts of the town, first calling to see Mrs. Consul General Hitz, knowing that she, with her sprightly children, had been residing here several months; but we were disappointed in finding that they were in Paris on their way home. The Cathedral is the most prominent building in the city. It dates back to the tenth century, and possesses a good deal of interest. It contains among other monuments one to Victor Amadeus VIII., Duke of Savoy, and one to Otho of Grandson. There are also on the walls many memorial inscriptions, one of which, in French, recites that Henrietta, wife of Stratford Canning, English Ambassador to Switzerland, died June 17, 1817; amiable as she was young and beautiful, and as happy as it is permitted to mortals to be. On this account, however, not less prepared to enter heaven, if innocence and a sincere piety may have any merit before God. Lausanne is noted as having been the residence of both Voltaire and Gibbon, and that the latter, whose house we saw, wrote here the concluding chapter of his great work on the "Decline and Fall of the Roman Empire." The city stands some fifteen minutes' walk from the lake. It covers three ridges and the intermediate valleys, and most of the streets are rather steep; but the situation, affording as it does charming views of the lake and adjacent scenery, is very beautiful. There is an old Castle here with watchtowers on its four corners. It is now used for public offices. Many of the houses have a very ancient look.

Ouchy is the port of Lausanne, and here is situated the principal hôtel, the Beau Rivage, one of the largest and finest public houses probably in Switzerland. It is near the lake shore, and the grounds around it are laid out in the most tasteful manner. We left our Pension Beau Séjour on the 23d, at ten o'clock, expecting to take the boat for Vevay at half past ten; but when we reached the steamboat landing, right in front of the Beau Rivage Hôtel, we learned that the boat had been gone half an hour. We had to wait till noon, therefore, for the next boat — a disappointment, as we wished to visit Vevay and the Castle of Chillon that day, and stop over night at Villeneuve, the end of the steamboat route from Geneva. It so happened, however, that it was a very fortunate disappointment, showing that

> "There is some soul of goodness in things evil,
> Would men observingly distill it out."

We knew before that ex-President Thiers was sojourning at the Beau Rivage Hôtel, but being naturally disinclined to disturb him in his retreat, we did not intend to call on him. Finding, however, that we must wait two hours for the boat, it occurred to us that we would inquire at the hôtel whether such a call would be proper, and on being assured that it would, we sent up our card to him. His

French waiter, immediately brought back word that
Monsieur Thiers was at present engaged, and wished
to know if we were stopping at the hôtel, and if we
would not be good enough to call in the afternoon.
We explained why it was not convenient to wait,
and the messenger soon returned with a request for
us to walk into Monsieur Thiers' private parlor, a
large and handsomely furnished second-story room,
looking out upon the lake. We took seats, and in a
few moments the venerable ex-President entered
from an adjoining front room and received us very
cordially, taking a seat near us. We addressed him
in English, when, raising one hand to his ear, he
intimated that it was difficult for him to understand,
and we then spoke to him in our broken French.
He said he had been stopping some time at Vevay,
but that he enjoyed better health at Ouchy. He
complained of bronchitis, but his appearance was
that of perfect health. He is a short, thick-set man,
with a large head, gray eyes, hair nearly white,
wears large-bowed spectacles, stands erect, and his
expression, free from anything like hauteur, is altogether pleasant. Meeting him under such circumstances, we made our call, of course, very brief; but
in the few moments' conversation we had with him,
President Buchanan's name being mentioned, he remarked that he knew him, of course, but not person-
ally. On our taking leave he accompanied us to the
door, extending to us a pleasant good-bye, and we
left highly gratified with our call—the result of one
of those happy accidents which in the end turn out
to be "blessings in disguise," and which we shall
ever look back upon with profound pleasure. He is
beyond question one of the most remarkable men as
well as one of the greatest statesmen of the age, and

there is no person living whom we would have preferred to see and speak with.*

According to an authority before us, it was, while detained by stress of weather, at the Anchor Hôtel of Ouchy that Lord Byron composed his "Prisoner of Chillon," "and where, from his window, he could observe the Castle thus immortalized rising white on the eastern verge of the lake. He visited every locality," in this part of Switzerland, "known in history or tradition; and in one of his published letters says: 'I inclose you a sprig of Gibbon's acacia, and some rose leaves from his garden, which, with part of his house, I have just seen.' Moore has well observed that this circumstance in the life of the immortal bard has added 'one more deathless association to the already immortalized localities of the lake'—

'Rousseau, Voltaire, our Gibbon, and de Stael—
Leman! these names are worthy of thy shore!'"

In less than one hour after leaving Ouchy we found ourselves at Vevay, where we spent three hours—long enough to walk all through the little town and get a lunch at the Hôtel Monnet before the arrival of the next boat. At Vevay there is a very ancient and noted society called the "Abbaye des Vignerons," whose object it is to encourage and superintend the culture of the grape vine with a view to the raising of the best grapes and the pro-

---

* The announcement of the sudden death of this great man, which occurred at Paris on the 3d of September, 1877, touched us the more deeply from this personal interview. It was with lively satisfaction that, on the day of his funeral, we observed the United States flags at half-mast over the Government Departments—a fitting recognition of his distinguished character and services, and of the cordial relations between the two countries.

duction of the finest qualities of wines. At certain periods they have a great fête, at which premiums are distributed to the most meritorious wine-growers; and on these occasions sometimes as many as sixteen thousand spectators, from all parts of Switzerland, are present; and they are entertained with processions, dances, songs, banquets, and dramatic exhibitions of a most unique character, embracing "a medley of heathen ceremony and scriptural scenes from the Old Testament, mixed up with customs still observed in the Canton."

"Clarens, sweet Clarens, birthplace of deep love,"

is the next village southeast of Vevay, and then comes Montreux, both, like Lausanne and Vevay, beautifully situated on the east shore, or near the shore of the lake, with a southern exposure. Next is Chillon, which can hardly be called a village, as we remember to have seen little more than scattering dwellings along the road which leads by the Chateau. As we were now soon to cross the mountains to Chamouni, and thence to take the diligence to Geneva, on going aboard the boat at Lausanne, we had our baggage checked direct to Geneva. From Vevay we proceeded to Chillon, where we landed, and our party of four (Mr. Evans and daughter being still with us) were in about twenty minutes conveyed in a rowboat to the Castle of Chillon, too late, however, to be admitted that evening, although the boatmen, who were in for a job, assured us that we should be in time. Arranging for an early admission in the morning, as we desired to take the first boat for Villeneuve, we walked a short distance to the nearest public house—a small hôtel or pension built against the perpendicular side of a cliff, the top of which, where there was a vineyard, being reached by long ladders from the side of the highway. Here we had comfortable accommodations in rooms fronting on the lake; and the charge therefor was so ridiculously low that we give it: For supper, lodging, and breakfast, our bill for each person was just three francs and a half — seventy cents! In the morning by seven o'clock we were at the Castle, which resembles some of the smaller castles on the Rhine, and which we entered over a bridge. Until the invention of gunpowder it is said this Castle was considered impregnable, being entirely surrounded by water, which is very deep against the walls on the lake side.

> "Lake Leman lies by Chillon's walls;
> A thousand feet, in depths below,
> Its massy waters meet and flow;
> Thus much the fathomed line was sent
> From Chillon's snow-white battlement,
> Which round about the wave enthralls."

We were conducted over nearly the entire structure, going first into the dungeon where Bonnivard, prior of St. Victor, the "Prisoner of Chillon," made immortal by Byron, was confined six years, about 1536, and where we saw the ring in the stone pillar to which Bonnivard was chained. The name of Byron, cut by his own hand, appears on this pillar, or on one near it, and in an adjoining dungeon we saw the stone bed on which prisoners had to sleep, if they slept at all, on the night preceding their execution. The rooms occupied six hundred years ago by the Duke and Duchess of Savoy are now uninhabitable, and the banquet room is filled with old flags and other ancient relics. Other rooms contain cannon and a variety of other war implements.

On our way by Villeneuve, a large village, at which we did not stop, at the end of the lake, to Bouveret, we passed in the steamer near a diminutive island, only about large enough to support one or two trees, and this was the only spot of land within sight of Bonnivard, through the narrow opening in his dungeon wall. We reached Bouveret, a woe-begone looking little village, at nine o'clock in the morning, where we had to wait until noon for the train to Martigny, arriving at the latter place about half past one. This is the point of starting up over the mountains for the valley of Chamouni, and we had the afternoon for preparation and rest. Between Bouveret and Martigny we passed near the Gorge du Trient and the Falls of Sallenche in plain sight. This cascade has a fall of one hundred and twenty feet, ending almost in spray, and is very beautiful. The Gorge, so far as the splitting of the mountain is concerned, is quite as wonderful, perhaps, as the Tamina Gorge at Ragatz. In 1867 the writer walked into the Gorge du Trient half a mile or more on a narrow suspension foot bridge over and along the rushing river Trient—a principal tributary of the Rhone—the mountain opening just enough to allow the waters to pass between walls we should judge to be four hundred feet in height. In many places the space was so narrow and the walls so projecting that we could not see the sky above us. It is this Gorge, no doubt, of which Byron wrote:

> "Now where the swift Rhone cleaves his way between
> Heights which appear as lovers who have parted
> In haste, whose mining depths so intervene
> That they can meet no more, tho' broken hearted;
> Though in their souls, which thus each other thwarted,

Love was the very root of the foul rage
Which blighted their life's bloom, and then departed —
Itself expired, but leaving them an age
Of years all winters — war within themselves to wage."

CHAPTER XXIX.

CHAMOUNI, September 27.— There is little of interest at Martigny, a village of some thirteen hundred inhabitants, but the surrounding scenery is grand. It is situated at the foot of the mountains where special conveyances are engaged for Chamouni, either by Tête Noir, or Col de Balme, as the traveler may choose. By the former route one may go in a low, narrow carriage, but by the latter, which we took, transportation is only by mules or donkeys. Having the whole afternoon at our disposal before starting on our route the next morning, we amused ourselves as best we could by walking around town and out over the river Dranse in the suburbs toward the Castle of La Batie, situated on a high bluff a mile or so from the village. The ruins of this old Castle add much to the picturesqueness of the place. The monks of St. Bernard have a convent here, but we remember to have seen no elegant buildings. We sought out the postmaster for some postage stamps, and seeing that he was engaged in making wine, we expressed a desire to see the wine press. He cheerfully acquiesced, and took us to the mill, a short distance from his office, where we were treated to a ladleful of the unfermented juice out of the wine vat. It tasted like sweet cider. The press resembled the old-fashioned cider press. On our way back to our hôtel we were entertained by the violent antics of a donkey that took it into his head to run off with a load of fodder, regardless of sidewalks and frightened women and children. He was soon overtaken, however, and received a sound lashing for his ill-behavior. Our attention was also attracted by a peasant woman carrying a large basket of clothes on her head, and her bonnet or hat under one arm, while she was leading a goat and knitting all at the same time. Such industry surely ought to reap a suitable reward.

Having made our arrangements for guides and mules the preceding evening, we were ready to proceed on our journey at half past seven on the morning of the 25th instant. Our traveling companions were now increased to six. At least we formed a party of eight, who, with guides and mules, were to jog along together over the mountains. Each couple had two mules and one guide between them, except a Mr. Hoskins and wife, from London, who hired but one mule, Mr. Hoskins walking the whole way. An Irish member of Parliament, Mr. Brooks, and his wife, and Mr. Thomas Evans and daughter, previously mentioned, were the other two couples. The guides generally held the reins of the ladies' mules, but the gentlemen managed their own, or rather left the animals to do as they pleased. It was amusing to watch their perambulations. The writer's mule, like all the rest, we have no doubt, was very clever, in the English sense of that word at least. He had a decided penchant for going as near the edges of precipices as possible without falling over, and especially when we came to the short turns in our zigzag course. Several times in such places we drew a taught inner rein on him, and instead of mending his ways he would stop stock still, as much as to say, "If you think you know better than I do, you should dismount and we will change positions with each other! Remember I am an old hand at this business, while you are evidently a novice, else you would leave me to paddle my own canoe, or, what amounts to the same thing, do my work in my own way." There was such a calm determination in his bearing that we felt satisfied it would not only be useless, but dangerous, to contend, and remembering, too, that "discretion is the better part of valor," we yielded gracefully to superior wisdom—a course we had no cause to regret, for we were borne along safely on the very edges of some of the most frightful precipices imaginable. For nearly two hours of the first part of the journey it was so foggy that our view was entirely obstructed; but after that, until we reached nearly to the summit, where there is a small inn, the fog having passed off, we were favored with many views that filled us with delight. It began to rain just before we arrived at the inn, and continued for two hours and a half while we remained there for dinner and for the rain to cease. All this time, when we fondly anticipated enjoying a prospect nowhere else to be seen, we were enveloped in the clouds, and we wished now that we had gone upon the Rhigi. We caught our first sight of Mont Blanc a few minutes before it set in to rain, but the clouds were already resting on its base and upon all the adjacent mountains, so that the view was anything but satisfactory. Our inn was a poor concern—far inferior to the old Tip-top House on Mount Washington—but it was much better than none, notwithstanding soup was about the best food to be had there. It served, too, to shelter us from the storm, which raged fiercely until three o'clock, when we started to descend. The path was now so steep, and slippery by the rain, that it required no argument from the guides to convince us that our safer course altogether was to descend the mountain on foot, as they advised; therefore, all except Mrs. Brooks chose this way, and walked and slid for two hours until we reached the level ground of the valley. More than once some of our party, both ladies and gentlemen, suddenly found themselves tripped up and sliding at full length down steep places over the wet turf, which we occasionally sought in order to avoid the mud and roughness of the mule path. To support each other, some of our couples walked hand-in-hand; and as we were traveling for pleasure, we made light of our mishaps, as it was natural under such circumstances for young people to do. On the way, high up on the side of the mountain, where there was some verdure, we came to a flock of sheep and goats, attended by a shepherd. Hastening on, we at length reached the valley, where we were glad to remount our mules, which had been brought along by our guides. A ride of two or three miles, more or less, took us to a small settlement where hackmen were anxious for us to employ them to take us the rest of the way, five miles, to Chamouni; but as this was to be an additional expense, and as we had paid for our mules to carry us through, we decided to keep our saddles and go ahead. This decision did not find favor with our guides, who evidently wished us to make the change, so that they themselves might ride the mules into town. It was now sundown, and it commenced to rain again, and soon to pour in torrents, which did not cease until after we reached our Pension Couttet in the village of Chamouni, near the foot of Mont Blanc and of the Mer de Glace. Luckily, before sailing from New York, we purchased for ourselves each a gossamer water-proof, the lady's with cape and hood— the weight of both was just two pounds—and these, with an umbrella, shielded us in good degree from the storm.

The next day was clear and pleasant. Here we were in a valley three thousand feet above the level of the sea, shut in closely on three sides by high mountains, the monarch of all, Mont Blanc, towering over twelve thousand feet above us. "Nothing short of actual observation can convey any adequate idea of the solitary grandeur and gigantic proportions of Mont Blanc." In a straight line from Chamouni to its summit the distance is only about ten miles, and in the sunlight, or in a bright moonlight, it appears to be even nearer; but travelers who ascend to the top are obliged to walk between forty and fifty miles to accomplish the journey. Dr. Paccard, a physician of Chamouni, was the first to make the ascent, on the 7th of August, 1786. In the following year De Saussure, attended by a servant and eighteen guides, also made a successful ascent, carrying meteorological instruments, and surprised and delighted the civilized world with a report of his experience and observations. Notwithstanding many persons have since lost their lives by this hazardous undertaking, no year now passes without its safe accomplishment by a greater or less number of enterprising travelers. With few exceptions, however, visitors are satisfied with a trip over Montanvert to the Mer de Glace. and to the summit of Mont Brevent, or to Flegère. high above the valley on the west or southwest of the village. In 1867 the writer visited those three places, one day walking up Montanvert, across the Mer de Glace, and back to Chamouni by the Mauvais Pas, or dangerous foot-path, cut in the side of a nearly perpendicular mountain. On the upper side of this footway, which extends a distance of many rods, there is an iron railing to hold on by. Montanvert is ascended by a zig-zag mule path in about two hours. Coming to the sea of ice, we expected to see a smooth, transparent surface, but such was not the case. One writer has described its exterior mass as "congealed waves which, from the heights of Montanvert, appeared like furrows in a plowed field," but which, on approaching them, are found "to rise in abrupt ridges from twenty to forty feet," with a rough surface.

> "Wave upon wave! as if a foaming ocean,
> By boisterous winds to fierce rebellion driven,
> Heard — in its wildest moments of commotion —
> And stood congealed at the command of Heaven."

The principal danger in crossing upon the ice is that one is liable to fall into deep chasms and wells near which he is obliged to pass. "The clefts, which have proved fatal to so many adventurers, are extremely variable in width, of enormous depth, and changing, as they descend, from a beautiful light green to an intense blue. They are occasioned by the rocky or unequal surface over which the glacier progressively descends, the sudden changes of atmospheric temperature, and the brittle material of which they are composed." We remember that we had to walk several yards on a foot-way of not more than two feet in width between two of these deep crevices in the ice, having only our umbrella for an alpenstock. The narrow ridge had been hacked by the guides to afford a safer foothold; but it would have been a very dangerous passage for any one of unsteady nerves. "The wells, which we observe scattered over these fields of ice, are produced by detached masses of granite, which, heated by exposure to the sun, melt and penetrate into the glacier, leaving the vertical aperture through which they descended filled with water. Within the substance of this glacier, as well as on its surface, numerous fragments of rock are deposited, which the storms and avalanches have detached from the higher mountains and transported to their present situation. On the borders and at the base of the glaciers these stones are accumulated in such masses as to form cairns of a hundred feet high." At the foot of this glacier is the Crystal Grotto, a tunnel caused by the melting of the ice, and from which issues a constant stream of water. It is described as very beautiful. "Its partition walls, as if cased by the finest pier-glass, multiply and reflect each other in such endless succession as to produce the most striking illusions, and conduct the imagination through a long labyrinth of gorgeous apartments, such as might embellish the wildest Arabian tale." On the border and within one foot of this wonderful sea of ice, we plucked fragrant wild flowers; as did also our dear companion, on the present visit, whom we entrusted to make the trip to the Mer de Glace and back direct without crossing, in the care of Mr. and Mrs. Hoskins.

Mont Brevent is a very high mountain, fronting Mont Blanc. Starting at seven, it took till noon to reach the resting house at the terminus of the mule path, from which point we were obliged to go on foot; and it was nearly two o'clock when we arrived at the Tip-top House. On this part of the route we had to cross a field of snow, from which we made snow-balls which we carried to quench our thirst, for the day was very warm; and beyond this field our path was up the side of a ledge so steep that for some distance we had to incline forward and hold on by our hands, steps being cut in the rocks to avoid falling over backward. Then further on for a quarter of a mile our way was over a bed of loose rocks, large and small, till at length we reached the highest point. From this dizzy height we observed plainly, with a good field glass, two parties who had just attained the summit of Mont Blanc, which, with the rugged peaks of many other mountains before us, and the valley between, afforded, we imagine, one of the wildest and grandest views in the world. After enjoying this grand picture of the Alps for an hour or more, we began our descent, which was more dangerous even than the ascent; but we all got over the fearful pass in safety, and rollicking across and down the steep fields of snow, we soon came to the mule station, from whence we returned, also on foot, by the way of Flegère to our comfortable quarters in the village.

CHAPTER XXX.

"Above me are the Alps,
The palaces of Nature, whose vast walls
Have pinnacled in clouds their snowy scalps,
And throned Eternity in icy halls
Of cold sublimity, where forms and falls
The avalanche — the thunderbolt of snow!
All that expands the spirit, yet appalls,
Gathers around these summits!"

ARGENTIÈRE is a small hamlet through which we passed on our way to Chamouni, where we still remain, September 27th. It is situated at the foot of a glacier about five miles from the latter place, and, like Chamouni, is a pleasant summer resort for travelers. The Mer de Glace extends to within a few miles of the village of Chamouni on the north, and on the other side, nearer, at the foot of Mont Blanc, is the Glacier de Bossons, to which we one day started to walk, but were overtaken by the rain and were obliged to relinquish the undertaking. Our effort, however, was not without compensation, as our walk took us into the country by several cabins occupied by the peasantry and their cattle, and the rain furnishing us a good excuse to enter, we had the opportunity of observing somewhat of the domestic life of these humble people. In a rough shed by one cabin they were breaking and hatcheling flax, as we used to see it done on the farm long years agone. We were more interested at another cabin, into which we were driven by the rain, now increased to a fierce storm, at the point where we were compelled to turn about. It was the home of an old mountain guide, now eighty-five, whose name is Couttet, a near relative of our landlord of the Pension Couttet, who has also been employed many years as a guide and resigned with marked rewards of merit. While the rain was pouring, this veteran guide related to us something of his history, giving account of the many times he had pioneered travelers, among whom were Ruskin and Albert Smith, of English fame, to the summit of Mont Blanc and safely down again. There is but one door to his cabin, and we sat on stools in the narrow hallway, out of one end of which, extending nearly along the whole front of the building, there is a door to the rooms occupied by himself and daughter, and from the other end a door to the apartment devoted to their cattle. When the cattle came home for shelter we had to rise to let them pass. The daughter looks as coarse and sunburnt and almost as old as her father. Both were very kind to us, and appeared very thankful for the few sous we were happy to give them for their hospitality. Having no idea of being caught in such a storm, we were not well prepared for it, and when we reached our boarding house we were pretty well drenched.

GENEVA, OCTOBER 6.—At half-past seven on the morning of September 28th, Mr. Evans and daughter having preceded us a day or two earlier, we left Chamouni by diligence and arrived in Geneva at half-past two. For two-thirds of the way or more, until we come in sight of the Jura mountains west of Geneva, the scenery is of the wildest character. The road runs between high mountains for many miles along the banks of the Arve —

>"Born where the thunder and the blast,
>And morning's earliest light are born,"

as Bryant writes of it, thus continuing:

> "Not from the sands or cloven rocks,
>   Thou rapid Arve! thy waters flow;
> Nor earth, within her bosom, locks
>   Thy dark, unfathomed walls below.
> Thy springs are in the cloud, thy stream
>   Begins to move and murmur first
> Where ice-peaks feel the noonday beam,
>   Or rain-storms on the glacier burst."

In some places the river passes through deep gorges and over steep, rocky beds, surging along with fearful force and velocity. It was a grand sight to look from the top of the diligence — it was two stories high — away down into these gorges, as we were carried along right upon the edge of the precipice. We passed through several villages, and at one point, where we crossed the river on a stone bridge five hundred feet in length, we obtained a magnificent view of Mont Blanc. The view of this "Alpine Monarch" from this bridge is said to be the grandest and most satisfactory anywhere to be had of it. Not far from Cluses we passed near the mouth of the Grotto of Balme, which extends into the mountain nearly two thousand feet, and is regarded as a great natural curiosity. Here and there along the road are shrines, similar to what we saw by the highways in other parts of Switzerland, as well as in Austria. Generally they consist of a small structure just large enough to hold a figure, either in sculpture or painting, of the Crucifix or the Virgin; but sometimes only the Cross is presented. It is difficult to give a faithful description of this day's journey; suffice it to say, that but for the rather too cold weather in the morning, the ride all the way would have been unsurpassed in everything calculated to enhance our enjoyment.

Italy being our next objective point, we are now

comfortably settled in Geneva, probably for a month, the winter season being the safest if not the best time to visit that land of the vine, olive, and fig-tree. Through the kind attention of our Consul, Hon. Charles H. Upton, and his estimable wife, we are pleasantly situated in a private boarding house, or pension, fronting on Lake Leman. The city is built on both sides of the lower end of the lake, or what might as well be called the Rhone — for the lake is only an expansion of the river — which is narrowed here, and, joining the Arve one mile below, flows on to the sea. Like all the Alpine streams from the snowy regions, the waters of the Arve have a milky appearance, and it is curious to observe how they retain this color in contra-distinction to the dark waters of the Rhone at the junction of the two rivers. The two flow rapidly along, side by side, in the same channel, for a mile, more or less, before they mingle and the Arve loses itself in the Rhone. This is one of the interesting sights of Geneva. At a point just above where the two rivers unite there is a bridge over the Arve, leading to a beautiful estate on its southwestern banks — a pleasant resort in hot days. The Rhone runs with great force through the city, dividing and forming a considerable island in the southern part thereof. This island is covered with buildings, most-ly, we believe, manufacturing establishments, the machinery in which is moved by water. Two sub-stantial bridges connect the island with the main land on both sides. The river is spanned by two other fine long bridges nearer the lake, and from one of these is a foot-bridge to Rousseau's Island, a small spot of ground in the river, ornamented by shade trees and a handsome bronze statue of that distinguished Frenchman. The statue is on an elevated base in a sitting posture. It has for sentinels a flock of beautiful swans, whose lodge is near by. They glide gracefully over this part of the lake and river, sometimes also flying from one point to another. They are so fascinating to grown as well as little children that they are seldom without crackers and sweet cakes on their board, and they appear to be free from care and in the enjoyment of perfect happiness. The tongue of slander nor the sting of ingratitude ever disturbs their perfect composure: Who would not be a swan? Bath houses and wash sheds are erected over the river far enough from the shore to have the advantage of the swift stream. The latter face the shore, and at all times of day washerwomen, in long rows, may be seen hard at work washing clothes in the river. Their washboards reach into the water, and after applying a liberal quantity of soap and rubbing the clothes, throw them over a projecting bar arranged to secure them, and the rapid stream does the rinsing. The borders of the lake and river for miles around are protected by a substantial wall raised to a level with the streets, and the lake steamers and sailing vessels come directly up to this wall as their place of landing. Further up there is a breakwater extending out from either side of the lake, notwithstanding which, however, when what is called the *bise* takes place, which we have felt, the waters are thrown over into the streets. The *bise* is a violent north wind, which, sweeping down from the whole length of the lake, powerfully agitates the waters, as the waves of the ocean break upon the coast in a storm. The manner of setting the sails on the sailing vessels, called "mouches" (flies) here, gives them the appearance at a distance of enormous birds about to alight on the water with their wings extended upward.

We were surprised on the first of October to see wild strawberries on our table for dessert. They were about the size of the field strawberry of New England, but more oblong and pointed in shape, and not as sweet. We did not learn where they came from, but probably from the sunny side of the mountain or valley, as we observed here and there one on the Col de Balme and in the valley of Chamouni. They are, no doubt, sold at a moderate price, else grapes, which are plenty at from six to eight cents per pound, would be served instead. Delicious plums, too, are here in abundance and cheap. Peaches are scarce, and the only really fine ones we have seen we found in Vienna and Munich.

The "English Garden" is a small inclosure in front of the eastern part of the old city, extending for a short distance along the foot of the lake. In this garden, laid out in grand walks bordered by shrubbery and flowers, with scattering trees, there is a neat cottage building, where there is a "Relief of Mont Blanc," presenting a correct description in miniature of this monarch of mountains, the top of which is to be seen to good advantage from the west side of the river or foot of the lake. Early after sunset in Geneva, on clear evenings, many lovers of the grand and beautiful go to this locality to feast their eyes upon the splendid sight of Mont Blanc, looming above all other mountains and smiling still in the varied hues of a bright sunshine. It is indeed a most charming picture.

We have been happy to meet here our Minister, Hon. Mr. Rublee, and also our battle-scarred veteran, General Heintzelman, with his pleasant wife and daughter. We have passed an hour most agreeably at Mr. Bremond's manufactory of music boxes and other musical instruments, where we saw and heard various kinds of music boxes, *chairs, books,* and *bottles,* and charming artificial singing birds. Take a seat in his chairs, handle his books, or go to turn over his bottles, and they will at once strike up and discourse sweet music. Some of his instruments are in the shape of a cathedral of beautiful carved work; others of a rustic sawmill, arranged with spiral glass tubes moved by the machinery to represent the fall of water, and others in the usual form of music boxes, finished in the highest style. You can have your choice in kind as well as price—paying for each instrument from fifteen francs up to two thousand dollars at your pleasure. Apropos of this establishment, Mr. Upton told us of a good pun which our genial and witty "Grace Greenwood" threw off a few days ago when she with a party of friends was here. They were on the way to visit the establishment; but some of the gentlemen having to walk while the rest rode, Mr Upton, who was in the carriage, gave those on foot the direction by saying they would know the house by the sign of a lyre on its roof. "Yes," quickly added Grace; "and when you see that *lyre,* it will tell the *truth.*"

CHAPTER XXXI.

GENEVA, OCTOBER 30.—We have now been here a month, and the weather, a large part of the time, has been wet and disagreeable. Nevertheless, Geneva is an agreeable stopping-place, even in the wet season, to travelers going to or returning from Italy; and there is always a large number of strangers here. There are, we know not how many, first-class hôtels here, and many excellent private boarding houses, all within easy distance of one another; and one never need be at a loss for pleasant company, leaving out the resident population, among whom are many cultivated and refined people. We have in our boarding house Rev. Abel Stevens, author of the "History of Methodism in the United States," and his amiable wife, whom, among others here, we have found exceedingly pleasant company; and in the family of Mr. Consul Upton, near by, we are always made to feel as though at home. Then the Rev. Leonard Woolsey Bacon, pastor of the American church and editor of the *Swiss Chronicle* here, who with his family, consisting of his wife, eight children, and two interesting lady cousins, resides at Petit Saconnex, gives a reception every Thursday evening from four to ten o'clock, to which all Americans especially are invited. We have spent one evening most agreeably with them. Their residence is in the country, about two miles from our boarding house. Refreshments were set out at six o'clock. After this we had several pieces of music by two of Mr. Bacon's sons and their teacher, on the violin, Mr. Bacon himself, who is an accomplished musician and composer, accompanying them on a violoncello. Following these, Madame, wife of General Fluck, of the Austrian army, also present, performed a number of pieces on the piano in a superior manner. Thus, with music and conversation, these evenings are very enjoyable.

One day we went to Ferney, which is in France, a distance of some five miles from the city, to see Voltaire's chateau. Only two rooms, the parlor and a bed-room, both on the ground floor, are shown to visitors, and these remain just as he left them at his death. His parlor stove is quite a huge affair, and his lounge and most of the other furniture are rather common, but some of his chairs were handsomely embroidered — the work of his niece, whose portrait on the walls of one of the rooms shows her to have been a beautiful woman. His own portrait and marble bust are also preserved here, as well as the portraits of Frederick the Great and Queen Catherine II. of Russia. There are likewise engraved likenesses of Milton, Racine, Corneille, Newton, the Calas family, Washington, and Franklin. That of Washington is unlike any other we have ever seen, and it is probably the only one of the kind extant. Of the Calas family, the likenesses of the mother, one son, two daughters, and man and maid servant are given. The history of this family is doubtless known to most of our readers. Jean Calas, the head of the family and a Protestant, was cruelly executed in 1762, at Toulouse, on the charge of murdering one of his own sons to prevent his secession from Protestantism; and subsequently, through the efforts of Voltaire and others, a reversal of the judgment of guilty against him was obtained; he and the family were declared innocent, and a pension of thirty thousand francs was granted to the family by

Louis XV. The only remaining descendant of this family now resides in Geneva, and is supported mainly by charity. In Voltaire's bed-room are two other small paintings; one a portrait of his washerwoman, and the other, a handsome face, of his chimney sweep in an Italian hat. The floor of the parlor is of wood, handsomely inlaid. In this room is an urn containing the ashes of Voltaire's heart. The house has beautiful surroundings, and it must have been a very fine one in its day. We walked through the long arbor where he used to go for exercise, and in which, we were told he sometimes did his writing. Near the northern entrance to the chateau is a small building with a clock-tower, and the name of Voltaire appears under the clock-face. This, we understood, was his church, but we think it is not used for religious services now. From this point a magnificent view is obtained of Mont Blanc. In the evening we went to hear a lecture by Monsieur Taine, the celebrated French author, before the College of Geneva. It was upon the life and manners of the French people before their revolution, from the time of Louis XI. to Louis XVII. The public hall was crowded by attentive listeners, among whom we observed Père Hyacinthe. Monsieur Taine is a man, we should judge, about fifty years of age. His height is about five feet, ten inches, frame spare and muscular, and his movement active. He wears his whiskers and beard, which are black, with a slight mixture of gray, cut short.

We have been several times to hear Père Hyacinthe, who conducts his services and preaches in the French language. Although we could not understand him as well as we could wish, we felt sensibly the influence of his magnetism and eloquence. He is undoubtedly an accomplished elocutionist and orator, and, without being a very large man, his presence is at once commanding and graceful. We sat near his wife and little son Paul, of whom they are said to be very proud, as they have a right to be, for he is a fine-looking boy, and may live to become as eloquent as his namesake. The congregation was comparatively small.

There is a beautiful Greek Church here, richly frescoed in the interior, and the floor is covered by a handsome carpet, on which the people either stand or kneel, there being few or no seats. On a Sunday we were present for a short time near the close of the services, which were peculiar. The music, entirely vocal, was very fine. The Cathedral Church of St. Peter, where we have also attended Protestant services, is by far the more important. This church dates back to the eleventh century, and is fraught with many stirring events in the history of Geneva. Without going further back, when the Roman Catholics held sway here, years before John Calvin made his appearance, Farel and other Protestant reformers had succeeded in abolishing Romanism from the city, and St. Peter's, we believe, has ever since been in the possession of the Protestants. The same pulpit from which Calvin preached still remains in its place. Expelled from France, of which country he was a native, he was passing through Geneva as a fugitive when, being recognized by his Protestant brethren, he was prevailed on to remain, and finally became the dictator of the city. In an old French volume which a friend loaned us to read here, it is stated that when Calvin first came here he was a young man, and that he was so pale and sickly in appearance many thought he had but a few years at most to live.

In the Rath Museum there is a collection of fine pictures, among them one representing "The Death of Calvin," and another, "Bonnivard in Castle Chillon." In the Academic Museum are many fine specimens of Zoölogy and Geology. Immense pieces of white and smoked crystal quartz in their native state excited our wonder and admiration.

One pleasant afternoon we took a walk to the Chateau Diodati, situated about one mile and a half from the city on the southeast side of the lake. In 1816 this Chateau was the residence of Lord Byron, and this is where he wrote some or all of his "Manfred" and portions of "Childe Harold." It is snuggled in among the trees, with a balcony on the lake side, the room in which he wrote looking out also upon the lake. We saw his bed, table, chairs, and other furniture used by him in this room. There are many charming residences on both sides of the lake, among them the princely chateau of Baron Adolphe Rothschild on the northwest side, in or near Little Saconnex. Just in the suburbs of the city is a large old mansion, now in a dilapidated condition, with a large lawn in front. It was at one period the residence of Voltaire, and for a few days in 1867 the writer and his younger son occupied a chamber in it as boarders—the family with whom they were boarding having removed there. We observed nothing remarkable about it except that the dining-room, very high posted, as were all the other first story rooms, was unusually spacious, and the large panels of its walls were embellished with landscape paintings. Had these paintings the power of speech they could, without doubt, narrate many an interesting story in the gay life of Voltaire and his congenial associates.

We have made here the acquaintance of a very pleasant gentleman and his accomplished wife, by the name of Saltzman. He is a retired watch manufacturer. In company with Mr. Consul Upton, wife, and sister, we had the honor one day of dining with them. We mention this for the purpose of introducing a touching personal incident of the occasion. We will premise by saying that when the writer was at Geneva in 1867, Mr. Upton had two interesting daughters, Lucie and Estella, both young ladies grown. The latter, however, was then a suffering invalid, and died not very long afterward. Lucie subsequently married a Greek gentleman of fine character and went with him to reside in Greece, where they were blessed by the birth of a son, and, sorrowful to tell, the mother soon thereafter followed her sister to the spirit-land. At the dinner table Mr. Upton was led to speak of a melancholy pilgrimage he had not long before made to the home and grave of this cherished daughter; and he repeated, in a tone and with a pathos we shall never forget, some lines he had written in allusion to this sad journey over the sea. At our special request he sent us the next day a copy of those lines, and we give them as they appear before us in his own plain hand:

A CONCEIT.

Float me safely, dark blue waves,
O'er the Mediterranean sea —
A living tie between two graves,
I go, their spirit-tie to be.

From where Estella lies in gloom,
A rose, an autumn rose, I bear,

To softly lay on Lucie's tomb,
Whose leaves would else have perished there.

*   *   *   *   *

Now tell me, tea-rose, whisper low!
Have the dear sister-spirits met?
And are they where bright flowers grow?
And are they where no cheeks are wet?

Be still, my heart! I cannot hear
What the fluttering leaves would say.
Oh, coward heart! you doubt, I fear,
And I, in anguish turn away.*

CHAPTER XXXII.

TURIN, NOVEMBER 4.—We have now fairly entered upon what we undertook not without some apprehension of sickness—a trip to Italy. We have heard a great deal about the deadly malaria of the Campagna, and of the debilitating and often fatal Roman fever, and we should leave a

---

* We should not have ventured thus to raise the vail which concealed this sacred reminiscence from the public eye, but that we are obliged to record here, as we do in deep sorrow, the death of our dear friend, the author of this little poem—itself a gem. He died suddenly, supposed from heart disease, on the night of June 17, 1877. Mr. Upton had held the office of United States Consul at Geneva since his appointment by President Lincoln in the spring of 1861. In addition to this, he was from time to time called on to perform the duties of United States Minister for Switzerland during the absence of that officer; and on the 23d of January, 1877, after the Swiss mission had been reduced to that of a Chargé d' Affaires and Mr. Rublee had resigned, Secretary Fish gave him the appointment, outside of his consulship, of Chargé d' Affaires *ad interim*, and he held this office until his death. Admirably qualified by his ability, education, and courtesy of demeanor for any such position, he was ever most faithful to his trust.

truth unspoken did we not frankly admit this apprehension. It was this concern of mind, no doubt, that superinduced this child's prayer one night as we lay more asleep than awake:

> Great Father, guide us on our way,
> And keep us safe from every harm;
> We crave Thy care from day to day,
> To cheer and keep from false alarm.

Oftener than otherwise when one in sleep or in a dreamy state thinks he has said a wise or witty thing, on awakening he is surprised to find it the very opposite; but those lines appeared so fully to express our feelings and desires that, simple as they are, we put them in our note book, without, however, the remotest idea of their ever going further. If any apology is needed for copying them here, it may be found in the patent fact that we started out and have continued on a somewhat familiar plane with our readers in all that we have had to say.

Much of the time while we have been in Geneva the weather has been rainy, and it rained when we left there at half-past six on the morning of the 2d instant. We at first thought of taking Cook's tour tickets, which were offered at only about half the regular fare; but we were obliged to decline them because they were limited to ninety days—the length of time Mr. Seward said it would take to put down the rebellion. Before starting, on the day before, we procured from a restaurant a plump roast chicken, some nice bread, and a bottle of *vin ordinaire*. for our next day's lunch on the train—preferring to take our meal quietly in our compartment to running the chance of "a hasty plate of soup" at a restaurant outside. Knowing that we were to have the company of Mr. and Mrs. J. S. Stickney and

Rev. Mr. Sumner, a young Congregational preacher from Chicago, they, on our advice, in like manner, secured the requisite materials for "internal improvement." Rev. Mr. Frazier, from Philadelphia, on his way to Egypt, and a German gentleman were the only other occupants in our compartment. Wet as it was when we left Geneva, before we reached Culoz, two and a half hours' ride, we came out into fair weather, such as we had seldom seen for a month. The road runs along the slopes of the Jura mountains on the right bank of the Rhone, which flows through a narrow rocky valley between the Jura and Mont Vouache, where it is commanded by a French fort high up on the right. As the clouds overhead broke away, they settled down for many miles on the top and side of the Jura mountains, presenting, as the sun shone upon them, one of the most beautiful pictures of the kind we ever beheld. They were fleecy like cotton, and as from our elevated position we could see the top as well as the side of the clouds — the sky beyond forming the background — we could hardly find words to express our admiration of the tableau. Our special companion remarked that "the mountains seemed to be reluctant to lose their soft enveloping curtain so gently obscuring their peaks." The scenery all the way between Geneva and the Mont Cenis Tunnel — there must be at least twenty other tunnels on the whole route — is strikingly interesting, some of it being almost as fine as is to be seen anywhere in Switzerland. There was an examination of baggage at the French frontier, and then again at Modane, just before entering the great tunnel, near the eastern end of which, but some two hundred feet below in the valley, is a small village, where there is a railroad junction. Our track led along the side of the mountain and directly above this village, where we had to pass over a bridge, which had evidently just been destroyed by a flood and temporarily reconstructed sufficiently to allow the train to pass. As we were on a curve, and moved very slowly, we could see the danger to which we were exposed, since, had this temporary structure given way, we should inevitably have been precipitated to the bottom of the valley. Just before reaching this bridge, we saw the guard and one or two passengers alight and run ahead as though they were apprehensive of danger, and we think it was wrong not to have allowed all the passengers to do the same. The entrance to the tunnel does not differ from those of other railroad tunnels. There is a double track, and at short intervals lamps on high posts mostly between the tracks, but occasionally at the side; and if our eyes did not deceive us, there is a narrow foot way, also at one side. We were on the left track, and passed a lighted hand car with several roadmen on it in one part of the tunnel. We were not in the least disturbed by either smoke or gas, nor did we observe any unusual closeness in the air. While passing through, all in our compartment, except the German gentleman, united in singing the "Rock of Ages," "Nearer my God to Thee," "Shall we Gather at the River," and "The Morning Dawn is Breaking," the last at Mrs. Stickney's suggestion, just as the twilight began to pierce the darkness at the further end of the tunnel. We entered the tunnel, which is eight miles long, precisely at five minutes past five and emerged from it at twenty-eight minutes past five, thus occupying twenty-three minutes in the passage. On the ascending grade into the heart of the mountain the train moved much slower than on the descending grade. At the highest point we were four thousand feet above the level of the sea. It was about half-past nine in the evening when we reached Turin; and, as luck would have it, we were obliged to go to our hôtel without our baggage, except what we had in a shawl strap. Intending to return by Geneva, we left one of our valises there, taking the other, a good sized one, along with us, and this, we found had been checked through by the express train, which parted from our train at Culoz, arriving at Turin two or three hours in advance of us. The baggage by the express train, not claimed, had been locked up for the night, and the officers of the customs had gone home; so we were obliged to wait for our valise until morning, when, with the least possible examination by those polite gentlemen with cocked hats and military cloaks, it was delivered to us.

On the third, Messrs. Stickney, Sumner, and Frazier, having gone to the valley of the Waldenses, we, in company with Mrs. Stickney, were driven for one hour through the most interesting parts of the town and across the Po, over a bridge we should think to be four hundred feet in length. This is an arched stone bridge, and a short distance further up the river there is a suspension bridge for foot passengers only. We passed many fine monuments, one of the most elaborate being that to Cavour—born 1810, died 1861. We cannot fully describe it. It consists in part of a statue of himself with that of a beautiful woman, partly kneeling, with her left arm around his waist, and eyes raised toward his face. Other figures surround the base. We have a good photograph of it. To show the contrast between Turin and Washington, we may be pardoned for saying that the whole charge for the hour's ride — our carriage was a nice one with four seats handsomely lined and cushioned — was just one franc and a half, with the addition of three sous *pour boire!* We are also agreeably disappointed in the beauty of the city, which is generally laid out in squares, with streets of good width, and many public squares well paved and adorned by equestrian and other monumental statues, and flanked by magnificent palaces. What we especially like about the streets is that, while they are paved for the most part with cobble stones, there are four rows of smooth stone slabs placed just wide enough apart for carriage wheels, and the sidewalks are paved with similar slabs. The buildings generally are high and handsome, and the city has altogether a modern appearance. We have seen no narrow, dirty streets, such as we find in all the old cities we have visited. On some of the streets and open squares are long rows of shops, entered from high and airy arcades.

From 1859 to 1865 Turin was the capital of Italy and the residence of the King, whose Palace here is always ready for him whenever he visits the city. We have been conducted through the Palace, which is a plain brick edifice sumptuously furnished, and we avail ourselves of the note-book of our "better half" for a description of what we saw. The pillars of the gateway to the Palace are decorated by two groups in bronze of Castor and Pollux, and in a niche in the Palace hall is an equestrian statue of Duke Victor Amadeus I.— the statue being of bronze and the horse marble, beneath which are the figures of two slaves. We were met first by an officer wearing a long cloak, one corner of which was thrown over his shoulder, and a three-cornered hat, adorned with a large bunch of black rooster's feathers, falling gracefully over his side face. He walked up and down without saying a word; but another officer, dressed in red, white, and gold, pointed to the beautiful marble entrance, which is quite beyond description. There are six white marble steps to the first landing, from which other wide marble steps lead to the second story. The ceiling is beautifully frescoed. On the walls of the stairway are fine paintings. One represents Tasso, richly dressed in black velvet, being introduced to the Court; and another, "The Receipt of the Declaration of War by Spain." We walked first into the footmen's room, elegantly furnished with rich paintings on ceiling and walls; then into the pages' room, equally elegant, and next to the throne room, and so on until we had passed through some twenty rooms in all. Over the throne is a canopy of red velvet shaded to orange. The doors are richly gilded and the ceilings of the rooms, some of which are lined with red velvet, are beautifully frescoed, while the window curtains are of silk lace. There are many fine paintings in the different apartments, the floors of which, of inlaid wood, are so smooth that we were obliged to slip or slide over them. Among the paintings is a magnificent one of "Solomon on his Throne." In the dining room there is a crystal chandelier, and there is another in the large ball room, which is splendidly finished with Doric columns and heavy gilt cornices. The Queen's Chapel is small but elegant. The furniture of all the rooms is very rich, none of it more so than a number of mosaic tables, which are surprisingly beautiful. The Palace also contains an extensive library.

There is an Armory, Museum of Natural History, Museum of Antiquities, and an extensive Painting Gallery here; but we did not take the time to visit them, since we expect to see everything of this kind in other Italian cities.

CHAPTER XXXIII.

MILAN, NOVEMBER 5.—We left Turin yesterday forenoon, and arrived at Milan in time to ride an hour around the city, visiting the Cathedral of St. Ambrose and the celebrated picture of the "Last Supper," by Leonardo da Vinci. The Cathedral was founded by St. Ambrose in the fourth century, and the guide-books tell us that the gates are those which he closed against the Emperor Theodosius after the cruel massacre of Thessalonica; also, that the Lombard Kings and German Emperors formerly caused themselves to be crowned here with the Iron Crown, which is still preserved at Monza. The interior is richly adorned with fresco and other paintings, mosaics, statues, etc. "The brazen serpent on a column in the nave is said to be that raised by Moses in the wilderness." We had not time to investigate the truth of this statement, and therefore accepted it as authentic without controversy. It is no doubt just as true as that a certain silver case in the Cologne Cathedral contains the bones of the three wise men who came from the East to Bethlehem to offer their presents to the infant

Christ, and which precious remains, it is said, were presented to the Archbishop of Cologne by the Emperor Barbarossa when he captured them with the city of Milan. We were shown here, also, some very curious old parchment books of the fourteenth century, and sat in a marble arm-chair made at the time the church was founded.

The painting of the "Last Supper" is in the refectory (now a cavalry barrack) of the suppressed Monastery of the Church of Santa Maria delle Grazie. There is nothing very remarkable in the church, but we viewed this picture with great interest, notwithstanding it has been much defaced. Roscoe, in his "Life of Leo X.," speaking of Leonardo da Vinci, observes: "By his astonishing skill in music, which he performed on a kind of lyre of his own invention, and by his extraordinary facility as an improvisatore, in the recitation of Italian verse, no less than by his professional talents, he secured the favor of his patron (Lodovico, 1492,) and the applauses of the Milanese Court. Lodovico had, however, the judgment to avail himself of the opportunity afforded him by this great artist, to enrich the city of Milan with some of the finest productions of his pencil; and if the abilities of Leonardo were to be estimated by a single effort, his panegyrist might perhaps select his celebrated picture of the "Last Supper" as the most valuable of his works. In this piece it was doubtless the intention of the painter to surpass whatever had before been executed, and to represent not merely the external form and features, but the emotions and passions of the mind, from the highest degree of virtue and beneficence in the character of the Saviour to the extreme of treachery and guilt in that of Iscariot; while the various sensations of affection and veneration, of joy and of sorrow, of hope and of fear, displayed in the countenances and gestures of the disciples, might express their various apprehensions of the mysterious rite. In the midst sits the great founder, dispensing with unshaken firmness, from either hand, the emblems of his own approaching suffering. The agitation of the disciples is marked by their contrasted attitudes and various expressions. Treachery and inhumanity seem to be concentrated in the form and features of Judas Iscariot. In representing the countenance of Christ he found, however, the powers of the artist inadequate to the conception of his own mind. To step beyond the limits of earth, and to diffuse over those features a ray of divinity, was his bold but fruitless attempt. The effort was often renewed, and as often terminated in disappointment and humiliation. Despairing of success, he disclosed his anxiety to his friend and associate, Bernardo Zenale, who advised him to desist from all further endeavors, and in consequence of which this great work was suffered to remain imperfect." The size of this picture is fifteen by thirty feet.

In the evening we went into the great Cathedral, which, by many travelers, is regarded as the most majestic and beautiful in the world. It had been a great day there, but we arrived only in time to see a long line of priests leaving for their cloisters, and the removal from the altar of a number of silver saints—statues, of full size, in solid silver—all of which we saw in the sacristy to-day, after which we spent an hour or two on top of the building, the whole of which, including the roof, its ninety-eight pinnacles, and its innumerable statues, is of white marble. Some travelers have stated the number of statues in the interior and on the outside as high as seven thousand, with places for three thousand more. Here is a true picture by Tennyson:

> "O Milan, O the chanting quires,
> The giant windows' blazoned fires,
> The height, the space, the gloom, the glory!
> A mount of marble, a hundred spires!
> I climbed the roofs at break of day;
> Sun-smitten Alps before me lay.
> I stood among the silent statues,
> And statued pinnacles mute as they.
> How faintly-flushed, how phantom-fair,
> Was Monte Rosa, hanging there.
> A thousand shadowy-penciled valleys
> And snowy dells in a golden air!"

The interior is hardly less imposing than the exterior. "Its double aisles, its clustered pillars, its lofty arches, the luster of its walls, its numberless niches filled with marble figures—give it an appearance novel even in Italy, and singularly majestic." Its works of art, consisting of paintings, statuary of various kinds, bronze as well as marble, monuments to distinguished persons, etc., with nearly four hundred representations of Scriptural subjects on the stained glass of the choir windows, afford boundless satisfaction to the visitor. We should not forget to speak of one other thing we saw on our visit here: Within a circular railing, twenty feet or more in circumference, near the altar, a white covering had been spread on the floor, and a choir boy was engaged in gathering into a bag thousands of soldi or sous that had been thrown in there by the faithful worshipers, literally covering the floor with them.

In the Picture Gallery here are many noted paintings of Rubens, Tintoretto, Paul Veronese, Bellini, Giotto, Leonardo, and other distinguished artists.

Among these we were particularly impressed with one by Bellini, representing "St. Mark Preaching at Alexandria," and another by Paul Veronese, depicting "Christ in the House of the Pharisee."

The extensive arcade recently constructed here is a magnificent improvement. It takes in parts of four streets, forming a cross, entirely spanned by glass roofs. The buildings below the base of the arches are five stories high. There is a dome in the center, and therefrom wings extend the length of a square in each direction. Within this arcade are a large number of the finest shops, and in the evening when we were there it was thronged with people. The dome, which is much broader than that of our Capitol, in like manner with ours was lighted by a circular row of gas jets.

VERONA, NOVEMBER 6.—We reached Como from Milan last evening. It is a charming place. This morning, after visiting an interesting old cathedral, the market, etc., we took the steamer for Varenna, a tumble-down village on the east side of the lake, some three hours' sail, via Bellagio, another delightful summer resort on a point of land between Lake Como and another part of that lake called Lake Lecco. The scenery was charming, but the season, of course, was too far advanced to show all its beauties. We had for companions Mr. Stickney and wife and Rev. Mr. Sumner, all of whom had traveled with us from Geneva. At Varenna we hired a comfortable two horse carriage and rode over a smooth turnpike for two hours and a half, along the lake shore to Lecco, where, after a good dinner at a hotel, and a view of this singular old town, we took the cars for Bergamo, on the main line from Milan to Verona and Venice. This turnpike, much of the way, was cut out of the mountains, and at two points it runs a considerable distance through tunnels. Other portions are bordered by grape vines, olive and mulberry trees, with occasional fig trees and box-wood growing spontaneously. The carriage ride was very romantic, and we all enjoyed it better even than the sail on the lake. When we reached Bergamo it had commenced to rain, and the night being dark we were shut out from all view until we arrived, near midnight, at Verona, where we now rest.

Having, in the early part of October, 1867, made the trip from Milan to Venice by daylight, in company with his son Henry Franklin, the writer is enabled to give a brief description of the route. When at a little past six in the morning we took the cars at Milan the ground was covered with frost. At ten we were at Brescia, the ride thus far being through flat, wet country, possessing little interest, except the city of Bergamo, a walled town on the side of a hill, which we passed at half-past eight, and which presented a novel appearance. At eleven we were at Desenzano, on Lake Garda, a beautiful sheet of water stretching off to the mountains on our left. All the way from Milan are forests of mulberry trees. They have the shape of an apple tree, and here and there the peasants were carefully picking the green leaves from their limbs. There were here also many grape vines running in festoons from one mulberry tree to another. We next came to Peschiera, where there are formidable fortifications on the left, embracing a village, which faces Lake Garda, and the whole is upon a small island. There is also a strong fort on the right. Our time being limited, we stopped at Verona only to dine, and did not leave our seats at Padua; but near the station at the latter place we saw men engaged in expressing the juice from cart loads of grapes by trampling upon them barefooted and bare-legged. These vehicles served both for carts and vats—the cart-body being made tight so as to hold the wine until drawn off. This is probably the primitive mode of making wine.

CHAPTER XXXIV.

*Please you, I'll tell you as we pass along,
That you will wonder what hath fortuned.*
—*Two Gentlemen of Verona.*

VERONA, NOVEMBER 8.—Yesterday (Sunday) we attended service at two of the Roman Catholic churches, both very ancient, and also the Waldensian Protestant Mission, where we arrived in time to hear part of a sermon by the Italian pastor, Rev. Stefano Revels. As he preached in the Italian language we were able to comprehend but very little of what he said; but, nevertheless, we were impressed with his apparent solemnity and eloquence of manner, and enjoyed the sweet singing of the choir. The service was in a small room entered through two others, one of which is used for their Sunday School, and over the door of which, in Italian, is this verse: "Know ye not that ye are the temple of God, and that the spirit of God dwelleth in you?" The following verses were on the walls of the lecture room: 1—"Jesus saith unto her, Go call thy husband and come hither." 2—"For we are

His workmanship, created in Christ Jesus unto good works." 3—"Search the Scriptures; for in them ye think ye have eternal life." 4—"Jesus said unto her, I am the resurrection and the life: he that believeth in me, though he were dead, yet shall he live." After dinner, on our invitation, Mr. Revels and his young English wife called and passed an hour with us at our hotel. He is evidently well educated, speaking English fluently, and is earnestly engaged in his mission. He says there are fifty-nine thousand Roman Catholics, one thousand Jews, and only five hundred Protestants in this city. He makes it a large part of his duty to visit from house to house, where he is always kindly treated, but generally told by the families that they look to their priests for spiritual guidance and prefer that he should not trouble himself to call. Occasionally he meets a person who acknowledges to him secretly that he believes the Protestant to be the true religion, but says at the same time that were he to come out openly and declare such to be his belief, he would be cast off by both priest and people, and consequently unable to get any employment. The priests warn all against listening to the Protestant instruction, and they take and burn all the Bibles they find presented to them. Mr. Revels said there is about one priest here to every thirty of the inhabitants, and that while some of them are rich, a great many are miserably poor and shockingly careless of their personal cleanliness, their under clothing being the color of mummy wrappings. He was stationed several months at Lucca, near Pisa, a town of twenty-one thousand inhabitants, one-tenth of whom he said were priests. There are three Roman Catholic seminaries there, and the preponderance of that sect is so great in that town that they call it "Sacristel de Roma." Among the Waldenses he said there are a few men possessing property to the value of ten thousand dollars, and these are esteemed very rich; but that they are very miserly, and will try to split a soldo (one sou) to make two of it. A man with five cows, a few chestnuts, and a few walnuts is considered well off. Of the general morals of the Waldenses he spoke very favorably, stating that of the number incarcerated for crime they were only as one to sixty or seventy of the Roman Catholics. He appeared greatly encouraged by the spread of the Protestant faith in Italy, where, he said, there were already forty Protestant churches, embracing not less than three thousand Sunday School children. Besides this, there is one other small Protestant Mission in Verona.

Turn we now to romance and ancient story:

> "Two households, both alike in dignity,
>   In fair Verona, where we lay our scene,
> From ancient grudge, break to new mutiny,
>   Where civil blood makes civil hands unclean."

It seems like a dream to be here amid the scenes which must have been familiar to Romeo and Juliet, if indeed any such persons ever lived here. At any rate, we are assured that the play of "Romeo and Juliet" is founded on events which actually occurred here; and, without stopping to question the truth of the romance, we have paid a visit to the tomb which, for one franc, is shown as that of Juliet. It is in a rough garden entered from a dirty side street, and the forlorn looking Italian woman who let us in appeared as though she pitied us on account of our gullibility. A ragged boy ran ahead to show us the way to an old monastery, not, we believe, now in use, connected with which is a decayed chapel, containing a rude sarcophagus in red Verona marble, called Juliet's tomb. Hanging on the wall over the sarcophagus was a wreath of faded flowers, all of which is shown by a photograph in our collection. The origin of the story of "Romeo and Juliet" is in doubt. Its material incidents, we are told by writers upon Shakspeare, are to be found in romances written before his time; but it was left to his genius to give them immortality. "'Romeo and Juliet,'" says Schlegel, "is a picture of love and its pitiful fate in a world whose atmosphere is too rough for this tenderest blossom of human life. Two beings, created for each other, feel mutual love at first glance. Every consideration disappears before the irresistible influence of living in one another; they join themselves secretly, under circumstances hostile in the highest degree to their union, relying merely on the protection of an invisible power. By unfriendly events following blow upon blow, their heroic constancy is exposed to all manner of trials, till, forcibly separated from each other, by a voluntary death they are united in the grave to meet again in another world." Thus much of these unhappy lovers. To acknowledge that no tears were shed by us at Juliet's tomb might indicate an unpardonable degree of hard-heartedness—

> "For never was a story of more woe
> Than this of Juliet and her Romeo."

On this point, therefore, we leave our readers in the dark.

The founding of the city of Verona is assigned to the Gauls, but later the Romans held sway here. There is an amphitheater here in tolerable preservation, supposed to have been erected about the year 284, under Diocletian. It is calculated that it would accommodate twenty-five thousand spectators seated and seventy thousand more standing. Its arcades are now occupied as traders' shops.

The most imposing monuments here to individuals are the tombs of the Scaligers, or della Scala family, who, from 1262 to 1389, were Presidents of the Republic of Verona; and a full-length marble statue of Dante on a lofty pedestal. Dante is represented in a long robe coming to his feet and closely buttoned over his chest, with a long cloak fastened closely around the neck—the left side hanging gracefully over his arm, while with his left hand, in which he also holds a half-closed book, the other side is raised in folds to his right elbow. On his head is a kind of skull-cap. Resting his right elbow on his left hand and the forefinger of his right hand against his chin, he appears in the attitude of listening or of meditation. His expression is stern and forbidding. This statue stands in the center of the Plazza del Signori, so called from its having been the place of residence of the Scaligers. We wish it were in our power to describe the tombs of the Scaligers. They consist of a number of Gothic structures situated in front of the little Church of Santa Maria l' Antica, and are very striking in their appearance. The ladder which forms the crest of the family "recurs frequently on the elaborately executed railings. The largest of these monuments is that of Can Signorio. It consists of a sarcophagus resting on a pedestal supported by columns of moderate height, over which rises a canopy crowned with an equestrian statue of the Prince. On the square column in the middle are six Christian Heroes; in niches higher up are the

Christian Virtues." Another sarcophagus also with a canopy and equestrian statue is that of Mastino III. Between these two principal monuments are four large sarcophagi, the first three dating from 1311. The last is that of Can Grande II., who was assassinated in the public streets by his brother, Can Signorio, in 1359. Over the church door are the sarcophagus and equestrian statue of Can Grande, Francesco della Scala; and adjoining it, on the wall of the church, those of Giovanni della Scala and Mastino I.

The two distinguished scholars, Julius Cæsar and his son, Joseph Justus Scaliger, claimed to be descendants of this famous Scala family. The father was born at Padua in 1484, and died at Agen, France, 1558. He was a doctor of medicine and philosopher, and was remarkable for his prodigious memory. Joseph (born at Agen, 1540, died in Leyden, 1609) was acquainted with all the languages, ancient and modern, and with the idioms of the East as well as of the West. His contemporaries called him "an abyss of erudition," "the ocean of sciences," "the last effort of Nature." His letters are spoken of as a veritable treasure. Hallam pronounced him and Isaac Casaubon "the two greatest scholars of the sixteenth century," and Niebuhr says of him that he "stood on the summit of universal solid philological learning in a degree that none have reached since." Whether descendants of the old lords of Verona or not, the names of Julius and Joseph Scaliger are handed down to us inscribed high on the scroll of scholastic history.

The Cathedral of Santa Maria Matricolare is the most imposing of the churches. It dates back to the time of Charlemagne. Though bearing the marks of age, some portions of it are still beautiful. Among the paintings is an "Assumption," by Titian; and of the monuments, one to the poet De Cesuris and one to Pope Lucius III., who was buried here when he died in 1185. There are several other fine churches here, but we did not take time to visit them all. Portions of the old walls and some of the old gateways of the city still stand as interesting relics of the old times; and we can go in no street or square here that we do not see more or less to attract our special attention. The river Adige, spanned by several fine bridges, runs rapidly through the city, the streets of which are liable to be sometimes overflowed by the rushing floods from the Alps, which now loom up near us covered with snow.

CHAPTER XXXV.

"There is a glorious city in the sea,
The sea is in the broad, the narrow streets,
Ebbing and flowing; and the salt sea-weed
Clings to the marble of her palaces.
No track of men, no footsteps to and fro,
Lead to her gates. The path lies o'er the sea,
Invisible; and from the land we went,
As to a floating city — steering in,
And gliding up her streets as in a dream,
So smoothly, silently — by many a dome,
Mosque-like, and many a stately portico,
The statues ranged along an azure sky;
By many a pile in more than Eastern pride,
Of all the evidence of merchant kings;
The fronts of some, though Time had shattered them,
Still glowing with the richest hues of art,
As though the wealth within them had run o'er."

THIS IS VENICE; but when Rogers wrote this description the city was not approached by a railway. Now, on the western side, one of the main small islands of the city is connected with the mainland by the railroad from Padua and Verona—the distance from the shore about two miles by a bridge built on over two hundred arches across the lagoons which surround the city on all sides. We were safely landed on this little island at half past three on the afternoon of the 8th of November, having come in about four hours from Verona, our last stopping place. Officers of the customs were on hand to make the least possible examination of our luggage, and other officials in uniform handed us tickets for whichever conveyance—gondola or omnibus boat—we might choose to convey us to our hotel. Being a party of five, we chose an omnibus, which, although built in the same form, is considerably larger than the gondola, and has a more spacious cabin at the stern. For a charge of one and a half lira (thirty cents) each, we were rowed with our light luggage along the Grand Canal and through the narrow winding *streets* for half an hour or more to the Victoria Hotel, where we concluded to stop. As in the case of all buildings here rising up from the sea, the steps of the hotel extend into the water, and we disembarked upon them directly from the boat. Along some portions of the Grand Canal, which winds through the city, there is a quay of good width, mostly, we understand, of modern date; and this is a great improvement, inasmuch as it serves not only as a protection to the buildings, which everywhere have a rusty appearance from the action of the salt water upon them, but it also affords an agreeable promenade.

Mr. Rogers' description of the city as he saw it is true to life. An American traveler calling on him in London, in 1852, three years before his death, took occasion, in the course of their conversation, to say that Mr. Rogers' volume of poems had been his constant companion in his travels, when the latter at once spoke of his residence on the continent with Lord Byron, and quoted part of his own lines on Venice. "Byron," said he, "repeated them to me one morning as we sailed up the Grand Canal, telling me they were very fine, and written, he believed, by Southey, forgetting that the real author was by his side."

The city is compact, and the land streets, lanes, and alleys are so narrow, generally not over four or five feet in width, while many are much narrower; and the one hundred and forty-seven canals, only wide enough usually to allow gondolas to pass one another, are likewise so confined that one here feels as though he were in a wilderness. Madame de Staël made this observation: "A sentiment of sadness seizes the imagination on entering the city. You take leave of vegetation — not even a fly is to be seen; all animals are banished, and man alone remains to struggle against the sea. Silence is profound in this place, whose streets are canals, and the noise of the oars is the only interruption to this silence. It is not the country, since not a tree is to be seen here; it is not a city, since one hears here not the least movement; it is not even a vessel, since one advances not." She adds: "You find persons here who have never been from one quarter of the city to another, who have never seen St. Mark's square, and to whom the sight of a horse would be a veritable marvel. These black gondolas, which glide upon the canals, resemble coffins or cradles — the last and first habitation of man. In the evening one sees only the reflection of the lanterns in the gondolas, whose black color prevents their being descried. One might say that these were shadows gliding in the water guided by a small star." We have translated these remarks from a French volume of "Corinne" before us, because they give, in the main, a vivid description of this wonderful "city in the sea" as it struck us on the occasion of our present visit, and as it appeared to the writer when here for a day in 1867. We are not able, however, either to confirm or deny the statement that there were no flies in Venice, although we can conceive of no good reason why they should not exist there, as well as in any other city. As regards horses, it is doubtless true that none were seen there in Madame de Staël's time, as the number now there does not exceed a dozen, and these are kept on a small island laid out as a riding park, which we visited, at the extreme eastern end of the city. In this park there are clusters of trees, and there may be seen here and there one in the city; but generally one beholds only a wilderness of houses closely packed. One may walk over the three hundred and seventy-eight bridges to almost any part of the city; but to a stranger, as we have observed before, it is like being in a maze, so numerous and irregular are the streets and lanes, many of which are arched ways under the second stories of houses, and only just wide enough for two to pass. By "spotting" corner shops and signboards we soon learned the way to Piazzo San Marco, the great central point of the city. It is in form oblong, about five hundred and seventy-five by one hundred and eighty-five feet, with an open space, called the Piazzetta, (little square,) leading to the quay on the east side. The celebrated Church of St. Mark faces the eastern end of the square, and next to it stands the Palace of the Doges, facing the same way and extending along the Piazzetta to the quay, presenting also a beautiful front toward the sea. Here, on either side of the Piazzetta, is a splendid granite column—one bearing the "Winged Lion of St. Mark, the emblem of the tutelary Saint of Venice, the other surmounted by St. Theodore on a crocodile, the patron of the ancient Republic, placed there in 1326." The gondoliers have their headquarters here. Nearly opposite to St. Mark's is the campanile of that Church, a square tower three hundred and twenty-two feet in height, and affording a magnificent view of the city, country, and Adriatic sea for many miles around. This tower is probably one of the easiest of ascent of any in Europe, the way up being by an inclined plane rising by one step at each corner. The bell man at the summit, provided with a telescope, keeps constant watch, and in case of fire gives instant alarm by telegraph or by ringing the bell. While we were there the band, which performs here several times a week in the daytime as well as on specified evenings, was discoursing sweet music in the square below. Opposite the campanile is the clock tower, on the platform of which are two bronze figures in the shape of men, which strike the hours on a bell, as though animated by life; and by means of revolving machinery and transparencies the time both of day and night is always apparent on the face of the clock.

The Church of St. Mark dates back eight hundred years. Its form "is that of a Greek cross, with equal arms, covered by a Byzantine dome in the center and one at the extremity of each arm." Over the vestibule are smaller domes, and "externally and internally the Church is adorned with five hundred columns of marble, the capitals of which present an exuberant variety of styles." The vaulting is of marble mosaics on a gold ground, and the floors, which have become very uneven, are of tesselated marble. They were being repaired when we were there. Over the main entrance are the four celebrated horses in gilded bronze, supposed to have been constructed in the time of Nero. "Constantine caused them to be conveyed to Constantinople, whence the Doge Dandolo brought them to Venice in 1204. In 1797 they were carried by Napoleon to Paris, where they afterward occupied the summit of the Triumphal Arch in the Place de Carousel." In 1815 they were restored to their former position by the Emperor Francis. The Church contains a large number of statues, both in marble and bronze, of noted persons, and other monuments, as well as relics, including a crystal vase with the "Blood of the Saviour;" a silver column, with a fragment of the "True Cross," and a cup of agate, with portions of the "Skull of St. John."

We visited several other churches, in all of which there are many things to interest the traveler. In none were the attractions greater than in the Church of the Franciscans, built in the thirteenth century, and which is one of the largest and most beautiful in the city. It contains many paintings, sculptures, and monuments—among the latter a fine monument to Titian and one to Canova, of which, as well as of the Church, interior and exterior, we have photographs.

CHAPTER XXXVI.

VENICE, NOVEMBER 12.—We have now been here about four days, and have seen the principal objects of interest in the city, which is between seven and eight miles in circumference. Of the three hundred and seventy-eight bridges here, nearly all are quite narrow and are reached by steps, rendered necessary to allow the gondolas to pass under them. Three of the bridges only span the Grand Canal. Two of these are of iron, and the third, the famous Rialto, is of marble, built in 1588-'91 by Antonio da Ponte. This "is called after the largest island (isola del Rialto, from *il rivo alto*, the deep stream.)" Entered by flights of steps from a small open square at either end, it has three passages, along which are rows of shops, and in rainy weather there is a busy provision market in gondolas under it. It looks beautiful at all times, but especially at night, as we saw it one evening when we went out to get a view of "Venice by moonlight" and to hear the lively singing of the gondoliers. These gondoliers are an institution in themselves; but they are governed by strict laws. The charge for a single trip, or for not exceeding one hour in the common gondola, accommodating two or three passengers, with one rower, is one franc, and five sous for each additional hour; in addition to which the gondolier expects a small fee *pour boire*. For five francs one can have a gondola and rower for the whole day. The number of gondolas here is not far from four thousand, all painted black, in obedience to an ancient law, to guard against extravagance. The gondoliers are very expert in their vocation; and it requires a good deal of skill on their part to avoid collisions. When about to turn a corner they cry out—"*Già è*," (boat ahead,) "*Premè*," (pass to the right,) "*Stali*," (pass to the left;) and these, or similar warnings, are about all you hear from them, unless you ask them questions; nor do they make scarcely any noise with their oars. In gliding along through the narrow canals, the people being shut up in their dwellings, the silence is usually as profound as it would be were you being rowed on a river or lake through a dense forest. To one first making such an excursion it is, indeed, a novel experience.

Yesterday, when we were in a gondola on the Grand Canal, we came to a point where there was a funeral, the gondolier said, of an English gentleman who died at the hotel where the ceremonies were being performed. In front of the hotel there was one handsomely ornamented gondola, with an ornamented hearse, and some twenty or more common gondolas, arranged several abreast in four or five platoons. Some of the attendants were in uniform, and the gondoliers were dressed in their best. We did not wait to see the procession start. The Venetian cemetery is on the small island of Murano, a little north of the city.

We stopped at a glass factory, and were kindly shown through all the workshops as well as the rooms in which the various articles made here are stored when finished. Here glass mosaics of almost every description are manufactured, embracing necklaces, pendants, bracelets, brooches, table leaves, etc., and all kinds of fancy articles, wine glasses, beads, and we know not what else.

We have passed many hours in the Palace of the Doges and the Academy of Fine Arts, where we saw an endless number of pictures, statues, rare books, old manuscripts, old coins, and other wonderful things impossible to enumerate. Among the pictures seen in the Academy are "The Assumption," by Titian, famous everywhere; and "The Entombment," also by Titian, and on which he was engaged, but had not entirely finished, at the time of his death (1576,) in the ninety-eighth year of his age. On the frieze of the Palace are the portraits of seventy-six Doges, and on the walls twenty-one pictures "painted to commemorate the achievements of the Republic, especially against Frederick Barbarosa." At the head of the Giants' Staircase we stood on the spot where the Doges used to be

COURT OF THE PALACE OF THE DOGES.

crowned. This staircase, erected in 1482, is a beautiful structure. In one of the rooms is Tintoretto's "Paradise," in size eighty-four by thirty-three feet six inches, said to be the largest oil painting in the world. There are several rooms devoted to painting and sculpture. Among the more noted paintings are "The Last Judgment," by Giovane; "Forest Landscape," by Paul Veronese; and "Christ in Glory," also by the last named artist. Of the sculptures in marble, "Apollo Reposing," "Gaul in his Last Desperate Struggle," "Gaul Sinking from Exhaustion," "Dead Gaul Lying over his Shield," are regarded as among the most meritorious. There is a curious old map of the world here, the work of Fra Mauro, a Camaldulensian monk, in 1459. In an upper room, called the Sala della Bussola, "once the ante-chamber of the three Inquisitors of the Republic," there is an opening in the wall, "formerly decorated by a lion's head in marble, into the mouth of which documents containing secret information used to be thrown." The library is remarkable for age and valuable historically. One of the books, kept in a private apartment and shown specially, is well worth seeing. It is called "The Golden Book," in which the names of the nobili were entered, and contains among many other beautiful pictures twelve representing the months of the year. Its form is large octavo or small quarto, and it is six or eight inches thick. The text, beautifully written, in Greek or Hebrew, is illuminated with gold on each page, all, like the pictures, done by hand—the work, we understood, of monks. We were conducted across the Bridge of Sighs, over which so many unfortunates have passed to their death; but there being persons in the prison, which is still used for convicts, the door on the prison side is kept locked, and we were not admitted. With Byron we could each say:

> "I stood in Venice on the Bridge of Sighs;
> A palace and a prison on each hand."

This bridge extends to the prison from the second story of the Palace, and is lighted by two or more square grated windows. In the ground or underground story of the Palace there are dungeons—one for political and the other for brigand prisoners—and these we were allowed to examine, being conducted into them by the custodian, who carried a torch or lamp to light the way. The first had a raised wooden floor for a bed and the second only a flat stone two or three inches above the cold stone floor of the dungeon. There are holes in the wall through which the food was passed to the prisoners, who were kept always in total darkness—the attendant waiting upon them without a light. Near the dungeons are places for confession, and by a grated window near by, a narrow stall where those condemned to death were beheaded. In the floor at the end of this small space are holes, which we saw, through which the blood of the slain ran into the water below, and their bodies were taken into gondolas and buried in the sea. We also saw where the machinery was fastened for the strangulation of prisoners sentenced to that mode of taking leave of this world.

There is a spacious area formed by one side of St. Mark's and three inner walls of the Doges' Palace; and within this are two wells with bronze curbs breast high. From the number of men and women —many more of the latter than the former—who come here for water, one might suppose the whole city is supplied from this source. These poor creatures come with two heavy copper buckets, holding eight or ten quarts each, hooked upon a flat hooped stick resting on one shoulder, and with a rope ten or fifteen feet in length and a hook at one end, with which to lower the bucket and draw it up by hand. Every one has his or her cord, which is kept ever in hand, and each well is large enough in circumference to allow ten or a dozen persons to draw water at one and the same time. Deep grooves are worn in the bronze curbing by these ropes. These water-carriers are very expert at their business; and we stood for some time admiring the manner of filling their buckets. On being lowered, the bucket, by sudden jerks, was set to tilting so that on touching the water it was instantly filled. We wonder if Rachel drew water in this way?

After all, one of the most charming sights of Venice is the hundreds of tame doves that are fed every day in the Piazza San Marco — some accounts say at the expense of the city, and others that "an old lady, widowed and childless, left a large amount to be expended for this purpose, she having been much interested in their welfare during her life." Bædeker says that "according to tradition, Admiral Dandolo, while besieging Candia at the beginning of the thirteenth century, received intelligence from the island by means of carrier pigeons, which greatly facilitated its conquest. He then dispatched the birds to Venice with the news of his success, and since that time their descendants have been carefully tended and highly revered by the citizens. They nestle in the nooks and crannies of the surrounding buildings, and are generally seen in great numbers in the evening perched on the façade of St. Mark's." But whether fed by the city or not, they are not likely to go hungry, for we have never been in the Piazza that we have not observed several tourists who, like ourselves, bought corn and fed them for the pleasure of it. Any number of Italian boys stand ready with their cornucopias of grain for sale; but, as a matter of economy and not to be restricted, we usually filled our pockets at some grocery store on our way to the square, which is the great place of resort for all Venice. The moment the doves saw we were provided they would flock by hundreds around us, and fly up and eat from our hands; sometimes as many as six or eight resting on our hands, wrists, and arms at the same time, all eager for their repast. They appeared to like our holding them by the *toes*, as they found it difficult to balance themselves when others were alighting on their backs or necks. We caught one for a moment, but she got away and flew off, evidently indignant at our ill manners. We felt guilty.

CHAPTER XXXVII.

FLORENCE, November 15.—We came here by way of Padua, Ferrara, and Bologna. We did not stop at Padua, but we had a view of the town from the railroad station. It has much the look of Verona, and, like that city and Mantua, on the road to Modena, it has been made famous by Shakspeare. During the reign of Augustus it is said to have been the wealthiest town in Upper Italy. "From the middle ages down to the present day Padua has been celebrated for its University, which was founded by Frederick II. in 1238. The town, a quiet place of fifty-one thousand inhabitants, occupies an extensive area. Its narrow streets and arcades are interspersed with spacious gardens." Ferrara is a very old town, in which Ariosto and Tasso flourished, to the former of whom, in one of the public squares, there is a high monumental column surmounted by his statue. It was the birthplace of Girolamo Savonarola, and Titian also resided here for a time.

Near one of the churches we saw a number of very beautiful marble monuments and statues, mostly modern, among which is one erected in 1872 by a Mr. Hardcastle, of Boston, to the memory of Alfred Lowell Putnam, a Bostonian, who died there on the 2d of October, 1855. We do not remember to have heard of him before, but he was probably an artist or scholar. For several centuries prior to 1600, when the family became extinct, this city was governed by the house of Este. Roscoe, in his "Life of Leo X.," relates of this family a story, the interest and brevity of which will justify its repetition here. He writes that in the early part of the year 1505 died Ercole of Este, Duke of Ferrara, after having governed his States with great credit, both in war and peace, during thirty-four years. His son, Alfonso I., husband of the infamous Lucretia Borgia, succeeded him. The reign of Alfonso I., Roscoe observes, was marked by a most tragical event, which endangered his safety and destroyed or interrupted his domestic tranquillity. Besides his two sons, Alfonso and Ippolito, the younger of whom, Ippolito, had been raised to the dignity of a Cardinal, the late Duke had left by his wife Leonora a son named Ferdinand, and by a favorite mistress an illegitimate son called Don Giulio. Attracted by the beauty of a lady of Ferrara, to whom they were distantly related, the Cardinal and Don Giulio became rivals in her affections; but the latter had obtained the preference, and the lady herself, in confessing to Ippolito her partiality to his brother, dwelt with apparent pleasure on the extraordinary beauty of his eyes. The exasperated ecclesiastic silently vowed revenge, and availing himself of an opportunity, while he was engaged with Don Giulio in the chase, he surrounded him with a band of assassins, and, compelling him to dismount, with a diabolical pleasure saw them deprive him of the organs of sight. The moderation or negligence of Alfonso in suffering this atrocious deed to remain unpunished excited the resentment not only of Don Giulio, but of his brother Ferdinand, who, uniting together, endeavored by secret treachery to deprive Alfonso at once of his honors and his life. Their purposes were discovered, and after having confessed their crime they were both condemned to die. The fraternal kindness of Alfonso was not, however, wholly extinguished, and at the moment when the axe was suspended over them he transmuted their punishment to that of perpetual imprisonment. In this state Ferdinand remained until the time of his death in 1540, while Giulio, at the expiration of fifty-four years of captivity, was once more restored to liberty.

Bologna is a fine city with irregular streets and long arcades, but the display of shops is not as fine as we have seen in many other cities. As usual, we started out for some of the churches, and went into one building called the "Seven Churches," a series of small places of worship, and one large Cathedral, adorned with pictures and statuary. In the latter is a recess in the wall, with iron railings in front, and in it a reclining figure representing the body of Christ. There were wreaths of flowers on and near this statue and lighted candles or tapers before it. Of course it is intended to represent Christ in the sepulchre. In front is a *Prie Dieu*, provided with stationary forms of prayer in large print, which some forlorn-looking persons were repeating with eyes devoutly fixed on the sepulchre. Some of the paintings, one in particular—"A Madonna"—in this Cathedral are very fine. The spacious square on which this church stands is used for a market place. It was crowded with sellers and purchasers, the former crying their commodities in all sorts of ways, and making a noise, as it struck our ears a little way off, like the sound of rushing waters. A great many of the Italians we see are wretchedly clothed, and look as though their blood had all been drawn from their veins.

On our way from Bologna our party had for company in our compartment only a Flemish gentleman and his wife and an elegant Italian lady and her little daughter Ada, a sweet child about five years old. This lady could speak no language but her own, nor could any of us either speak or understand more than a few words of Italian. For several hours Ada afforded us all a good deal of pleasure, as she would sit in our laps, singing songs to us, and, in her own tongue, make her remarks on whatever struck her attention. Her mother gave her to eat, first, a handful of boiled chestnuts, which are a great article of food here, especially among the poorer classes, then some grapes, and finally some chocolate candy. About an hour before reaching Pistoria, her stopping place, all at once Ada commenced crying and rolling up her eyes, and soon to vomit, when her mother, thinking she was throwing up blood, became so distracted that she had to be restrained to keep her from springing, child in arms, out of the window. She had given Ada a slate pencil, and as it could not be found she thought the child had swallowed a piece of it, and cried in an excruciating manner that she was dying. All the light we had was shed by a small oil lamp overhead, there was no means of giving the alarm to stop the

FLORENCE.

train, even if it had been of any use to do so, and we were driving along one half the time in tunnels—there are forty-five of them between Bologna and Florence—no dwelling near, nor could we get liquid of any kind to give the child. It is needless to say that we were all not a little concerned, both for Ada and her mother, for it was plain the child was very ill, her pulse being so low that the Flemish gentleman, who held her in his lap, said he could not feel it beat. She lay as if in a stupor; but having satisfied ourselves that what she had thrown up was not blood but chocolate, and having found the pencil her mother had given her to play with, our fears were somewhat allayed. At length we came to a station where the train stopped, and the lady with her child changed her seat to another compartment that she might be in company with some of her own country people. With us she was indeed a stranger in her own land; and had she been traveling in a country where not a word of her own language was spoken or understood, she could hardly have been more helpless. Before leaving, Ada began to revive a little, and when we reached Pistoria her mother came, much to our relief, and reported her out of danger, expressing many *grazias* for our sympathy and efforts to assist her in her trouble.

Florence is most beautifully situated. To-day, pioneered by Rev. Mr. Merriman, President of Ripon College, who had preceded us here, we took a pleasant walk to San Miniato, an elevated part of the city on the south side of the Arno, a fine plateau, in the center of which is the new monument of Michael Angelo, which was unveiled with great pomp and ceremony a few weeks before our arrival. The central figure is a colossal statue of his "David" in bronze, below which, at the four corners, are copies, also in bronze, of four others of his celebrated statues —"Day" and "Night," "Morning" and "Evening" —all elevated on an elaborate base of granite or marble. A short distance beyond this monument and higher up is a National Observatory, near which stands the observatory or tower from which Galileo made his astronomical observations. On our way back to our hotel, on the north side of the river, we passed through one of the old gate ways of the city, several of which, as well as portions of the old city wall, remain as grim monuments of ages far back in the past. Just before coming to the river we found ourselves in front of the house in which Elizabeth Barrett Browning lived and died. It is one of a continuous block, and over the main doorway, in Italian, is an inscription showing it to have been her residence.

Just after twilight last evening we heard from our sitting room singing or chanting in the street, and looking to see the occasion of it, a sight so novel met our eyes that the writer seized his hat and ran into the street to obtain a better view of what was passing. It was a funeral procession, and a few minutes brought him to the head of it. All were on foot. First, three men in masks supporting a high banner surmounted by a cross; next, two lads in white frocks; then, in double file, some sixteen priests in long white robes and broad-brimmed chapeaux, chanting the litany; next, the coffin, covered with a pall and borne by four men in close masks, three pall-bearers on either side and two in the rear, also wearing masks; and these were followed by one hundred men, more or less, in citizens' dress, all, except those who bore the coffin and the standard-bearer, carrying torches. This singular mode of burial, it seems, dates back to the year 1240, the date of the origin of the Society of the Misericordia, to which these masked members belong.

CHAPTER XXXVIII.

FLORENCE, NOVEMBER 16.—We spent this forenoon in the Church of Santa Maria Novella, which was completed in 1470, and "from the elegance of its form and proportions" Michael Angelo called it La Sposa, the bride. It contains many very striking fresco paintings, representing "Heaven," "Hell," "The Last Judgment," etc., and there are also some old and some modern paintings on canvas, possessing much merit. In the painting of "The Last Judgment," which is some twenty feet square, various modes of punishment and torment are depicted—some poor creatures being in a lake of fire, only their lower limbs visible, showing that they were plunged head foremost into the seething lake; others in the most terrible outer darkness of despair, we cannot tell in how many forms; but the kind of sins for which each group was suffering was set down in words. The arch fiend himself, or his executioner, in the form of a raging lion, appeared in the midst of the largest group, and as he had the head and shoulders of Judas in his mouth, the inference was that all were to be thus devoured. So far as Judas was concerned, no one seemed to have any sympathy for him.

In the afternoon we visited the studios, all near

together, of Powers, Ball, and Fuller, the latter of whom died a year or two ago. The two brothers, sons of the late Hiram Powers, have their studio in the same place where the writer saw their father in 1867. The elder brother has just completed a beautiful bust of a maiden, giving it the name "Star of Bethlehem," and the younger is engaged on a bust of General Grant. Whether either son will ever become as famous as their father, time will tell. They evidently possess a good deal of artistic talent. They continue to multiply, as they find sale therefor, the more popular statues and busts modeled by Hiram Powers; for instance, those of "Washington," "Franklin," "Eve," "The Greek Slave," "Faith," "The Fisher Boy," "Genevra," "America," "Diana," "Charity," "Proserpine," "Clytie," "Hope," and others. We were highly gratified with a view of all these works of art. We were equally well pleased with the works exhibited in Ball's studio, where we were happy to meet his young and promising pupil, Daniel French, who has already made his mark by his statue of "The Minute Man," lately erected in Concord, Massachusetts — a work regarded by the best judges as possessing great merit. We were delighted with Ball's "L' Allegro" and "Il Penseroso," two revolving busts, with children's faces, a joy to behold; and his statue (full size) of "St. John" is one of the grandest we have anywhere seen. It represents the Apostle as standing with eyes raised toward heaven — in his right hand a pen and in his left a book — as if listening to the words: "And I heard a voice from heaven saying unto me, write, Blessed are the dead which die in the Lord from henceforth." The statue in which we were more interested, perhaps, was one of Lincoln and the half-kneeling freedman at his feet, his chains broken and eyes fixed in wonder on the land of liberty. Leaning on a pedestal, Lincoln holds his Emancipation Proclamation in his right hand, and is imagined as saying, "And upon this act I invoke the considerate judgment of mankind and the gracious favor of Almighty God." The likeness is excellent. A colossal statue after this model has just been cast in bronze, in Munich, where we saw parts of it at the foundry there, and it is to be erected in Washington City. It cannot fail to be admired. Fuller has left many meritorious works, the most striking of which, perhaps, that we saw is a reclining statue of a mother and infant, illustrative of a passage in Moore's Lalla Rookh—"Paradise and the Peri:"

> "My child she is but half divine,
> Her father sleeps in the Caspian water.
> Sea weeds twine
> His funeral shrine,
> But he lives again in the Peri's daughter.
> Fain would I fly from mortal sight
> To my own sweet bowers of Peristan;
> But there the flowers are all too bright
> For the eyes of a baby born of man.
> On flowers of earth her feet must tread,
> So hither my light-winged bark hath brought her.
> Stranger, spread
> Thy leafliest bed
> To rest the wandering Peri's daughter."

The mother, the child on her breast, reclines in a fairy "light-winged bark," with a graceful swan for its figure-head. Another beautiful statue is that of "Little Nell," and one of "Blind Lydia," the Pompeian damsel, is also touchingly striking. We have called once at Gould's studio, where we were much pleased with what is, perhaps, his masterpiece, a charming figure of a maiden, styled the "West Wind," the light drapery of which has the appearance of being pressed closely around and back of the form by a strong current of air.

The Pitti Palace, aside from its Picture Galleries, is a magnificent edifice. It was the residence of the King when the seat of government was in Florence. The rooms, some twenty or more, which we saw, and their furniture are very fine, and in some of these rooms there are a considerable number of excellent paintings, one of which, in size eight by fifteen feet, represents in a vivid manner "The Battle of St. Martins." There are here four or five ebony secretaries richly inlaid with lapis lazuli and other precious stones, and many tables inlaid in the same manner, all surprisingly beautiful. A writing table of modern make commanded our admiration on account of its ingenious construction. Its shape is oval and its size that of a common center-table, say three feet and a half long. The guide unlocked what we supposed to be a drawer, but which proved to be the back of a comfortable chair, the withdrawal of which caused the leaf of the table to separate in the middle, presenting a complete writing table, readily adjusted to the proper inclination, with all the necessary compartments of a writing desk. On either side of the seat were drawers, and altogether we thought it the most complete escritoir we had ever seen. Moreover, it is a card table as well.

One day we visited the Museum of Natural History, where we saw two telescopes and other astronomical instruments used by Galileo, and at the same place one of his fingers, which had been preserved in alcohol and kept in a glass vessel. It was so shrunken that one would not have taken it for a finger, nor do we understand what the object could be in preserving it, unless to show that "the earth moves"—backward. It is anything but a pleasant sight. Not more disagreeable though than any number of wax forms we saw here, showing the construction of man, beast, bird, and fish in all their minutest details. The horrible sights in the Medical Museum at Washington fall far short of what is to be seen here. The collection of stuffed skins of animals, birds, and various other creatures is very good.

We have been to the Protestant Cemetery, which is on the eastern edge of the city, to see the graves of Elizabeth Barrett Browning, Theodore Parker, and Hiram Powers, whose remains lie buried here. It occupies an elevated spot, one acre or more in extent, and is enclosed by a high iron railing. It is adorned by rows of yew and other trees, shrubbery and flowers, and commands a charming view of the hills of Fiesole and vicinity. Inside, near the gateway, is a small building, occupied by the attendant, who opened the gate for us. There is a gravel walk from the gate through the center of the grounds to the top of the hill, and Mrs. Browning's tomb fronts the left side of this walk near the center. Her monument is of white marble, the upper and more elaborate part, somewhat in the form of a sarcophagus, resting on six small marble pillars. On the front is her profile in *bas-relief*, under which, on the left, are the letters "E*B*B*," and on the right "OB* 1861*." This is all we could see as indicating for whom the monument was erected. There are other carvings of an appropriate character, representing the lyre, harp, flowers, etc. Gathering clover leaves and two or three wild flowers growing near her tomb, we passed on to find the grave of Theodore Parker, which is a few steps beyond on the side hill at the right. It is indicated by a plain head and foot-stone of granite or gray sandstone, and bears the simple inscription: "Theodore Parker. Born at Lexington, Massachusetts, United States of America, August 24, 1810: Died at Florence, May 10, 1860." Over the grave of Hiram Powers—born July, 1805; died June, 1873—is a raised white marble slab, bearing his name and date of birth and death. His grave is on the same side of the main walk with Mrs. Browning's, but higher up and further toward the west. The most prominent monument here is one to the memory of "Frederick Guillaume, Roi de Prusse, MDCCCLVII." It is a shaft of white marble, twenty feet high, surmounted by a marble cross, the base being of granite. Under his name is the following: "Je suis la ressurrection et la vie. Celui qui croit en moi vivra quand même il seroit mort.—St. Jean, xi., 25." There is a beautiful monument here, also, to the memory of Samuel Reginald Routh, of Farleigh, England, who died at Florence, June 21, 1860, in the forty-seventh year of his age. The inscription states that it was "erected by those who loved him living, who mourn him dead, and who hope through the mercy of God to rejoin him in heaven." "For in Thee, O Lord, do I hope: Thou wilt hear, O Lord my God.—Psalms, 38, 15." This monument is also of marble—a square base, six feet in height, with ornamental corners, and supporting a life-size standing figure of a woman, tastefully draped, with eyes raised toward heaven. Another very striking monument is "Sacred to the memory of Arnold Savage Landor, Esq., born 5th of March,

1818; died 2d of April, 1871." It is likewise of marble, raised some five feet, bearing a life-size statue of a woman, supposed to represent the widow, kneeling on a *Prie Dieu*, and resting her head on her left hand and holding a wreath in her right, her whole expression full of grief. On the front is carved the family coat of arms. To us there is always a sort of fascination in monumental inscriptions, and we copied those of several other monuments here; but we reproduce only one more—"Henry Florence, son of John A. C. and Susan Gray, of New York, aged nine months:

"Fare thee well, our youngest treasure!
On the soil that gave thee birth;
By the rippling Arno's water,
Rest thee in Italia's earth,
While the memory of thy sweetness
Cheers a distant home and hearth—
Cheers us while our sad hearts tell—
The dear Lord doeth all things well."

We do not present this for any special merit, but to show what only a parent's heart, who has been called to part with dear little ones, can feel, that, no matter how young, the loss of a sweet child is always sorrowful. "To-morrow," once wrote one of our distinguished historians and statesmen, who had just lost a dear infant—"to-morrow we intrust her to her resting-place, and the next day we must take up our solitary journey on the paths of life."

CHAPTER XXXIX.

FLORENCE, NOVEMBER 17.—Yesterday afternoon we went first to the Medicean Chapel connected with the Church of San Lorenzo. This is a magnificent octagonal room, very high in the walls, and lighted from an arched roof, which is adorned with fine fresco paintings in style not unlike the frescoes in the rotunda of our Capitol, and the walls are lined with marble and inlaid stones of various kinds, polished so brightly that they reflect the pictures from above almost as perfectly as the best mirror could do. In point of magnificence and beauty it is far ahead of either the Marble Room in the rear of our Senate Chamber or the Bank Room of the Treasury.

We next went into the Sagrestia Nuova, also connected with this Church, a small building planned by Michael Angelo for its monuments, which were executed by him, and which are regarded as masterpieces of art. These are the monuments of Giuliano and Lorenzo de Medici and the "Madonna and Child." There are also statues here of "San Damiano" and "San Cosimo"—one on the right and the other on the left of "The Virgin." There are allegorical figures on Giuliano's monument, or as composing a part of it, representing Day and Night, and on Lorenzo's representing Aurora and Twilight, or Night and Morning. They are in the human form in reclining positions, and are the originals of those forming a part of the new monument to the great artist on San Miniato. In allusion to these statues Rogers wrote:

> "There, from age to age,
> Two ghosts are sitting on their sepulchres;
> That is the Duke Lorenzo, mark him well!
> He meditates, his head upon his hand.
> What from beneath his helm-like bonnet scowls?
> Is it a face or but an eyeless skull?
> 'T is lost in shade; yet, like the basilisk,
> It fascinates and is intolerable.
> His mien is noble, most majestical!
> Then most so, when the distant choir is heard
> At morn or eve."

Lorenzo and Giuliano de Medici were brothers, and from the latter part of the fourteenth till the early part of the eighteenth century the Medici family held the scepter of power almost continuously in Florence. The elder of these brothers was called "Lorenzo the Magnificent," and was regarded as among the ablest and best sovereigns of his time. Leo X., whose pontificate "is celebrated as one of the most prosperous in the annals of the Romish Church," was his son. During the reign of Lorenzo, in 1478, there was a conspiracy, instigated by Sixtus IV., to assassinate Lorenzo and Giuliano and get possession of the government. The place selected for this atrocious deed was during service at the great Cathedral of Santa Maria del Fiore, otherwise called the Duomo, in Florence, and it was intrusted to the archbishop and several priests. Giuliano not making his appearance at church as soon as expected, two of the conspirators, Francesco de Pazzi and Bandini, went to his house "to insure and hasten his attendance." He accompanied them; "and as he walked between them they threw their arms around him with the familiarity of intimate friends. but, in fact, to discover whether he had any armor under his dress, possibly conjecturing from his long

delay that he had suspected their purpose." The
signal of attack was to be the ringing of the bell,
when the priest should raise the consecrated wafer —
"the people bowed before it, and at the same instant
Bandini plunged a short dagger into the breast of
Giuliano. On receiving the wound he took a few
hasty steps and fell, when Francesco de Pazzi rushed
upon him with incredible fury and stabbed him in
different parts of the body, continuing to repeat his
strokes even after he was apparently dead. Such
was the violence of his rage that he wounded himself deeply in his thigh. The priests who had under-
taken the murder of Lorenzo were not equally successful. An ill-directed blow from Maffei, which
was aimed at the throat, but took place behind
the neck, rather roused him to his defence than
disabled him. He immediately threw off his cloak,
and holding it up as a shield in his left hand, with
his right he drew his sword and repelled his assail-
ants. * * Bandini, his dagger streaming with the
blood of Giuliano, rushed toward Lorenzo; but meeting in his way Francesco Novi, a person in the
service of the Medici, and in whom they placed
great confidence, he stabbed him with a wound in-
stantaneously mortal. At the approach of Bandini
the friends of Lorenzo encircled him and hurried
him into the sacristy, where Politiano and others
closed the doors, which were of brass." While this
bloody scene was being enacted in the Cathedral,
"the archbishop and about thirty of his associates
attempted to overpower the magistrates and to possess themselves of the seat of government" at the
Palace; but being foiled at every point, the conspirators now sought to save themselves by flight. In
this they were equally unsuccessful. The archbishop

and nearly every other prominent actor with him were seized and hung through the Palace windows. Thus the conspiracy was an entire failure; but the people deeply mourned the death of Giuliano.

To return to the Church of San Lorenzo, where there are many other things of interest, among them two oblong pulpits, which are entered only by a ladder or moveable steps. On these pulpits are bronze *bas-reliefs* representing the "Passion and Resurrection of the Saviour"—"The Descent from the Cross" and "The Entombment" being regarded as the finest.

On our way home we stopped a few moments at the Baptistery, near the great Cathedral, and examined closely the celebrated bronze doors, of which there are plaster castings in the Corcoran Art Gallery. These are on the side facing the Duomo. On two other sides of the Baptistery there are also bronze doors, we believe, of the same size, but less elaborately constructed. In the interior are some pictures, statuary, etc. One extensive piece of statuary, in rear of the altar, representing some Bible scene, and the mosaic work in the dome, are surpassingly fine. Here priests and their attendants are every day engaged in christening and registering the names of newly-born infants; and the proceedings appeared to us more like an ordinary business transaction than a solemn religious ceremony.

On entering the Duomo, which is a most imposing structure, looming high up above all the surrounding buildings, except the Campanile, which is about the same height, we were surprised at the plainness of its finish internally, and at the absence of remarkable works of art. There are, however, many monuments, statues, and paintings here, of more or less merit. The dome is said to have served as a model to Michael Angelo for that of St. Peter's in Rome, which it exceeds in size. The Campanile, or belltower, erected in 1334-'6, is two hundred and ninety-two feet in height, and is regarded as one of the finest existing works of the kind. It is sometimes called "Giotto's Tower," he being the architect who commenced its construction. It is square in form and four stories high, the lower story being decorated by statues and figures in *bas-relief*. It is stated that Giotto intended to surmount it by a spire of one hundred feet, but that Gaddi, who completed it after his death, abandoned this project. Longfellow, in a short poem, thus refers to it:

> "In the old Tuscan town stands Giotto's tower,
> The lily of Florence blossoming in stone —
> A vision, a delight, and a desire —
> The builder's perfect and centennial flower,
> That in the night of ages bloomed alone,
> But wanting still the glory of the spire."

On a beautiful afternoon a party of us rode to the site of the old Roman city of Fiesole, situated on a high hill some three miles northeast of Florence, where the remains of the city walls, built two thousand years ago, are still to be seen, as well as the vestiges of an amphitheater supposed to date back also to that period. The Cathedral which we entered there has been built over eight hundred years, and other buildings near by, occupied as a convent, are equally ancient. What was once a city is now only a scattered village. Hallam describes it as "a villa overhanging the towers of Florence, on the slope of that lofty hill crowned by the mother city, the ancient Fiesole, in gardens which Tully might have envied. With Fieino, Landino, and Politiano at his side, he delighted his hours of leisure with the beautiful visions of Platonic philosophy, for which the summer stillness of an Italian sky appears the most congenial accompaniment." The view from Fiesole is very fine when the weather is clear; but we thought the picture of the place itself, with the charming residences and gardens of the dwellers on the slope of the hill as we approached it, was finer still. In the spring, when the foliage is fresh and green, it must be beautiful indeed. It is reached from Florence only by a zigzag turnpike.

CHAPTER XL.

FLORENCE, NOVEMBER 23.—On the morning of the 18th instant we were prompt at breakfast in order to be early at the Painting Galleries, and by nine o'clock we were at the Uffizi Gallery, fifteen minutes' walk from our boarding house, No. 7 via Palestro; but, very much to our disappointment, we found a notice on the door stating that the hour of opening was eleven A. M., notwithstanding Bædeker's Hand-book says nine A. M. Since the latest edition of this book, however, we understand a law has been passed in Italy providing for an admission fee to all the public Galleries on every day of the week except Sunday and Thursday, but whether the hours of exhibition are to be different on the free from the paying days we do not know. The admission fee here is one franc, or, what is the same, one lira; and it is evidently the purpose of this poor

Italian Government to reap a handsome income in fees from the thousands of travelers who flock here every year. Seeing we had nearly two hours to wait, we crossed the Ponte Vecchio (bridge) and passed the intervening time in the Royal Palace heretofore briefly described. At the appointed hour we were on hand at the Uffizi Gallery door, and save a short time for lunch we occupied the day until three o'clock in that and the Pitti Gallery. In this time, however, we could give little more than a glance even at a very small part of the pictures, statuary, and other rare objects of art here; and it would be folly to attempt to give an intelligent description of them. The Uffizi Gallery is on the north and the Pitti Gallery, adjoining the Royal Palace, on the south side of the Arno, which divides the city, and both are connected by a covered way, which crosses above the street, and, turning at right angles, runs over the tops of the buildings along the river side a considerable distance to the Ponte Vecchio; thence again turning a square corner, extends over the long rows of jewelers' shops, by which the bridge is lined on either side from one end to the other, and ascends by steps to the Pitti Gallery, looking out on the southeast side upon the beautiful Boboli Garden. These shops in themselves, like many others along the Lung Arno and in other parts of the city, of similar character, are a sight to behold, brilliant as they are with all kinds of the most attractive jewelry that can be made of gold and precious stones. Nowhere else have we seen such quantities of turquoise, lapis lazuli, agate, jasper, and onyx, not to mention diamonds. The Florentine mosaics, a specialty, are very beautiful.' It is a walk of ten minutes from one Gallery to the other through the covered passage or corridor, which is well lighted. On the walls of this corridor are gobelin works, some oil paintings, many engravings, and an endless number of drawings, many of the latter regarded as very valuable, being the works of Michael Angelo, Giotto, Leonardo da Vinci, Tintoretto, Albert Dürer, and other old artists. The inlaid marble tables, of which there are several in these Galleries, like those in the King's Palace, are superb beyond description. Villages, landscapes, birds, musical instruments, people, and other objects are represented in them in a wonderfully perfect manner. One of them is said to have kept twenty-five men busy twenty-two years in its construction — a work for one man of five hundred and fifty years! In one of the rooms are the marble statues of "Venus di Medici," "The Wrestlers," "Young Apollo," "The Dancing Fawn," and "Slave Whetting his Knife"—all originals, and plaster casts of which are common. Here, also, are Titian's "Venus" and Raphael's pictures of "The Madonna with the Goldfinch," "St. John as a Boy," "St. John Preaching in the Desert," and his "Portrait of Pope Julius II.," as well as many others of his celebrated paintings. Correggio's "Madonna Adoring the Child," and Raphael's "Madonna of the Chair," or "Sitting Madonna," both original and both universally copied, are among the most attractive pictures of the thousands of fine paintings in these Galleries. In a corridor of the Uffizi Gallery is a cabinet of gems, consisting of costly jewels and numerous other valuable articles of *virtù* not unlike what we saw in the Green Vaults at Dresden. Since our first visit we have been several times to these Galleries, and were we to go there every day for a year we should hardly be able to examine critically all that there is here to be seen. We could but think that were the collection of pictures reduced by casting out no small number of nude figures, inferior "Madonnas," "Holy Families," and "Saints," it would be a great improvement; and the same thinning out of the statuary could not, we think, be any matter of regret.

We spent the afternoon of the 22d instant in the National Museum, which building, in the olden times, was the Hall of Justice, and is itself an object of more interest, perhaps, than what it now contains. The sides of the walls in the court are covered with coats of arms of the different podestàs, or principal officers of the city, and inscriptions of various kinds are inserted in the walls under the two stages of arcades which extend entirely round the court, in the center of which is a well like those in the court of the Doges' Palace in Venice. In the lower story is a collection of old armor, the most formidable weapon being a large brass cannon of the sixteenth century, bearing the coat of arms of the Medici. It is highly ornamented, and at its breech is a complete bust, intended to represent St. Paul. What he could have had to do with such a monster of destruction does not appear. Near by were several pyramids of cannon balls, cut out of granite, and a weapon resembling the Gatling gun, quite remarkable. This gun has nine barrels, with a groove for the priming, the ignition of which by a flint lock served to discharge all the barrels at once. Unlike the Gatling gun, however, this was a hand weapon, the barrels and stock being about the length of those of a horse pistol. Among the works of sculpture here is Michael Angelo's

"Dying Adonis;" "Adam and Eve," formerly of the Garden of Eden, by Bandineli; and "Virtue Triumphant," by Giambologna. This last is a stalwart and rather fierce-looking damsel, very much in the dress of her sister Eve—rather too scant, we could not help thinking, for a virtuous lady triumphing over vice—with her foot on the neck of an unfortunate young man, also lightly clad, who had evidently in some way gotten into a bad scrape. There is also a celebrated statue of "Mercury," by Giambologna, and one of "David," by Verrochio. If this last had been named "Isaac" we should never have known the difference. We gaze with wonder at many a statue and many a painting, which we might pass with only a glance but that it has some great name and is said to be the work of some famous artist. We were interested in two small pieces of sculpture in bronze, representing "Abraham's Sacrifice." This subject was given to artists on trial as competitors for the doors of the Baptistery; and these two specimens were by Ghiberti and Brunellesco, the former of whom was successful, as he was evidently entitled to be. In one of the rooms is a large collection of fancy ivory carvings of a most ingenious character. For instance, you see a ball three or four inches in diameter with half a dozen or more balls, all separate, one within the other, neatly carved by some instrument or instruments admitted through small openings on four sides, or opposite points of the sphere. Various other devices are chosen to show the ingenuity of the artist and excite the wonder of the beholder. A most wonderful piece of wood carving is also exhibited in the same room; and then there are anatomical statuettes in wax and bronze, a series of sculptures representing "The Combats of Hercules," a cabinet of fine crystals, etc. It would require a volume to describe the numerous articles in this collection.

We have been gratified by a visit to the house of Michael Angelo, situated in via Ghibellina, near the Piazza Santa Croce, where there is a collection of his pictures, designs, manuscripts, and other interesting relics. It is shown for a fee of half a franc. We saw his canes and his two-edged sword, which bears the arms of his family, the portraits of many of whom hang upon the walls. Some of his tableware is highly prized as being very beautiful. There is a bust of him in bronze, from a cast taken after death. Models of some of his most celebrated works are likewise preserved here. In an out-of-the-way corner of the house is a little closet, with only one small window, where, we were told, he used to conceal himself whenever he wished to avoid intruders. When closed there was no sign of any door to this snug retreat. He never married. Being asked why he preferred to remain single, he answered, "My art is my wife, and gives me as much trouble as married life could do; and my works will be my children."

Some of our party rode one day to La Certosa, three miles out of town, to visit there an old Carthusian Monastery, "which is approaching dissolution and contains twelve inmates only." These monks were dressed each in a long white flannel robe with a pointed hood and tied around the waist with a thick cord, suspended from which was a string of beads with a cross. They wore sandals strapped to their feet, without stockings. They have an herb garden and pharmacy, and sell medicine, perfumes of various kinds, and delicious chartreuse, a bottle of which we secured for home consumption. The Monastery is quite a curiosity. When Pius VI. was banished from Rome by the French he had his residence here, and the room he occupied is shown to visitors. The Villa of Galileo is passed on the way to Certosa. It was here or at his prison in Florence that Milton visited Galileo near the close of his life, and wrote: "There it was that I found and visited the famous Galileo, grown old, a prisoner to the Inquisition for thinking in astronomy otherwise than the Franciscan and Dominican licensers thought."

CHAPTER XLI.

FLORENCE, DECEMBER 8.—On the 24th ultimo we went again to Powers' studio to take another view of the many beautiful statues and busts there, and to obtain photographs of some with which we were most pleased, that we might be able the more readily to recall them hereafter. One of the most charming of these, by Hiram Powers, is that of "Genevra," so named, no doubt, from the circumstance that this was the name of a Florentine lady who was the heroine of a romantic story related by Bocaccio. This story, as given in "Walks in Florence," is as follows: "Genevra, a daughter of the noble house of Amieri, or Admari, was beloved by Antonio Rondinelli, whose family belonged to the popolani, or plebeian order, which had led an attack against the nobles in 1343. The father of Genevra accordingly refused his consent to her marriage with Rondinelli, and obliged her to accept as a husband Francesco Agolanti, who was of equal birth with herself. During the plague of 1400 she was seized by the fatal malady and fell into a swoon, which her husband mistook for death, and she was buried in the family vault in the cemetery, between the Cathedral and Campanile. In the middle of the night Genevra recovered her senses, and was terrified when she perceived, by the clear moonlight which penetrated the apertures between the stones, that she was lying in a vault. She succeeded in bursting the bandages which confined her, and contrived to raise the stone above, and to make her escape. She first directed her steps toward her husband's home, and in order to reach it she had to pass along the narrow way called from that time forth the via del Morte. Agolanti, looking out when she knocked at the door, supposed her to be a spirit come to torment him, and refused her admittance. She then proceeded to her father's house, near St. Andrea behind the Mercato Vecchio; but, again rejected, she returned to the via Calzaioli and sat down on the steps of the Church of San Bartolommeo, to reflect where to go next. Gaining courage, she sought the house of Rondinelli, near the street which to this day bears the name of his family. Here she was received by his parents, and the tribunals having decided that the marriage of a woman who had been dead and buried was annulled, she was permitted to marry her former lover." Of course, a walk through the via del Morte, or street of Death, and to other points mentioned in this romantic story, possessed additional interest on account of these associations.

At our quiet boarding house we have a parlor

in common with Mr. and Mrs. Stickney and Rev. Mr. Sumner, and every morning join with them in family worship. On the 25th of November, Thanksgiving Day in the United States, we assembled as usual after breakfast, and gathering around us all our relations (in photograph) we could command, the Thanksgiving Proclamations of the President and Governor of Connecticut were read, and the hymn, "Praise God from whom all blessings flow," was sung as a part of the morning services. At eleven o'clock we all went to the American Union Church, where we had an excellent discourse on "Cheerfulness" by the pastor, Rev. J. E. Kittredge, and a good Thanksgiving poem by Hon. Charles Thurber, from Brooklyn, N. Y., some time a sojourner in this city. The address was a strong and eloquent plea against all moroseness and morbid feeling, and for a bright and joyous life—driving away all dull care as far as possible. The poem contains many happy hits in allusion to politics and other current matters in our own country, pointedly condemning all action tending to weaken the credit of the United States in the eyes of Europe. Besides congregational singing, the gentleman who presided at the cabinet organ sang with a fine voice an appropriate hymn, and Miss Emma Abbott, a professional singer, gave us the hymn, "Nearer my God to Thee," with touching effect. One of the walls of the old hall in which these services were held is curved, and on inquiring why it was so constructed, we were informed that it was for the purpose of "keeping the devil out," and that many, if not most, of the old buildings here have at least one such wall—the result of this strange superstition. A somewhat similar superstition seems to prevail in Germany, where, as we observed in our travels, it is the custom, when the roof of a new house is raised, to erect a tree on the ridge-pole; and this is believed to be a security against any intrusion thereafter of his Satanic majesty. Another singular superstition, which prevails in Italy among the lower classes, is that an "evil eye," often detected in a crowd, or in passing along the street, may be turned away from you by closing the two middle fingers and thumb of one hand and pointing with the index and little finger at the "evil-eyed" person. The inference is that the "old boy" is shy of forked instruments. We know that travelers resort to this method, with good effect, to disperse Italian beggars when too troublesome.

It is gratifying to see, everywhere we have been in Italy, that there appears to be perfect religious liberty; and we were particularly struck by this fact on going to the American Episcopal Church here one Sunday, the room in which the Episcopal services were held being separated from an old Roman Catholic church only by a single wall, and the front doors of both buildings opening on the same street. Here was not only entire freedom of worship by sects in some things wide apart, but in bodily conjunction so close as to make one feel that only one step more is necessary to bring about a complete union on the true Christian basis.

The Church of Santa Croce, which dates back to the thirteenth century, stands on the Piazza Santa Croce, in which there is an imposing monument to Dante, consisting of his statue, nineteen feet in height, on a pedestal twenty-three feet high, adorned on its four corners with four shield-bearing lions. This Church is called the Westminster Abbey of

Florence. Besides many valuable paintings in fresco as well as on canvas, there are a great many monuments here of a striking character, among which are those of Dante, Machiavelli, Alfieri, Galileo, (died 1642,) and Michael Angelo, (died 1564,) the remains of the latter two of whom rest here. On Michael Angelo's tomb there is a bust, by Baptista Lorenzi, said to be a correct likeness of the great artist; and guarding the door are three statues, in mournful attitude, representing "Painting," "Sculpture," and "Architecture." The position of this tomb is said to have been selected by Michael Angelo himself, that he might see from his last resting place the dome of the Cathedral, "the delight and study of his mind." The Bonaparte family own a chapel in this church, and there are monuments in it to Carlotta Bonaparte, who died in 1830, and to Clara Bonaparte, whose death took place in 1845. Within one square of our boarding house there is a splendid mansion fronting the Arno, the residence of a nephew of Napoleon I. It occupies, with its garden and outhouses, an entire square.

We have been into several other churches here, all of them more or less attractive on account of their age and the many interesting objects they contain.

Fronting on the Piazza della Signoria, one of the largest squares of the city, and the scene of Savonarola's martyrdom in 1498, is the Palazzo Vecchio, "originally the seat of the Republic, and subsequently the residence of Cosmo I., erected in 1298." It is an interesting old edifice, containing many fine frescoes. Also, fronting on the same square is the Loggia dei Lanzi, erected in 1376. Under the portico, among other statuary, is John of Bologna's group in marble, called the "Rape of the Sabines," and another group, by Fedi, called the "Rape of Polyxena." Fedi is an Italian artist here, whose studio we have visited. He is an enthusiast, and seemed to take great pleasure in showing us what he had accomplished in works of art. Newman, an American gentleman devoted to painting in water colors, has a studio here, where we saw some excellent pictures; and we have been also to the studio of Ciseri, an Italian painter, whose remarkable oil painting of "The Entombment" hangs in the Crystal Palace, London.

We have been to McNamee's studio, a sculptor from Brooklyn, N. Y., to see his model, not yet completed, of his "Base Ball Player," on which he said he had been engaged four years. His living model was present and took the attitude being represented, that we might compare the one with the other. The model's right foot on tip toe is at the base, while his left, with the body, is stretched forward and arms extended to the utmost point—both hands ready to catch the ball—and head turned toward his left shoulder, looking with intense eagerness as if to follow the direction of the ball. It is a singular fact that this living model, an Italian of twenty-five or thirty years of age, from having been rather a frail young man when he first stood for Mr. McNamee, has by this exercise become powerfully muscular, and his left thigh, from the greater strain upon it, has increased in size three inches more than his right. Mr. McNamee has just completed a beautiful bust in marble of Miss Kinsley, of Brooklyn.

The Riding Park and open promenade lies west of the city, extending back on the banks of the Arno about two miles. One of the six or seven bridges over the Arno at Florence crosses from this Park, which on fine days is a great place of resort for all the gay people of the city.

Many odd sights appear in the market places, not the least being the market people themselves. Many of the poor people one is sure to find here have the most woe-begone look, more especially when the weather is cold. Evidently they are reduced to the greatest extremity, and are ready to seize on almost any kind of food to keep from starvation. We see them parting with their last soldo for a piece of warm chestnut bread and a mouthful of fried blood of fowls and animals, which are slaughtered and their blood saved and cooked on the spot. If the weather is cold, those of them who are able carry in their hands a scaldino, a small earthern vessel filled with a few live coals and hot ashes to keep from freezing to death. These vessels have handles, and we see the shivering poor carrying them in chilly weather wherever we go in the streets.

During the most of the three weeks we have been in this city the weather has been anything but pleasant, being either cloudy and raw or rainy. In the middle of last month it rained for a whole week almost incessantly, and the Arno became so swollen that the city authorities became alarmed and took measures to guard against an overflow, such as we are informed occurred here six years ago, when the Lung Arno, the street which runs the entire length of the city on the east bank of the river, was three feet under water.

We have lingered longer in Florence than we anticipated doing. Ho! now for the "Eternal City."

CHAPTER XLII.

> I am in Rome! oft as the morning ray
> Visits these eyes, waking at once I cry,
> Whence this excess of joy? what has befallen me?
> And from within a thrilling voice replies,
> Thou art in Rome. —*Rogers*.

YES, here we are in the "Eternal City!" but it seems more like a dream than a reality. Leaving Florence at half past eight on the morning of the 9th of December, we came in sight of the dome of St. Peter's at half past four in the afternoon. No other sign of the city was visible. The day was fair, and the sun, now but a little above the horizon, revealed a long, low range of clouds, which, lighted up by its rays, looked like a serpentine stream of fire. It was, indeed, a beautiful Italian sunset, and after two months of almost continual cloudy weather, it was not strange that we witnessed it with some degree of enthusiasm. On our near approach to the city we might easily have imagined ourselves as entering Washington from the north, the land being low and level, and no part of the city being in sight until we came within a short distance of its walls, which are in a dilapidated condition. In less than five minutes we were within the gates and at the railroad dépôt. A porter was ready at the car door to carry our light baggage to a carriage, which we entered, and gave directions to the coachman to drive us to the Hôtel della Pace, No. 8 via Sistina, where comfortable quarters had been engaged for us by friends whom we had met in Florence, and who had arrived there a few days before us. We shall have occasion to speak of these friends hereafter.

Our coachman started off with us, but before we reached the street from the dépôt his horse began to back and turn, and showed so ugly a disposition that we alighted, determined to try another team which should go forward instead of backward. If we were to have our necks broken, we desired at any rate to see Rome first. However, the driver having called two men to his assistance, we ventured to return to our seats, and the horse finding three too many for him, wisely concluded to behave himself, and we were soon landed at our hotel, where, thanks to our friends, we found a nice room with a wood fire awaiting us. The day had been quite cold, and we observed that ice had formed over shoal water and along the edges of the streams by the roadside; nevertheless we enjoyed every moment of the way, since every foot of ground over which we passed is historical territory. At Arrezzo, the ancient Arretium, where the Roman consul Flaminius lost his life in an encounter with Hannibal's army, we stopped long enough to gather leaves and touch the soil consecrated by the blood of the slain. Many of the towns we passed are built upon hills and strongly protected by thick walls. Orvieto is a most singular looking old place, situated on an isolated tufa rock, or ledge, over seven hundred feet above the river Paglia at its base. We could not see into it, as it is surrounded by a wall and entered from a steep paved road winding around the eastern side. "In the middle ages it was a stronghold of the Guelphs and often afforded an asylum to the Popes." We should have been glad to have stopped a day or two at every one of these old towns; but it was not in our programme and we must be content with a good look at the great cities.

No, we can hardly realize that we are in Rome, the seat of the long line of Cæsars, of whom we have read so much; the famous city to which St. Paul was brought a prisoner for trial, and where he "dwelt two whole years in his own hired house, and received all that came in unto him, preaching the kingdom of God, and teaching those things which concern the Lord Jesus Christ, with all confidence, no man forbidding him;" the city where he gathered about him his faithful friends, Timothy, Tychicus, Mark, Aristarchus, Demas, Epaphras, Luke, "the beloved physician," and, no doubt, scores of other humble followers. "The first hour after the sight of Rome greets you is, perhaps, the most memorable in the life of an educated man. It is impossible to describe it; it is impossible to convey an idea of the beauty of the picture Rome presents, seated on her seven hills, and surrounded by the exquisite mountain ranges of Soracte, Albano, and the Apennines on one side, and the broad plain and the distant sea on the other." So wrote the late Professor Felton in 1853, and so we feel to-day.

We have referred to friends who preceded us. They were the Rev. J. W. Parker, wife and daughter, from Washington, and Miss Kendall, of Boston, traveling with them. The next morning after our arrival Dr. Parker led the way by the Spanish Staircase for a look at the city from Pincian Hill, first, however, going to our banker's to register our names, and to the Piazza del Popolo, where we visited the Twin Churches Santa Maria in Monte Santo and Santa Maria de' Miracoli, and also the Church of Santa Maria del Popolo. There is little that is remarkable about the Twin Churches, except that they "are believed to occupy the site of the magnificent tomb of Sylla, who died at Puteoli B. C. 82, but was honored at Rome with a public funeral, at which the patrician ladies burnt masses of incense and perfumes on his funeral pyre." Santa Maria del Popolo was founded in 1099, and, it is said, occupies the site of the tombs of the Domitii, "the burial place of Nero, which was haunted by evil spirits." Tradition relates that these evil spirits came in the shape of a great number of crows, which alighted on a gigantic walnut tree that had sprung up from Nero's grave. "Pope Paschal II. dreamed that they were demons and that the Blessed Virgin commanded him to cut down and burn the tree and build a sanctuary to her honor in its place." The church abounds in sculptures, bronze figures, and paintings in the highest style of art.

In the Piazza del Popolo is an obelisk brought from Egypt by the Emperor Augustus, and erected in honor of Apollo. From this square three of the principal streets of the city radiate—the Corso in the center, the Babuino on the left, and the Ripetta on the right. The Corso is to Rome what Broadway is to New York. We walked to Mont Pincio by an old brick monastery which was the home of Luther when he lived in Rome. From this point we have a good view of nearly the whole city. It is on the northern border, just within the walls of ancient Rome, but it is not one of the "Seven Hills." "In early imperial times the site of the Pincio Garden was occupied by the famous villa of Lucullus, who had gained his enormous wealth as a General of the Roman armies in Asia." On the left side are several terraces with a zig-zag carriage-way and foot walk, "adorned with rostral columns, statues, and marble *bas-reliefs*, interspersed with cypresses and pines" and "lined also with mimosas and other flowering shrubs." From the furthest angle of the garden, northeast, "you look down from the parapet upon the Muro Torto, a massive fragment of the oldest Roman wall, which juts over, as if ready to tumble down by its own weight, yet seems still the most indestructible piece of work that men's hands ever piled together." This wall is very high. Beyond it is the villa Borghese with its spacious and beautiful gardens. From this eminence, on the opposite side, "the Eternal City is seen spread at our feet, and beyond it the wide-spreading Campagna, till a silver line marks the sea melting into the horizon beyond Ostia." Away across the Tiber, on the extreme eastern border, stands St. Peter's in all its glory; on the right and adjoining which are a series of buildings composing the Vatican; and about an eighth of a mile nearer, directly on the west bank of the Tiber, the round Castle of St. Angelo, built by the Emperor Hadrian for his family tomb, but now the stronghold of the city, rises high above the adjacent buildings. Nearer still, on the east side of the river, where much the larger part of the city lies, is the Capitol, like the city, ancient in appearance; and yet nearer, the Quirinal Palace, while beyond, in the southern suburbs, are the Coliseum, the Temple of Vesta, the Arch of Constantine, and the ruins of the Palace of the Cæsars, of the Temples of Saturn and Vespasian, and of Constantine's Temple of Peace. There in the center of the city is the Pantheon, erected by Marcus Agrippa a quarter of a century before Christ; a little to the left the Trajan Column, and out by the Roman Forum and Palatine Hill the eye traces the main avenue leading to the Appian Way, one of the great high roads into the Campagna.

These are only some of the prominent objects that meet the eye as we stand here exultant at the long-coveted sight.

No, it is not a dream! We have compassed the great deep; we have made our way through many lands; we have scaled the mountains of Switzerland; and Mont Cenis has given way to admit us into "Sunny Italy," where we now have the supreme satisfaction of beholding her Capital, the "Eternal City," with our own eyes! "Never mind, father," said Henry Franklin, near the close of October, 1867, when at Florence we were compelled, owing to the cholera and the hostile movements of Garibaldi, to turn our faces homeward without going to Rome and Naples—"never mind, father, it will be a good reason for coming again;" and so it was. Now the city is free from any unusual malady, Garibaldi, having entered Rome in triumph, is an invalid at his villa Casalini three miles outside its walls, and we see no obstacle to a complete enjoyment of our visit, which may extend to weeks. Indeed, our apprehensions of sickness have greatly diminished since our arrival, so comfortably are we situated and so cheerful everything appears around us. For the information of travelers who may come after us, we will remark that our hotel is well situated, and that we have a good room facing south, with board, including a bottle of wine at dinner, fire and lights, (two candles a week,) all for ten francs a day each, or four dollars a day for two. We require little fire, however, except after four in the evening, and this is provided by coke, first ignited and brought in a small cylinder, which is placed within a drum, a two-inch pipe being attached to the cylinder and leading out of doors. On retiring for the night we set this cylinder, which is closed by a lid, on the stone balcony outside. The drum is about three feet high and one and a half feet in diameter, having four two-inch pipes, for cold air, equi-distant from each other, opening at the bottom and also into the room near the top of the drum, which is closed by a close-fitting cover. It is a very economical arrangement for heating, and might be introduced to good advantage wherever fuel is dear. While thus briefly referring to our domestic comforts, we should not forget to mention the important fact that one of the walls of our room is crooked—a certain bar to evil spirits, according to Italian superstition.

CHAPTER XLIII.

ROME, DECEMBER 12.—Yesterday, the second day after our arrival, having the day before obtained at our banker's permits to the Sistine Chapel and Galleries of the Vatican, we started early for St. Peter's. Taking carriages—one lira, or nineteen cents, pays for a one-horse carriage carrying three persons to any part of the city—we were driven immediately to the main southern entrance of the Vatican; but learning that the doors of the Chapel would not be opened before eleven o'clock, we ascended the steps to St. Peter's, and were soon filled with wonder at the grand proportions and magnificent adornments of that mammoth edifice. Unequal to the task of presenting any satisfactory description of this building without the aid of competent authorities, we shall take the liberty of resorting to them for such assistance as we may find necessary, without stopping always to give credit. These, both in English and French, we have now before us, and in their descriptions they often necessarily employ, to a greater or less extent, nearly the same terms, and for the same reason, no doubt, which now controls us, not unfrequently the same words and sentences. Next to its unrivaled dome, what first strikes us on approaching St. Peter's is the spacious piazza in front with the magnificent colonnades, in the form of a half crescent, on either side, the Egyptian obelisk in the center, and two beautiful fountains, one on each side between the obelisk and the colonnades, in full play. The colonnades have two hundred and eighty-four Doric columns, are sixty-one feet wide and sixty-four high, and they inclose an area of seven hundred and seventy-seven feet. The length of each colonnade from its lower extremity to the portico of the church is eleven hundred and ten feet, and its greatest breadth seven hundred and eighty feet. On the roofs of the colonnades, which were erected in 1667, are one hundred and twenty-six statues of Saints. The obelisk was brought from Heliopolis by Caligula. Its whole height is one hundred and thirty-two feet, that of the shaft eighty-three feet. It was in this piazza that the great religious ceremonies used to be held; but since the Pope was deprived of his temporal power, we believe nothing of the kind has taken place here.

The first church built on the site of St. Peter's "was the oratory founded in A. D. 90 by Anacletus, Bishop of Rome, who is said to have been ordained by St. Peter himself, and who thus marked the spot where many Christian martyrs had suffered in the circus of Nero, and where St. Peter was buried after his crucifixion. In 306 Constantine the Great yielded to the request of Pope Sylvester, and began the erection of a basilica on this spot, laboring with his own hands at the work, and himself carrying away twelve loads of earth, in honor of the apostles." It was only half the size of the present Cathedral. It suffered severely in the Saracenic invasion of 846, and at the instance of Nicholas V. (1450) was almost entirely destroyed in the time of Julius II., prior to 1506, when the present edifice was begun from designs of Bramante. Of the old basilica, the crypt is now almost the only remnant, and "of the endless works of art with which it was filled" a few relics only have been preserved from destruction. "The façade of St. Peter's is three hundred and fifty-seven feet long and one hundred and forty-four feet high. It is surmounted by a balustrade six feet in height, bearing statues of the Saviour and the twelve Apostles." A wide flight of steps, at the foot of which are statues of St. Peter and St. Paul, lead by five entrances to the vestibule, which is four hundred and sixty-eight feet long, sixty-six feet high and fifty feet wide. "The magnificent central door of bronze is a remnant from the old basilica." On the right is a walled-up doorway, called the Porta Santa, only opened for the Jubilee, which formerly took place every twenty-fifth year. From the vestibule the church is entered through immense doorways, provided with heavy, stuffed leathern curtains suspended from the top. It takes a man's strength to lift aside these heavy curtains; and usually some poor beggar stands ready to perform this service, expecting, of course, a soldo for his proffered politeness. On entering, "the interior bursts upon our astonished gaze, resplendent in light, magnificence, and beauty, beyond all that imagination can conceive." So it struck us; nor can we wonder that Mendelssohn thought that St. Peter's "surpassed all powers of description." He said,—"It appears to me like some great work of Nature, a forest, a mass of rocks, or something similar; for I never can realize the idea that it is the work of man. You strive to distinguish the ceiling as little as the canopy of heaven; you lose your way in St. Peter's; you take a walk in it, and ramble till you are quite tired; when divine service is performed and chanted there, you are not aware of it until you come quite close. The angels in the Baptistery are enormous giants; the doves colossal birds of prey; you lose all sense of measurement with the eye, or proportion; and yet who does not feel his heart expand when standing under the dome and gazing up at it." Madame de Staël described the architecture of St. Peter's as "*musique fixée*" (frozen music.) "On each side of the nave are four pillars with Corinthian pilasters, and a rich entablature supporting the arches. The roof is vaulted, coffered, and gilded. The pavement is of colored marble inlaid. In the center of the floor, immediately within the chief entrance, is a round slab of porphyry, upon which the Emperors were crowned." Imagine our sensations as we stood upon this slab. "The enormous size of the statues and ornaments of St. Peter's do away with the impression of its vast size, and it is only by observing the living, moving figures that one can form any idea of its colossal proportions." Its length is six hundred and thirteen feet, and it has an area of two hundred and twelve thousand three hundred and twenty-one square feet. The height of the dome in the interior is four hundred and five feet. The letters of the Latin inscription in the dome, which are in purple mosaic upon a gold ground, are each six feet long, and the pen of St. Luke seven feet; yet from the nave below they appear to be of the natural size. There are in the dome colossal mosaics of "The Evangelists," also of "The Saviour," "The Virgin," "The Apostles," and on a level with the lantern, one of "God the Father." Around the shrine is a circle of eighty-six gold lamps, always kept burning. From this you look down into the confessional, where there is a beautiful kneeling statue of Pope Pius VI. The Church contains twenty-nine altars besides the high altar, and one hundred and forty-eight columns. The side chapels are splendid, and some of them are large enough for independent churches, and are provided with galleries for the choir. They are designated by different names. One derives its name from the *Pieta of Michael Angelo*, who had more to do, probably, than any other artist in bringing St. Peter's to its present state of architectural perfection. In the Chapel of the Holy Sacrament are the tombs of the Stuarts. On the right is the monument of Maria Clementina Sobieski, wife of James III., called in the inscription "Queen of Great Britain, France, and Ireland," and on the left is that of Canova to the three Stuart Princes, James III. and his sons Charles Edward and Henry—Cardinal York. "Distributed around the whole basilica are confessionals of every Christian tongue." They are inscribed with the names of the different languages. Beneath the dome there is an imposing bronze canopy supported by four richly gilded spiral columns, ninety-five feet in height, and under this the high altar. Near by, against the last pier on the right of the nave, is a bronze statue of St. Peter. "Its extended foot is eagerly kissed by Roman Catholic devotees, who then rub their foreheads against its toes." Of the many strange things here this proceeding was one of the first that attracted our attention. It is kept up almost continually. The toes of the statue, raised some five feet from the floor, are bright from this act of devotion, of which the great toe appears to receive the larger share and is considerably worn. Usually, before kissing, the devotee wipes the toes with a handkerchief, or oftener with the coat sleeve or wristband. "On high festivals the statue (sitting) is dressed up in full pontificals. On the day of the jubilee of Pius IX., (June 16, 1871,) it was attired in a lace alb, stole, and gold-embroidered cope, fastened at the breast by a clasp of diamonds; and its foot was kissed by upward of twenty thousand persons during the day."

While we were present religious services were being conducted in one or more of the chapels. At eleven in the forenoon we proceeded to the Sistine Chapel. At the foot of the *Scala Regia,* leading to the chapel and other apartments of the Vatican, we were met by the guard in military uniform, and the officer in command taking our tickets of admission, gave directions to a subordinate to accompany us up stairs to the chapel door, where we were admitted by the doorkeeper. The frescoes in this chapel are considered very remarkable. The painting of "The Last Judgment," by Michael Angelo, nearly fills one end of the room; and the ceiling, which is covered with Scriptural representations, contains what are regarded his most perfect works in fresco painting.

The chapel being closed again about noon, we returned and spent the time in the Cathedral until two o'clock, when we were admitted to and finished the day in the Raphael Gallery of Paintings, also in the Vatican, which is said to contain eleven hundred rooms, and to be the largest, but certainly not the most magnificent, Palace in the world. Among other famous paintings here we had the pleasure of seeing that of "St. Romualdo," by Andrea del Sarto; "The Coronation of the Virgin," by Jules Romano; "Last Communion of St Jerome," by Domenichino; Raphael's "Transfiguration," and his "Madonna di Foligno."

CHAPTER XLIV.

ROME, DECEMBER 14.—We have made an agreeable call at the office of the United States Legation, where we were pleasantly received by our Minister, Honorable George P. Marsh, whom the writer knew slightly as a Member of Congress from Vermont before the war. He received his appointment at the commencement of President Lincoln's Administration, and has conducted his mission in a manner highly honorable to himself and to his country. There is no doubt that he has had great influence with the Italian Government and people in softening old prejudices against freedom of thought and action in religion as well as in the encouragement of civil reform generally.

Last Sunday forenoon we attended the American Union Church, where we heard an excellent sermon by Rev. Mr. Langmuir, the temporary pastor, who hails from the United States. He read from a chapter in Acts, wherein St. Paul is referred to as coming to Rome. It seemed to us more real than ever before. The principal aim of his discourse was to impress upon his hearers the importance of attending religious services regularly, as well while traveling abroad as when at home. In the afternoon we went to St. Peter's to hear vespers. There were about twenty cardinals and some sixty priests who, with the choir, took part in the ceremonies, which were interspersed with reading and responses, singing by the choir, accompanied by the organ, and much bowing, turning, and kneeling. The cardinals occupied the highest seats, which are the back seats on the right and left of the altar, and the choir occupied a side gallery in front of the organ. The priests of lesser degree had seats in front of and below the cardinals, one of whom is a young man we should think not over twenty-five, belonging, no doubt, to some family of high rank and wealthy, as he was richly dressed. These services were in a side chapel, large enough to accommodate three or four hundred people.

On our way home from St. Peter's we stopped at the Church of the Trinità de' Monti to hear vespers by the French nuns. This church is situated by Pincian Hill, near the head of the Spanish Staircase, a magnificent flight of one hundred and twenty-five steps, leading up from the Piazzi di Spagna to via Sistina. We have seldom passed this point without seeing groups of curiously dressed persons of both sexes and all ages, who make a living by standing as models for artists or by being invited by strangers to photograph establishments to get their photographs taken. It may be a genteel way of begging. We understand they profess to be Neapolitans; but one thing about them is certain, they present a perfect picture of unconcerned laziness. On entering the church we saw one or two hundred nuns in front of the main altar — scholars with their attendants — who were taking part in the services by singing, being accompanied by the organ. Their singing was very plaintive and sweet. Three or four priests were officiating, being, with the nuns, shut off from the rest of the worshipers and audience by a high iron grating. At the conclusion of the service the nuns passed in regular order down the aisle to the steps of the altar, where each one courtesied or half knelt, and proceeded to a side door leading into the convent. They wore long white veils thrown over their heads, while the sisters, their attendants, wore black bonnets and black veils. "In the evening," Frederika Bremer observes, "people go to the Trinità to hear the nuns sing from the organ gallery. It sounds like the singing of angels. One sees in the choir troops of young scholars, moving with slow and measured steps, with their long white veils, like a flock of spirits."

In the evening, by special invitation, we all attended a reception at Mr. Van Meter's, who, with members of his family, is actively engaged here in teaching. He has one or more schools in the city, and one also at Frascata, which are supported mainly by contributions collected by him in England and the United States. A part of the evening was devoted to religious services, embracing the singing of Moody and Sankey hymns. Mr. Van Meter led in prayer and singing, his daughter performing on the piano, and reverend gentlemen present were called on by him for short addresses between the hymns. These social gatherings are held at his house every Sunday evening, affording a favorable opportunity for travelers to meet and exchange compliments, if not to become acquainted with one another. Mr. Van Meter invited us to visit his schools, and from what we have seen and heard we think he is doing a good work.

We have spent a forenoon in the Borghese Picture Gallery, said to be the best private collection in the city. This Palace is about three hundred years old. It is "an immense edifice, standing round the four sides of a quadrangle; and though the suite of rooms, which comprise the Picture Gallery, forms an almost interminable vista, they occupy only a part of the ground floor of one side. The picture rooms open from one into another, and have many points of magnificence, being large and lofty, with vaulted ceilings and beautiful frescoes, generally of mythological subjects, in the flat central parts of the vault. The cornices are gilded and the doorways are of polished and variegated marble, or covered with a composition as hard, and seemingly as durable." The Gallery is open free to the public from nine o'clock till two, except on Saturdays and Sundays. Among the celebrated paintings here are "The Entombment," by Raphael; "The Mourners over the Dead Christ," by Garofalo; "Portrait of Cæsar Borgia," attributed to Bronzino and also to Raphael; "St. Stephen," by Francesco Franzia; "Danæ," by Correggio; "The Flagellation," by Sebastian del Piombo; "David with the Head of Goliath," by Giorgione; "Sacred and Profane Love," by Titian; "Return of the Prodigal Son," by Bonifazio; "Christ and the Mother of Zebedee's Children," by the same artist; and "Earthly and Heavenly Love," thought to be one of Titian's greatest works.

On our way home we stopped at an old monastery and were shown into what we should style a dirty cellar, but which is called the Mausoleum of Augustus, which is now only a mass of ruins. The guide pointed out to us a four-gallon iron kettle, rusted full of holes, as the vessel which he said once held the ashes of Augustus, whose body at his death went through the process of cremation. We are bound to admit that the sight afforded us little satisfaction, especially as we ran great risk of taking a severe cold in going from a warm atmosphere into such a damp, chilling cave. We hope Augustus will not lay it up against us for cutting our visit short.

The Fountain of Trevi is a wonderfully perfect representation of Nature, heightened in interest by art. Its water, drawn "from a source far beyond the walls," of the city, "sparkles forth as pure as the virgin who first led Agrippa to its well springs by her father's door." It is said that all who drink from this fountain are sure to visit Rome again. "It is a great palace front. At the foot of the palatial façade is strewn, with careful art and ordered irregularity, a broad and broken heap of massive rock, looking as if it may have lain there since the deluge. Over a central precipice falls the water in a semi-circular cascade, and from a hundred crevices, on all sides, snowy jets gush up, and streams spout out of the mouths and nostrils of stone monsters, and fall in glistening drops, while other rivulets, that have run wild, come leaping from one rude step to another, over stones that are mossy, shining, and green with sedge, because in a century of their wild play, Nature has adopted the Fountain of Trevi with all its elaborate devices for her own." The water falls into a large marble reservoir.

One of our visits long to be remembered was to the Church of the Capuchins, or rather to the cemetery under it, but on a level with the ground outside. There are two or three famous pictures in the church; one, "The Archangel Michael Trampling upon the Devil," by Guido; one, by Gherardo della Notte, representing "Christ in the Purple Robe;" and "The Visit of Ananias to Saul," by Pietro da Cortona. The cemetery consists of four small rooms walled each on three sides, the other side being open to the passage way along by the front windows. The walls and ceilings are ornamented with the bones of about four thousand Capuchin monks, whose remains were buried here. Until within a recent period, when Victor Emmanuel's government prohibited any more burials here, in the case of a new interment, the bones of the monk longest buried were thus brought into requisition in order to make room for the latest corpse. There are no floors to these chambers, and the earth beneath, in which one body after another has been buried, was brought from Jerusalem. Besides the thousands of bones arranged in various artistic forms on the walls and ceilings, in the niches of the rooms there are mummy-like skeletons of several monks, said to have been among the most distinguished of the order. These are either seated or standing, "enveloped in their brown cowls, their cords around their waists, and with a breviary or withered bunch of flowers in their hands." In a word, they appear in the costume and appendages they wore when living. Altogether this was a sight that one would not care to see more than once.

CHAPTER XLV.

ROME, DECEMBER 18.—On the 15th we visited the Farnesina Palace, which is open to visitors only on the 1st and 15th of each month. We were admitted to only two rooms, and these contain what are regarded as some of "the most beautiful existing frescoes of Raphael and his school." One of these "represents the Goddess of the Sea borne over the waves in her shell; tritons and sea-nymphs sport joyously around her; *amorini*, discharging their arrows, appear in the air like an angel-glory." Another represents Diana in her car, drawn by oxen; and then there are twelve scenes from the story of Psyche, in which that mythological character, Venus, Cupid, Ceres, Jupiter, Mercury, and Olympus are conspicuous figures—all wonderfully beautiful. The rooms were very cold, and we cut our visit short.

We next rode to the Church of San Pietro in Montorio, "built by Ferdinand and Isabella of Spain on the site of an oratory founded by Constantine upon the supposed spot of St. Peter's crucifixion." It contains several chapels, richly furnished with paintings, some of which, such as "The Scourging of Christ," "The Transfiguration," and "The Virgin and Child with St. Anne," are very fine; and there are also monuments to various distinguished persons. "Here, in front of the high altar, the unhappy

Beatrice Cenci was buried without any monument." The custodian conducted us to the cloister, a small room under or adjoining the church, as having been built "on the spot where St. Peter's cross is said to have stood;" and with a cup attached to the end of a stick six or eight feet in length he drew from beneath the floor, through which there was an opening for the purpose, a small quantity of sand, which he distributed to the company present as a precious relic. Of course we received our share in a solemn manner and as solemnly handed to the obliging monk the accustomed fee without question. True, we knew that many authorities contend that St. Peter never was in Rome; but to have permitted any doubt that we stood over the exact spot of his crucifixion would have destroyed the main novelty of our visit; therefore we dismissed doubt—as far as possible. It is said that when St. Peter was brought to the place of execution he requested that "he might be crucified with his head downward, alleging that he was not worthy to suffer in the same manner his Divine Master had died before him," and that the officers granted this "extraordinary request."

In the afternoon, in company with Dr. Parker and party, we were driven by the Trajan and Roman Forums and many other interesting points, out through the Porta Capena, the old arched gateway by which St. Paul entered when he came to the city, four or five miles along the Appian Way. In some respects we were disappointed in the appearance of this famous turnpike. It is far from smooth and only of sufficient width for two carriages to pass comfortably. Walls, ten feet high on either side, for several miles obstruct the view. On the further end of our trip the walls are lower, admitting of a sight of the Campagna, with its crumbling monuments; and just beyond are the ruins of the old Roman acqueduct, the arches of which extend for miles around nearly to the walls of the city on the left. On our way we went into a little Church, called the SS. Nereo ed Achilleo. "The tradition runs that St. Peter, going to execution, let drop here one of the bandages of his wounds, and that the spot was marked by the early Christians with an oratory, which bore the name of Fasciola." In another small Church we were shown a copy of the footprints, in marble, "said to have been left by our Saviour, the originals being removed to St. Sebastiano." That we might be able to verify the fact, we purchased of a black-eyed maiden on the spot a photograph of these remarkable footprints. We passed, without entering, a small circular structure where St. Peter is said to have been imprisoned; and off a quarter of a mile or more from the main road we went into a dilapidated brick building, now used for a stable or storehouse, once the Temple of Bacchus—the tomb of Urbano. The Appian Way, as far as we rode upon it, is lined on either side with ancient tombs, raised by stones, brick, and mortar, some of them to a height of thirty or forty feet, all defaced by the storms and winds of two thousand years. One of the most prominent is that of Cecilia Metella. Everywhere the eye could reach are ruins of some kind; and Minister Marsh told us that one could not turn up the soil anywhere in the vicinity of the city without almost invariably bringing to light ancient relics of more or less interest. At a distance of sixteen miles eastward, toward mountains covered with snow, we could see the village of Tivoli, and nearer, a little toward the south, the village of Frascata and the smaller settlement of Albano, to which places the Roman people, who are able, go to escape from the summer heat and sickness of the city. Hearing that there had been recent robberies on the road, before starting on our trip we divested ourselves of our watches and other little valuables; but we are satisfied the precaution was wholly unnecessary. True, we passed two or three squads of banditti-looking fellows, who were at work on the highway; but had they a disposition to commit robbery, there was little time for it free from interruption, since sight-seers, as well as country people, are constantly passing and repassing during the day.

In the forenoon of the 17th we visited the studios of Rogers and Miss Hosmer, in both of which we saw many fine statues and other works in marble. Miss Hosmer appears to enjoy vigorous health, and said that, with ordinary care, any one may reside in Rome as safely, so far as health is concerned, as in most other cities. Mr. Rogers also seemed quite well. We should take him to be between fifty and sixty years of age. He expressed his intention of shortly taking up his residence in Washington City, where we are sure he would meet with a hearty welcome. We visited the studio, also, of a fine looking Italian gentleman who used to work for Crawford. It was full of beautiful statues, one of which, "You Can't Come In," represents a beautiful maiden just ready to take a bath in her room. She is evidently surprised by some intruder, and hastily gathers around her, as best she may, one of her garments not usually worn on the outside. In her confusion she leaves enough of her form uncovered to show that, sweet and beautiful as her face is, it cannot claim superiority, in that regard, over some other parts of her figure.

In the afternoon we went to the Barberini Palace to see galleries of pictures, among which is the famous "Portrait of Beatrice Cenci." But for her interesting history, we doubt whether this picture would attract such universal attention, although it cannot be denied that there is something about her expression which, closely observed, is calculated to excite more than passing interest. We had heard it stated that no artist was permitted to sit by and copy this portrait, and that the copies obtained had been executed by experts, who would carefully scan it and then hasten to their studios to convey their impressions to canvas. However this may have been formerly, it is not so now. The custodian showed us several copies for sale bearing a certificate under the seal of the proper authorities that they were directly from the original in the gallery, where we purchased a large photograph, which he assured us was likewise taken, as it evidently was, from the original. Of this portrait Shelly observed that it is "most interesting as a just representation of one of the loveliest specimens of the workmanship of Nature. There is a fixed and pale composure upon the features; she seems sad and stricken down in spirit, yet the despair thus expressed is lightened by the patience of gentleness." Hawthorne wrote: "The whole face is very quiet; there is no distortion or disturbance of any single feature; nor is it easy to see why the expression is not cheerful, or why a single touch of the artist's pencil should not brighten it into joyousness. But, in fact, it is the very saddest picture ever painted or conceived; it involves an unfathomable depth of sorrow, the sense of which comes to the observer by a sort of intuition. It is a sorrow that removes this beautiful girl out of the sphere of humanity, and sets her in a far-off region, the remoteness of which, while yet her face is so close before us, makes us shiver as at a specter." Dickens expresses a similar idea,—"Through the transcendent sweetness and beauty of the face there is a something shining out that haunts me. I see it now, as I see this paper or my pen." The other most noted picture in these Galleries is the portrait of the unfortunate Lucrezia Cenci, the stepmother of Beatrice, who suffered and was executed with her. The charge against them, believed to be true, was that they conspired together to rid themselves and the world of Beatrice's own father, not only on account of his debauchery and wickedness generally, but that his diabolism took form in "an implacable hatred toward his children," and especially toward Beatrice, in a manner too cruel and too base for utterance. These scenes occurred during the pontificate of Clement VIII., in 1599.

The Barberini Palace is extensive and grand, and contains not only a large number of rooms, filled with paintings and other works of art, but also an immense hall devoted mainly to statuary, and a library of valuable books and about seven thousand manuscripts, among which are letters of Galileo, Bembo, Urban VIII., and others. One wing of the building is now occupied by distinguished members of the Barberini family. Upon the grand staircase there is the representation of a lion in high relief, "found on the property at Palestrina. It is before this lion that Canova is said to have lain for hours upon the pavement, studying for his tomb of Clement XIII. in St. Peter's." In the hall of statuary are "four vast frescoes of the fathers of the Church—having been removed from the dome of St. Peter's, where they were replaced with mosaics by Urban VIII."

CHAPTER XLVI.

ROME, DECEMBER 22.—On the forenoon of the 18th the writer, in company with a fellow traveler, called on the Roman Catholic prelate of the American College, Father Chatard, formerly of Baltimore, for the purpose of obtaining a permit for one of the ladies of our party to visit his Holiness the Pope. Father Chatard received us very courteously, and after a pleasant chat we made known our business, when he inquired if the lady understood what would be required of her in case she should be admitted to the desired audience. At the same time, to remove any embarrassment she might feel, he went on to observe, we thought rather apologetically, knowing we were not of his religious faith, that she would be expected to appear without gloves, in a black dress, black veil over her head, and to kneel before the Pope on his approach for introduction. This, he said, was the prescribed etiquette, and he thought it much more simple than that which is required to be observed in presentations to Queen Victoria and most other sovereigns. We replied that this was all understood, and he promised to send us the solicited note of admission. It is said gloves are prohibited for fear of poison.

Now we hesitated about speaking of this purpose of calling on the Pope, for we have reason to think the lady in question is a little sensitive on the subject; but since we have commenced "telling tales out of school," we might as well acknowledge that but for two or three reasons the writer himself would also have applied for a pass. In the first place, he had left his dress coat, one essential article, at Geneva, nor was he the possessor of a white cravat, another necessary piece of apparel for such an occasion; but the most serious obstacle was *a stiffness of the knee joints*, the cause of which he failed to trace to a short but painful attack of rheumatism with which he had been afflicted some two months previous at Interlachen! The result was that he left without asking for a permit for himself, hoping sometime to meet his Holiness, who is no doubt a very good old gentleman and sincere Christian, where less ceremony may be required.

The 19th was Sunday, and we again attended services at the American Union Chapel, where we listened to another able sermon by Rev. Mr. Langmuir. After lunch we walked to Pincian Hill, the Hyde Park of Rome, where, in the course of the afternoon, thousands of persons assembled to promenade, on foot and in carriage, to enjoy the music of a fine band, and to see and be seen. We hoped to get a sight of King Victor Emmanuel,* who usually rides out on these occasions, but we were disappointed. We, however, saw Prince Humbert and the Princess Margherita, the latter of whom is very popular. Although the weather is said to be unu-

---

* He died, after a short sickness, January 9, 1878, and was succeeded by his son, Prince Humbert.

sually cold, tropical trees and plants are growing in the open air, and orange trees in the gardens are loaded with their golden fruit.

On the forenoon of the 21st we visited the museum of statues and cabinets of sculpture at the Vatican. The collection of statues and other objects of art here is as extensive as it is wonderful. It would be tedious to enumerate or attempt to describe at length. Many of the works here are famous everywhere; for instance, "The Laocoön," "The Apollo Belvidere," and "The Antinous," or "Mercury"—the latter statue being, "perhaps, the most beautiful in the world. It was found on the Esquiline, near San Martino al Monte." "The Laocoön" group was also "discovered near the Sette Sale on the Esquiline in 1506, while Michael Angelo was in Rome." This is believed to be the group described by Pliny as, in his estimation, superior to all other works both in painting and statuary. He remarks that "the whole group—the father, the boys, and the awful folds of the serpents—were formed out of a single block, in accordance with a vote of the Senate, by Agesander, Polydorus, and Athenodorus, Rhodian sculptors of the highest merit."

> "Turning to the Vatican, go see
> Laocoon's torture dignifying pain—
> A father's love and mortal's agony
> With an immortal's patience blending. Vain
> The struggle; vain against the coiling strain
> And gripe, and deepening of the dragon's grasp,
> The old man's clench; the long envenomed chain
> Rivets the living links — the enormous asp
> Enforces pang, and stifles gasp on gasp."

"The Apollo Belvidere" was "found in the sixteenth century at Porta d' Anzio and purchased by Julius II." "The Perseus" and "The Pugilists,

Kreugas and Damoxenus," by Canova, are also celebrated statues.

In the afternoon we spent the time at the Pantheon and two or three churches. The Pantheon is a Pagan Temple, having been erected by Marcus Agrippa twenty-seven years before the Christian era. Closed as a Temple in the year 399, it was consecrated as a Christian Church in 608. In form it is circular, with a portico one hundred and eight feet wide by forty-two feet deep. The portico is supported by sixteen Corinthian granite columns, thirteen feet in circumference and thirty-nine feet in height. Eight of these columns are in front and the others form three colonnades in the rear thereof. The walls of the building are of brick and twenty feet in thickness. The rotunda, which embraces the entire space within, is one hundred and forty-three feet in diameter and its height is the same. There are seven niches, in which are statues, in the walls, and on the outer circle also are chapels like those in common Roman Catholic cathedrals. In these chapels are a number of tombs, among them those of Raphael, Caracci, Zucchero, Peruzzi, Vaga, and Udine, all painters, and the remains of all of whom were interred here. The rotunda is lighted entirely by an aperture twenty-eight feet in diameter in the center of the roof. In allusion to this, Hawthorne evolves this beautiful picture: "'I like better,' replied Hilda, 'to look at the bright blue sky roofing the edifice where the builders left it open. It is very delightful, in a breezy day, to see the masses of white clouds float over the opening, and then the sunshine fall through it again, fitfully as it does now. Would it be a wonder if we were to see angels hovering there, partly in and partly out, with genial, heavenly faces, not intercepting the light, but transmuting it into beautiful colors? Look at that broad, golden beam — a sloping cataract of sunlight — which comes down from the aperture and rests upon the shrine at the right hand of the entrance.'" As there is no provision for closing this opening, the rain from above meets with no obstacle till it reaches the marble floor, in the center of which there are holes for it to pass off. This floor is now on a level with or below the ground outside, which, by the débris of centuries, has been raised to the extent of five steps, by which the Temple was originally entered. To us this is one of the most interesting places we have yet visited, because it takes us way back beyond the period when we commenced to reckon time. True, we may anywhere see things in Nature going back thousands of years, if not thousands of centuries, before this date; but here is the work of *men* who lived before Christ appeared on the earth — men who must have been the equals, at least in architecture and mechanics, of any living at the present day — perhaps their superiors.

Near the Pantheon we entered rooms, formerly above but now below the level of the earth, where St. Paul is said to have lived two years. The well, still supplied with water from which he quenched his thirst, was shown to us, and also the chain by which he was bound to his jailor to prevent his escape.

We have been again to the gallery of statuary in the Vatican and into a good many rooms filled with all sorts of old Roman relics, which were unearthed in and around the city. We saw, too, a large number of statues which we failed to see on our first visit. One of them is a fine full length statue of

Augustus, brought to light only a few years ago. From the Vatican we went through and to the top of the Castle of San Angelo, the circular military citadel, which next to St. Peter's and the Coliseum is perhaps the most prominent object in the city. From the roof we obtained a splendid view of both city and country. Directly by its walls we looked down upon the still open field, in which Cincinnatus left his plow to enter the public service. As previously observed, this structure, or rather the skeleton thereof, was originally the tomb of Hadrian and other Emperors. It has since been changed in form and much enlarged. We had to get a permit to enter it, and we were treated very politely by both officers and soldiers, who guided us through numerous apartments, including the room in which Beatrice Cenci was put to torture, but in vain, to make her confess. We also entered the dungeons in which she and her step-mother respectively were imprisoned. That of Beatrice was six to eight feet square, within walls about ten feet in height. Overhead, at one side, is a small window, through which a dim light might have entered, and on another side, also overhead, is a small aperture through which she received her food. We were obliged to bend ourselves nearly double in order to enter the dungeon through its low, narrow doorway. Our guide said she was confined here eleven months. In times of revolution this castle has been the refuge of the Popes, and we were shown an immense iron chest in which they kept their treasure. This chest is ten feet or more in length, six feet high, and three or four feet wide. One of the old Popes, the guide informed us, had at one time five millions of scudi in it to protect it from the revolutionists. From the

Castle to the Vatican are two passages, one over the other, constructed for the escape of the Popes, as they have several times been used, in times of danger. The upper passage is "open like a loggia, the lower covered, and only lighted by loop-holes. The keys of both are kept by the Pope himself."

CHAPTER XLVII.

ROME, December 23.—Since making note of our call on Father Chatard to obtain a permit for one of the ladies of our party to attend a reception of Pius IX., the atmosphere of Rome, or something else, has had quite an *oily* effect upon the knee-joints of the writer, as the stiffness(?) felt there some days ago yielded so much on the 22d that the other difficulties mentioned as in the way of his attending also having been easily surmounted, he was surprised to find himself on the way to the Vatican among the faithful of that occasion. The truth is he had a strong desire to see the Pope, and when the time came for his lady friend to go, she having received her promised pass, she was without an escort, and felt a delicacy about going in alone. What was to be done? Another lady of our party wished to go, but neither she nor the writer had a permit, and permits are usually obtained only on application several days in advance. Everything seemed to point to the writer as the proper escort. The excuse of no dress coat and no white cravat was immediately answered by an offer of the loan of the first by Mr. William H.

Ferry, Jr., nephew of Senator Ferry, and of the latter by our fellow traveler, Dr. Parker. Mr. Ferry was an independent gentleman, on his wedding tour with his charming wife, both at our hotel, and Dr. Parker, having resigned his pastorate of the Calvary Church, no doubt considered himself secure from a "church mauling" for so venial a sin, springing as it did from the goodness of his heart, that of proffering or consenting to loan a white neck-tie for such an occasion. Thus, the way being apparently clear, at least for a trial, a carriage was called, and the writer, with his two lady companions, was hastily driven to the office of Father Chatard and the case laid before him. He was exceedingly kind and courteous. He could not on so short notice give us regular permits, but he wrote and handed us a note to the doorkeeper at the Vatican, who receives the passes, adding that he himself would be present and give us a special introduction to the "Holy Father," as he styles the Pope. This not only made it all right for us, but very agreeable, and we went on our way rejoicing. We found no difficulty in gaining admission to the officiating priest whose duty it is to examine the passes, and, guided by ushers dressed in scarlet velvet, we were soon seated in the reception room, where we had to wait over an hour before the Pope made his appearance, owing, as we have since learned, to his having previously to receive a delegation of students from South America, who read to him an address, to which he responded. The reception room is a long corridor, with space for two rows of chairs, about one hundred, on either side, and for two or three persons abreast to pass between them. On the outside are large arched windows the whole way.

At the further end is an arm-chair for the Pope, with his bust in marble and coat of arms over it. At the opposite end is an iron rail gate with curtains thrown across, and this is the end at which the Pope—as well as the visitors—enters. The curtains were not entirely drawn aside until just before he made his appearance. He came in, accompanied by about a dozen cardinals or priests, and among them our friend, Father Chatard, who stopped and spoke to us as he passed down the corridor in the train of the Pope, who, on entering, saluted the company with a few words, which we did not exactly understand, but took to be a salutatory welcome. Immediately on his appearance inside the curtained gateway, we all rose from our seats, and the line of visitors opposite to us commenced kneeling and knelt as he approached them on the whole line. When he reached the end they all rose to their feet, and as he came back on our side the same ceremony of kneeling was observed. All took his right hand, or put one hand under his and kissed or raised it near their lips, while some of the more devoted did not stop at kissing his hand, but prostrated themselves before him and kissed one of his feet. Some of the women, evidently humble Italian or French women, were affected to tears. When he came to us, Father Chatard was at his side, and, kneeling also, introduced us. After we had shaken hands, Father Chatard informed him more particularly who we were, when his Holiness again took our hand and expressed his gratification at seeing us. Of course we reciprocated the compliment, which we have every reason to believe was sincere on his part, as it certainly was on ours, for we regard him as a very kind-hearted, good old gentleman. When he was through with his separate greetings and blessing—he breathed a short blessing on each one as he or she was presented to him, and also blessed beads, crosses, and other small articles which many of the guests brought for the purpose—he faced the audience and made a short speech in French. He commenced by invoking the blessing of God on all present, individually and collectively, and upon our countries respectively, representing as we did several nationalities. We were not able to comprehend all he said, as he spoke quite rapidly; but referring to his morning interview with the South American students, he said it had fatigued him, and he must therefore be excused from addressing us at length. In conclusion he said he earnestly hoped and prayed that we might all meet in heaven as we had met here. When he said this he raised his eyes toward heaven, and was very animated, as he was in fact throughout his speech, frequently bringing his cane down to the floor more fully to express his earnestness. His cane, the handle of which was ivory, he carried in his left hand. He wore a white silk cap, an inner robe of white cashmere, with a silk sash, and his cloak, or exterior robe, was scarlet merino or broadcloth. His hair is very white, his countenance benignant and very pleasant, and his whole appearance commanding. He has the shuffling walk of an aged person, but he does not show so much of the feebleness of age in his face as most men do at his time of life; he is now eighty-four. As soon as he had concluded his address, he retired with the members of his court, and the gratified visitors dispersed to their respective domiciles. To our collection of photographs we have added a remarkably correct likeness of him.*

In the afternoon we visited the Church of Santa Maria Maggiore, which, next to St. Peter's, is the most beautiful in Rome. It "was founded A. D. 352 by Pope Liberius and John, a Roman patrician, to commemorate a miraculous fall of snow, which covered this spot and no other on the 5th of August, when the Virgin, appearing in a vision, showed them that she had thus appropriated the site of a new temple." This is one interpretation of the legend. Another is that the Virgin appeared simultaneously to Liberius and John in their dreams, commanding them to erect a church to her on the spot where they should find a deposit of snow on the following morning. August 5th. There are long rows of magnificent marble columns, many imposing tombs, and the church abounds also in beautiful mosaics, illustrative of Scripture history and Christian doctrines. Among the tombs are those of Nicholas IV., Clement VIII., Paul V., Sixtus V., Clement IX., and "in front of and beneath the high altar Pius IX. has lately been preparing his own monument, by constructing a splendid chamber approached by staircases and lined with the most precious alabaster and marbles." In or near the high altar is a sarcophagus said to contain the remains of St. Matthew. Over this magnificent chamber is a canopy like that at St. Peter's. Among the illustrations in mosaic are representations of "The Throne of the Lamb," as described in the Apocalypse, Peter and Paul beside

---

* He died February 7, 1878. On the 20th of February, Cardinal Gioachimo Pecci was elected as his successor, and has taken the title of Leo XIII.

it; "The Annunciation," "The Angel appearing to Zacharias," "The Massacre of the Innocents," "The Presentation in the Temple," "The Adoration of the Magi," and "Herod Receiving the Head of St. John the Baptist." Some of the ceilings are richly frescoed. "It was in this church that Pope St. Martin I. was celebrating mass in the seventh century, when a guard, sent by the Exarch Olympius, appeared on the threshold with orders to seize and put him to death. At the sight of the Pontiff the soldier was stricken with blindness, a miracle which led to the conversion of Olympius and many other persons."

In the evening Father Chatard called and passed an hour with us all in Dr. Parker's private parlor. He is from Baltimore, where he was educated as a physician, but afterward studied for the priesthood, and has resided here since 1857. We should judge him to be from forty-five to fifty years of age. He is a tall, fine-looking man, and his long black robe with small cape gave him quite a dignified appearance. His cloak, which he laid off, is of fine broadcloth, reaching nearly to his feet, and his chapeau is of fur, with a wide brim, turned up with a silk cord to present three corners, like all the hats worn by the priests and students of the Roman Catholic Church here. He is at the head of the American College, and is evidently a gentleman of much influence in the Church. It having been represented in the United States that the Roman Catholics were educating here some two hundred negroes for the purpose of proselyting among their colored brethren in the Southern States, Dr. Parker inquired of him as to the fact. He replied that there was no truth in the report—that there were only two or three colored persons at school here, and that they were studying with a view to service in South America. He did not appear to feel any special interest in the colored over the white race, but, on the contrary, thought it no easy matter for both to occupy the same social platform. In this connection he related an amusing anecdote of the confession one day, we do not remember how long ago, at St. Peter's. The sight of a negro here is very unusual, and there are thousands of citizens, probably, who never set eyes on one. It happened that a negro priest, on a visit here, took a seat at St. Peter's in one of the confessionals to hear confessions. When thus seated the priests are concealed from view, and one may make confession without knowing to whom or to what kind of a person he is confessing. On this occasion a lady of noble birth knelt and made her confession to this black priest, and rising to retire, she happened to espy his face through a crevice in the door, when she became terribly frightened, declaring that she had been confessing to the devil! Father Chatard also narrated interesting incidents of the bombardment of the city at the time when Victor Emmanuel assumed possession. He said that he was awakened very early in the morning by an unusual noise, which he instantly became satisfied was the sound of battle, and being in a room into which shells might fall and explode, he immediately arose and went to the roof of the house, where he found several of his pupils on the same mission, to view the grand display of fireworks. He did not, however, deem it prudent to stop long, and they all betook themselves to a lower room, strongly arched, where they were safe from both shell and balls. About ten in the forenoon the cannonading ceased, a white flag having been raised from the dome of St. Peter's as a signal of the Pope's capitulation. He said the Holy Father desired to avoid bloodshed, and made only sufficient resistance to show that he yielded only to force. Less than fifty persons, we think he said, were killed on either side. We were highly gratified by this visit from Father Chatard, as we were likewise by his courtesy when we called on him. In reference to the surrender of Pius IX., our hostess, a very intelligent English lady, whose husband is an Italian, told us that the King entered the city early one morning without a guard, and that he was received by the people with unbounded acclamation. In answer to their greeting, as he rode through the city, he said, "I came just as soon as I could!" and he continued to repeat this response over and over again until he alighted at the Quirinal Palace.

CHAPTER XLVIII.

ROME, DECEMBER 24.—On the 23d, in company with Dr. Parker and party, we spent several hours roaming over and through the Palace of the Cæsars, or, more correctly speaking, among the ruins of many palaces once the abode of the Roman Emperors. Palace upon palace has been built here —one upon the ruins of another; but we know not why the term "Palace of the Cæsars" is used, unless it is because the present ruins, for the most part, are believed to be those of the Palace of Vespasian, which was built upon the top of the buried

Palace of Augustus, some of the ruins of which have been excavated, and are now entered from one of the halls of the Palace of Vespasian. New excavations constantly bring to light more and more of interest. In some of the rooms lowest down, the walls of which are standing, we saw fine artistic paintings on the plastering that must have been executed more than two thousand years ago. These ruins entirely cover Palatine Hill, many acres in extent; and on some days in the height of the visiting season there are no doubt scores of travelers here to examine them. What seemed strange to us was that on the day of our visit, in a place of so much interest, our party should have had it all to ourselves. Not exactly all, however, as we shall see. We were intently engaged in our investigations when, at some distance in a remote part of the ruins, we espied the tall figure of a gentleman in a long dark cloak and military cap. He stood erect with his back half turned toward us, and we could see that he was evidently deeply absorbed in study of the surrounding ruins, assisted by what we took to be a guide-book, which he held in his hands. His whole bearing was that of a military chieftain or other high officer of state; and it was a mystery how he could have reached his point of observation without having been seen by us before. Was it possible we could be deceived, or were we dreaming? It did indeed almost seem as though the spirits of the departed occupants of these buried palaces were present and watching our footsteps! We are not superstitious; but could it be possible that one of the Cæsars had been permitted to return and that he actually stood before us! In such case to whom could we resort for protection? True, we were a party of six; but four of these were delicate ladies. His Holiness the Pope was too far off and too feeble to come to our aid; and although we had found our only male associate, Dr. Parker, a most agreeable traveling companion, we could not dispel the apprehension that, under such circumstances, the fact of his being a Calvinist Baptist preacher, if known to any Roman Emperor present, whether in the flesh or in the spirit, would be almost sure to prove fatal to our whole party. But it was too much to believe that we were in this predicament, and we ventured to approach the distinguished stranger, when, much to our surprise, as well as pleasure, he proved to be none other than our own countryman, General M. C. Meigs, of the United States Army. Well, be it as it may, had he lived in Rome in the time of the Cæsars, who knows that he might not have been "the noblest Roman of them all?"

We were now at liberty to pursue our observations. In the basilica, which means "King's house," the ancient Law Court, we stood on the spot where St. Paul was tried and acquitted. A portion of the marble bar, or railing behind which the judges sat, is still to be seen, although the walls of the room are razed nearly to the ground. It is proper to remark that Hare, in his "Walks in Rome," says: "This basilica, though perhaps not then in existence, will always have peculiar interest as showing the form and character of that earlier basilica in the Palace of the Cæsars, in which St. Paul was tried before Nero. But it is quite possible that it may be the same actual basilica itself [as affirmed by other authorities] and that the Palace of Nero, which overran the whole of the hill, may have had its basilica on this site, where it was preserved by

Vespasian in his later and more contracted palace." "A leg of the Emperor's chair actually remains *in situ* upon the tribunal, and part of the richly wrought bar of the confession still exists." Early historians state that St. Paul was brought in fetters, under the custody of his military guard, and arraigned before the blood-stained adulterer, Nero; and that the prosecutors and their witnesses were then called forward to support their accusations, which had been sent by Festus in written depositions from Judea. As we all know, St. Paul was "accused of disturbing the Jews in the exercise of their worship, which was secured to them by law; of desecrating their Temple, and, above all, of violating the public peace of the Empire by perpetual agitation, as the ringleader of a new and factious sect." But, as already observed, "the trial resulted in his acquittal. He was pronounced guiltless of the charges brought against him, his fetters were struck off, and he was liberated from his long captivity."

In another section, just outside of the grand dining hall, or adjoining the spot where the hall used to be, the walls of which have disappeared almost to the ground, we saw the remains of the walls of a small room, which bore the suggestive name of Vomitorium, "with its basin, whither the feasters retired to tickle their throats with feathers, and come back with renewed appetite to the banquet." The half-section of the conduit to the sewer is still visible in the crumbling brick walls of this small apartment.

Near the basilica was a large hall, called the Tablinum, "a kind of commemorative domestic museum, where family statues and pictures were preserved." Opening from this gallery "was the Lararium, a private chapel for the worship of such members of the family—Livia and many others—as were deified after death. An altar, on the original site, has been erected here by Signor Rosa from bits which have been found." Next, "passing a space of ground, called, without much authority, Bibliotheca, we reach a small Theater on the edge of the hill, interesting as described by Pliny, and because the Emperor Vespasian — known to have been especially fond of reciting his own compositions—probably did so here. Hence we may look down upon the valley between the Palatine and Aventine, where the rape of the Sabines took place, and upon the site of the Circus Maximus. Beyond this, on the right, is (partially restored) the grand staircase leading to the platform once occupied by the Temple of Jupiter-Victor, vowed by Fabius Maximus during the Samnite war, in the assurance that he would gain the victory. On the steps is a sacrificial altar, which retains its grooves for the blood of the victims." At one point are the ruins of the Palace of Tiberius. Here there is a row of arches said to be those of the soldiers' quarters. Above these are several rooms richly frescoed. The Palace of Caligula was in the northwestern corner of the area. It was "built against the side of the hill above the Clivus Victoriæ, which still remains, and consisting of ranges of small rooms, communicating with open galleries edged by marble balustrades, of which a portion exists. In these rooms the half mad Caius Caligula rushed about, sometimes dressed as a charioteer, sometimes as a warrior, and delighted in astonishing his courtiers by his extraordinary pranks, or shocking them by try-

COLISEUM OF VESPASIAN

ing to enforce a belief in his own divinity." Other almost endless ruins, equally interesting, are described in the guide-books; but our stay was too short to allow of extended descriptions of our own, and what we have presented may afford a general idea of the whole.

From the site of these ruins we saw the Tarpeian Rock, not far off, by the Tiber. It is now only some eighty feet in height; but in the time of the Cæsars its height is said to have been one hundred and eighty feet. Immediately at the foot of Palatine Hill stands the Temple of Vesta, which appears to be in quite a good state of preservation. We did not enter it. On the opposite side of the street from the Palace of the Cæsars are the wonderful ruins of the Basilica, or House of Constantine. Some of the walls, still standing, of this edifice are seventy-eight feet high, with an arched span of eighty feet. From these ruins we passed to the Coliseum and the Roman Forum near by. One thing which struck us as remarkable is the enormous size of the Coliseum, covering six acres, and the vast extent of the Roman Forum and other ruins. One can get no correct conception of their dimensions from photographs. Under the walls of the Coliseum there are canals, by which the water from the Tiber is brought into the area. Some of our party went to see the Coliseum by moonlight—a good way to get the Roman fever—but they only followed in the footsteps of Lord Byron:

> "I do remember me, that in my youth,
> When I was wandering—upon such a night
> I stood within the Coliseum's wall,
> 'Midst the chief relics of almighty Rome;
> The trees which grew along the broken arches,

> Waved dark in the blue midnight, and the stars
> Shone through the rents of ruin; from afar
> The watch - dog bay'd beyond the Tiber; and
> More near from out the Cæsar's Palace came
> The owl's long cry, and, interruptedly,
> Of distant sentinels the fitful song
> Begun and died upon the gentle wind."

The work of excavation in the Roman Forum is still going on. "The level of the ancient soil is twenty-four feet below that of to-day." The ruins already exposed fill a very large space. The remains of walls and broken pillars show, to some extent, the shape and size of different halls and apartments on the ground floor. A few of the pillars and architraves, as seen in the photographs and engravings, rise high above the surrounding ruins, but look as if almost ready to fall. The street pavements, worn smooth by footsteps and carriage wheels before the time of Caligula, are of irregular cobble stones, some of them a foot or more in extent. We spent hours wandering over and through these wonderful and intensely interesting ruins. The Trajan Forum, with its famous historical column, where similar excavations have been made, is likewise a place of great interest.

CHAPTER XLIX.

ROME, December 27.—Christmas forenoon we drove to St. Peter's, expecting to see and hear something more than usually interesting, but were disappointed. There were services in which we understood one of the Cardinals represented the Pope, who, before he became a "prisoner," used to officiate in person on Christmas day. These services included high mass, in which there was good singing, but no better than we heard here on Sunday. From St. Peter's we went to the American Union Chapel, where we heard another excellent sermon from Rev. Mr. Langmuir, who took for his text the injunction, "Work out your own salvation with fear and trembling," etc. In the afternoon we were present at the dedication of a Protestant Church for Italians, the first of the kind in Rome *for the Italians* since the days of the Apostles. It is to be under the direction of the Rev. Dr. Vernon, a Methodist clergyman from Richmond, Virginia, who is to be assisted by an Italian preacher. Dr. Vernon made some remarks touching the cost of the building and the advantage of having a regular house of worship, erected for the purpose, as he said the Roman Catholic priests represent to their ignorant followers that holding religious services in any other house is no worship at all. Rev. Mr. Taylor, another American missionary here, made the principal address, and was followed by some observations from Rev. J. W. Parker, of Washington, and Rev. C. E. Sumner, of Chicago. The Roman Catholic priests, we are told, call the northern Italian invaders "Lombards," and confident of seeing them one day expelled, they tell their friends that when the "Lombards" are driven out, they will turn all the Protestant meeting houses into stables. Sunday afternoon we again witnessed the display of the aristocracy on Pincian Hill, but did not have the good luck to see the King, who was out for an airing with the rest. It was a beautiful afternoon, and the terraced streets, walks, and plateau swarmed with horses, carriages, and people, all to the music of the band.

On the morning of the 27th, in company with Dr. Parker and party, we engaged a carriage by the hour and were conveyed through St. Paul's Gate, about two miles beyond the city walls to the celebrated Church of St. Paul, erected to commemorate St. Paul's martyrdom, which took place on or near the spot where the church stands, and where it is said he was buried. It was founded in the year 380. Previously the small Church of Constantine occupied the same site. St. Paul's was improved from time to time until 1823, when it was almost entirely destroyed by fire. In point of magnificence and richness it is represented to have been one of the most beautiful churches extant. The work of restoration was immediately commenced, and though not yet completed, the interior in some respects equals St. Peter's in grandeur of appearance. The nave is three hundred and six feet in length and two hundred and twenty-two feet in width, with four ranges of polished granite columns, brought from the Simplon, near Lake Maggiore. These pillars, both in respect to size and length, we think are equal to those of the south and west fronts of our Treasury. There are other splendid columns of alabaster, said to have been presented by the Viceroy of Egypt, and large pedestals of malachite, presented by the

Emperor of Russia. Some of the mosaics, which are most remarkable, and other ornaments of the old basilica were rescued from the flames and have been introduced into the new church. Among the mosaics is a series of portraits of the Popes, and being above the long ranges of columns, they are five feet in diameter, but seen from the floor appear to be only about the natural size. The grand triumphal arch separating the transept from the nave is also a relic of the old basilica. "On the side toward the nave it is adorned with a mosaic of Christ adored by the twenty-four elders and the four beasts of the Revelation; on that toward the transept by the figure of the Saviour between St. Peter and St. Paul." In the altars and chapels are fine pictures, statuary, and other rare objects of art. Connected with the church is a monastery, but there are very few dwellings nearer than the city, this part of the Campagna having been almost entirely deserted owing to the deadly malaria which prevails here all seasons of the year. No traveler to Rome should leave without visiting St. Paul's.

On our way out we passed a small chapel, "which commemorates the farewell of St. Peter and St. Paul on their way to martyrdom." It bears the following inscription:

"In this place SS. Peter and Paul separated on their way to martyrdom.
"And Paul said to Peter, 'Peace be with thee, Foundation of the Church, Shepherd of the flock of Christ.'
"And Peter said to Paul, 'Go in peace, Preacher of good tidings and Guide of the salvation of the just.'"

Next we drove to the Temple, or Arch of Janus, only the walls of which remain, and on the opposite side of the road is the humble Chapel of San Giorgio in Velabro, founded in the fourth century. Here, too, is the Cloaca Maxima, or arched drain, constructed twenty-four hundred years ago "to dry the marshy land of the Velabrum." It was navigable its whole length by a boat. A section of it is still in use.

One of the most attractive objects on the road is the famous Pyramid of Caius Cestius, who died about thirty years before the Christian era. It is of brick encased in marble. Its height is one hundred and twenty-five feet, and its width at its square base one hundred feet. Near by this Pyramid is the Protestant Cemetery, where we stopped to visit the graves of Shelley and Keats. From a plain white marble slab, lying over the remains of the former, or over the ashes of his heart, "his body having been burned upon the shore at Lerici, where it was thrown up by the sea," we copied the inscription entire, as follows:

"PERCY BYSSHE SHELLEY, Cor Cordium.
"Natus IV. Aug. MDCCXCII. Obiit VIII. Jul. MDCCCXXII.

"Nothing of him that doth fade,
But doth suffer a sea-change
Into something rich and strange."

From an upright, plain marble slab at the head of the grave of Keats we copied the entire inscription as follows:

"This grave contains all that was mortal of a young English poet, who, on his death-bed, in the bitterness of his heart at the malicious power of his enemies, desired these words to be engraved on his tombstone:

"Here lies one whose name was writ in water.
"February 24, 1821."

Through the little Church of San Pietro in Carcere we entered the Marmertine prisons, "excavated from the solid rock under the Capitol." They consist of two chambers, one below the other, the lower originally being accessible only through a trap door overhead. Now there is a narrow staircase leading to this dungeon. It was here that St. Peter and St. Paul were imprisoned, so we are assured; and we were shown the chain which bound them to an iron post, still also to be seen in the room. Sometimes, it is said, they were chained to their jailor—their safety being thus secured, notwithstanding the jailor might fall asleep. There is a chair here in which we rested for a moment, on the assurance of the custodian that it was the same used by these illustrious Apostles. From a well beneath the prison floor we drank of excellent water. This fountain "is attributed to the prayers of St. Peter that he might have wherewith to baptize his jailors, Processus and Martinianus; but, unfortunately for this ecclesiastical tradition, the fountain is described by Plutarch as having existed at the time of Jurgurtha's imprisonment." It is supposed to have been from this prison that St. Paul wrote to Timothy,—"I suffer trouble as an evil-doer, even unto bonds; but the word of God is not bound."

We next went into San Pietro in Vincoli, another church full of interest. There are many figures in mosaic, some fine pictures on canvas, by celebrated artists, and several remarkable statues, the most famous of which is Michael Angelo's gigantic statue of Moses, which is called "The Glory of the Church." It forms part of the unfinished tomb of Julius II. "The figure is seated in the central niche, with long flowing beard descending to the waist, with horned head and deep-sunk eyes, which blaze, as it were, with the light of the burning bush, with a majesty of anger which makes one tremble, as of a passionate being, drunk with fire." We have a photograph of this statue, which we could not help thinking would present a better effect, being so much above the natural size, were it placed in an elevated position instead of resting on a base only three or four feet high. In niches on either side are statues of "Rachel" and "Leah," likewise by Michael Angelo; and there are niches for over thirty more. Relics, purporting to be portions of the crosses of St. Peter and St. Andrew are shown here.

In the afternoon we spent an hour in the Church of San Giovanni in Laterano, where we heard most excellent music by the choir, with organ and double bass viol accompaniment. We have seen nothing finer in any church than the twelve pillars supporting the nave, and, in niches, the marble statues of the twelve Apostles; and these are only a small part of the magnificent decorations of this church, which, after the time of Constantine the Great, is said to have been the principal church of Rome. It occurred to us that our sculptor, Mr. Ball, from Boston, might have taken his idea of his superb statue of "St. John" from the statue of that Apostle here, as they resemble each other. Both artists represent him as standing with a pen in his right hand and a book in his left, his eyes raised reverently toward heaven. "And I heard a voice from heaven, saying unto me, Write," etc. In the high altar, at which the Pope alone reads mass, there is a wooden table from the catacombs, which is said to have been used as an altar by St. Peter. We must content ourselves with speaking of only a few of the wonderfully interesting objects in this church. Indeed, one can enter hardly any of the old Roman churches without being at once impressed with their almost innumerable treasures, which are the accumulation of many centuries.

A short distance from the Church of San Giovanni in Laterano, in an old building which centuries ago formed part of the Lateran Palace, is the Santa Scala, or Holy Staircase, which our Saviour is supposed to have ascended and descended when they were in the house of Pilate at Jerusalem, from which place they were brought by Helena, mother of Constantine the Great. The steps, two of which are said to be stained by the blood of the Saviour, are of white marble, but to prevent further wear they are encased in wood. Through apertures in the casing we observed that they were much worn. It is allowed to ascend these steps, twenty-eight in number, only on the knees; and while we were present a dozen or more persons, men, women, and children, were slowly making the ascent, stopping on each step to breathe a prayer, and, on reaching the top, prostrating themselves over a brass cross fastened to the floor, and then continuing on their knees to the "Sancta Sanctorum," formerly a private Chapel of the Popes, across the hall. At the foot of the stairs, on one side is a marble group, representing "Christ before Pontius Pilate," and on the other, one representing "Judas Kissing the Saviour." On either side of the Santa Scala is a flight of stairs by which the devotees descend, and these are in common use for all. Whoever ascends the sacred steps on his or her knees is granted an indulgence from penance for nine years, so we were told on the spot; but the Schönberg-Cotta Chronicles say for a thousand years. According to this last authority, Martin Luther once undertook the ascent, when, as he was toiling up, he said he heard a voice as if from heaven, which seemed to whisper to him the words of his old battle-cry, "The just shall live by faith," and awakened as from a nightmare, he stood upright, and with firm step descended and walked away. Not so with those we saw, some of whom we observed stooped forward and kissed the steps in the most reverent manner. Pilgrims from a long distance come here to perform this act of devotion.

CHAPTER L.

ROME, JANUARY 1, 1876.—We begin to think there is no limit to the churches in Rome, and that if we expect to visit all of them we shall be obliged to extend our visit into months instead of weeks. We have already seen a great many, and we are becoming so familiar with them that we hardly realize how much of interest they possess. On the 27th of December we found ourselves at the Church of Santa Croce in Gerusalemme, situated quite near the city walls and right by the old Roman Aqueduct. It is remarkable principally for the relics which it contains, and which, if verified as genuine, would certainly be very wonderful. Among these is the "Title of the True Cross," "an imperfect plank of wood, two inches thick, one and a half palms long, and one palm broad;" "the finger of St. Thomas, Apostle, with which he touched the most holy side of our Lord Jesus Christ;" "one of the pieces of money with which the Jews paid the treachery of Judas;" "one bottle of the most precious blood of our Lord Jesus Christ;" another of "the milk of the most blessed Virgin," and a number of other equally wonderful things. Passing from the church, we gathered from the aqueduct walls some moss and leaves, as the most facile representatives of that ancient structure, for preservation.

On the 28th we went to see the Bambino at the Church of Santa Maria in Araceli, near the Capitol. It is a representation of the nativity of the manger. We made some notes of this exhibition, to which the whole of one of the side chapels is devoted; but the description of it by Mr. Story, the sculptor, is so perfect that we cannot do better than copy it: "In the foreground is a grotto, in which is seated the Virgin Mary, with Joseph at her side and the miraculous Bambino [infant Jesus] in her lap. Immediately behind are an ass and an ox. On one side kneel the shepherds and kings in adoration; and above, God the Father is seen surrounded by crowds of cherubs and angels playing on instruments, as in the early pictures of Raphael. In the background is a scenic representation of a pastoral landscape, on which all the skill of a scenic painter is expended. Shepherds guard their flocks far away, reposing under palm-trees or standing on green slopes which glow in the sunshine. The distances and perspective are admirable. In the middle ground is a crystal fountain of glass, near which sheep, preternaturally white and made of real wool and cotton wool, are feeding, tended by figures of shepherds carved in wood. Still nearer come women bearing great baskets of real oranges and other fruits on their heads. All the nearer figures are full sized, carved in wood, painted, and dressed in appropriate robes. The miraculous Bambino is a painted doll swaddled in a white dress, which is crusted over with magnificent diamonds, emeralds, and rubies. The Virgin also wears in her ears superb diamond pendants." This exhibition takes place only in the first week after Christmas, and on a stage erected for the purpose little maidens come and recite "sermons, dialogues, and little speeches" in explanation of the picture before them.

On the 29th we made a visit to Story's studio, where, among other meritorious works of his, we saw his "Cleopatra," a most beautiful statue chiseled out of the purest white marble. It is in a sitting posture, and looks every inch a queen. We also went into the studio of an Italian artist near by, where we found many interesting objects of art; and afterward made a second visit to the studio of Miss Hosmer. On the same day we were present at a school exhibition at Mr. Van Meter's, where little Italian girls from four to twelve years of age gave recitations in a very pleasing manner. Although the room was crowded with spectators, they were not in the least abashed, and their delivery and gestures were perfect. Ten or twelve of Mr. Van Meter's older lady pupils, now his assistants, were present and received each a copy of the Bible as a Christmas gift, while the little ones were overjoyed by presents of various kinds from the Christmas tree.

On the same day, in company with Mr. and Mrs. J. S. Lippincott, of Philadelphia, we passed some hours in looking at the pictures and other interesting objects in the Corsini Palace, which is open free to visitors every day except Sunday. With a large collection of paintings here are some which are quite noted. One of these is "A Madonna and Child," by Murillo, and another, also "A Madonna and Child," by Carlo Dolce. The latter, especially, is one of the most beautiful we have anywhere seen; and the galleries all abound in Madonnas, as well as in Holy Families, Crucifixions, Saints, and Martyrdoms. One of the most striking portraits here is that of "Clement XII.," the coloring and expression of which are so perfect that only a near view could convince that it is a stone mosaic and not an oil painting on canvas. From this palace we walked to the Janiculum, "a steep crest of a hill which rises abruptly on the west bank of the Tiber," and from which we had a fine view of the city and the Campagna in the direction of and beyond St. Paul's. "On this hill Janus is believed to have founded a city, which is mentioned by Pliny under the name of Antinopolis." Our objective point was the Church of St. Onofrio and adjoining convent. There is nothing very remarkable in the church; but the old convent is interesting as having been the residence of Tasso in his last days, and as containing the room in which he died on the 25th of April, 1595, in the fiftieth year of his age. We saw in this room his bust, a mask in wax said to have been taken from a cast of his face, his autograph, inkstand, crucifix, and other relics. We sat in the arm chair labeled as the one he usually occupied, but failed to experience on that account any poetic inspiration. On the invitation of Clement VIII., Tasso came to Rome in November, 1594, that he might be crowned as poet laureate on the Capitol. He expected the ceremony would take place immediately, but owing to the inclemency of the weather it was, much to his disappointment, postponed until late in the following spring. His feeble health admonished him that his end was near, and when he arrived at the monastery he said to the monks who received him, "My fathers, I have come to die among you!" and he wrote to one of his friends, "I am come to begin my conversation in heaven in this elevated place and in the society of these holy fathers." Upon receiving the Papal absolution on the day of his death, he exclaimed, "I believe that the crown which I looked for upon the Capitol is to be changed for a better crown in heaven." He was buried in the church, close by the high altar, and near the church entrance is a monument to his memory. In the garden of the monastery we stood under the old oak planted by Tasso, but which was partially destroyed by lightning or a hurricane in 1842. A young oak is growing beside it.

Most of the sojourners at our hotel and several of their friends stopping at other hotels here being desirous of calling on General Garibaldi, the writer dropped a note to him, asking him, if agreeable, that he would name a time when we might see him. He immediately answered through the post that he should be happy to receive us from two to four o'clock in the afternoon, but without naming any day. His note is written in Italian:

ILLUS. SIGNORE:
  Vi vedro suo piacere dalle 2 alle 4 P. M.
          Vi saluto,
 Roma, 28 — 12 — 75.   G. GARIBALDI.
Signore HORATIO KING,
  Roma.

Choosing the afternoon of the 30th to make the call, a party of fifteen of us took carriages and were driven to his Villa Cassalini, a pleasant country residence about a mile beyond the city walls. We were detained a few minutes in the corridor before being admitted, and were then invited by a young man, whom we afterward learned was the General's son, to walk up stairs. Here we were ushered into a spacious saloon which had been converted into a bedchamber, there being two single beds placed side by side in a corner of the room. In the center, covered with books and papers, was a long table, at the further end of which General Garibaldi sat in an easy chair. Waiting a moment under the impression that he would come forward to receive us, we soon observed that he was an invalid, and we all moved toward him, and were introduced — the writer first introducing himself and then the rest of the company separately. He was dressed in black pantaloons, a loose gray jacket, with a white flannel cloak thrown over one shoulder, and wore a black embroidered cap and slippers. He made no allusion to his health, but it was apparent that he was suffering from rheumatism or other malady rendering locomotion difficult if not painful. His slippers were slit as though his feet were swollen, and his hands were much cramped. He was, however, very cheerful, and expressed himself as very much gratified to see so many of his American friends, who, he remarked, appeared to represent, as they did, almost all parts of the United States. He said that he too was an American citizen — that he did not know Maine, but that he knew Boston, New York, Philadelphia, Washington, and the *Po-to-mác*, placing the accent on the last syllable. To one of our company who congratulated him on the progress of civil liberty in Italy, and who remarked to him as he held his hand on taking leave that *that* hand had had much to do in producing this happy result, he modéstly replied that he had done a little, but only his duty. We bade him adieu, all feeling that we had been in the presence of a man possessing many characteristics of greatness, by none of which were we more impressed than by his candor and unselfishness. He speaks English quite fluently, and repeatedly expressed his gratification at seeing us. The writer saw and heard him make an address in French on the occasion of his reception at Geneva in the month of September, 1867. There was a great crowd present, all eager to see him. He is of medium size. The likenesses we generally see of him are quite correct.

On the 31st we visited the Colonna Palace, occupied by the Prince of Colonna, who generously throws its galleries open free to visitors every day except Sundays and holidays. It is usual, however, in all such cases, to give the custodian a small fee. As in all the galleries, there are many fine pictures here, some statuary, and a few articles of rare old furniture among the numerous other objects of curiosity and art. We saw here a secretary, inlaid with ivory and precious stones, the making of which occupied thirty years. In the largest hall, on one of three or four steps up to a more elevated part of the floor, lies a cannon ball, which came through the window and lodged there when the French attacked the city in 1849. It split off portions of the marble step, making quite an indenture. A similar indenture from a like cause, and in the same siege, may be seen in the pedestal of one of the marble angels, several of which adorn the bridge of San Angelo over the Tiber near St. Peter's.

In the evening we went to the Church of Il Gesù, which was magnificently lighted, it being the occasion of a Te Deum, which takes place there every year on the 31st of July and 31st of December. It is "sung for the mercies of the past year," and formerly the Pope as well as cardinals and people of Rome were in attendance. The services were very impressive.

And now we must take leave of Rome for the present, and finish our sight-seeing here on our return from Naples.

CHAPTER LI.

NAPLES, JANUARY 7.—On the 3d instant we took the half past nine train from Rome and arrived in Naples about half past four in the afternoon, having for company Rev. Dr. Parker and party, Rev. Dr. Merriman, the genial President of Ripon College, Wisconsin, and Mr. and Mrs. Lippincott. The trip was void of special interest beyond the pleasure of passing the time in good company and seeing an old country new to us, with its peculiar people, along the road. We were most interested on arriving at the point where we obtained our first view of Mount Vesuvius, with its white smoke rising slowly, fold upon fold, and passing off to the northwest in fleecy clouds. We entered the city from the northeast, the central railroad station being on the eastern side toward Vesuvius. Taking carriages, we were driven immediately to a comfortable boarding house, previously selected, at No. 64 via Giovanni, a few steps from the Strada di Chiaja, one of the principal avenues on the bay. We had rooms looking out upon a spacious garden in which oranges and mandarins were ripe and ripening on the tall trees, and grape vines were green as in spring time.

Our first call on the 4th was at our consul's for letters from home. We found him (Mr. B. O. Duncan) a most courteous and intelligent gentleman, and, as we think, in all respects admirably qualified for his position.

In the afternoon we walked to Virgil's tomb, situated in a vineyard in which green peas, on stalks or vines as high as our heads, were nearly large enough to pluck for the table. This, in mid winter, was to us a rare sight. We entered from the street by an old rickety door, opening upon a long flight of steps, from the end of which we continued to ascend and wind around in a narrow path until we reached a commanding eminence. Here we came to a mean shanty, which appeared to be the domicile of the gardener and his wife; and the latter, a stalwart washerwoman, leaving her work strung on lines in every direction, presented herself before us and sang a song in a voice that might have been heard a mile. It was in Italian, of course, but we understood it plainly enough as a bid for soldi, which, we are bound to say, neither the beauty of her person nor the sweetness of her voice could draw from our purses. And now, guided by the gardener, who was also the gate-keeper, we descended the west side of the hill fifteen or twenty rods to a rough board gate, which he consented to open on the payment of half a franc each by our party. A few steps beyond we came to what is generally believed to be the Tomb of Virgil. It is anything but attractive, either externally or internally. It has a chamber about fifteen feet square, with three windows and vaulted ceilings; and in the walls, upon which there are appropriate inscriptions, there are ten recesses for cinerary urns.

The two following days we passed most of the time in the National Museum, which is open daily from nine until three—free on Sundays and Thursdays, and with an admission fee of one franc on other days. This in many respects is perhaps the most interesting Museum in the world. The objects here of most interest are relics from Herculaneum and Pompeii, of which there is a very large collection. Then there is what is called the Borgia and Farnese Collections, and any number of relics from Capua, Cumæ, Pozzuoli, Stabiæ, Naples, Lucera, Minturnæ, and other places. The ground floor is devoted mainly to ancient mural paintings from Pompeii, Herculaneum, Stabiæ, etc., and to ancient statuary. Here is the original group of the "Farnese Bull," so celebrated as having been carved out of a single block of marble. It was the work of Appollonius and Tauriscus, the Rhodian sculptors. "The two sons of Antiope, Amphion and Zethus avenge the wrongs of their mother by binding Dirce, who had succeeded in withdrawing the affections of Lycus from Antiope, to the horns of a wild bull. Antiope in the back ground exhorts them to forgiveness, and not in vain." The "Farnese Hercules," also rescued from the "Baths of Caracalla," is another piece of sculpture here regarded as quite remarkable. Other noted statues here are the "Venus of Capua," "Psyche of Capula," and "Æschines," a beautifully draped figure. In one room is an equestrian statue of Nero, found in the Forum of Pompeii. The collections of bronzes and terra cottas are almost unlimited, and, in respect to the marble statuary and paintings, it would be tiresome to enumerate.

Few things struck our attention more keenly than the many common household articles, such as pots, kettles, and other vessels, which have been brought from Herculaneum and Pompeii. Some of them contain charred wheat, beans, almonds, plums, figs, olives, egg shells, and other things. Here, too, are fifteen loaves of bread burned to charcoal, but perfect in shape as when they were deposited in the oven, where they had been lying nearly two thousand years, and where they were found. A large number of papyrus books, or rolls, charred and ready to fall to pieces, likewise possess much interest. Great pains have been taken, and with some success, to learn their contents. In the Hall of the Flora there is a historical composition in mosaic, which was found, in 1831, in the House of the Faun at Pompeii. It formed a portion of the floor, and is from six to ten feet square. It is a representation of "The Battle of Alexander" at the moment when, his helmet having fallen from his head, he is charging Darius with his cavalry, "and transfixes the General of the Persians, who has fallen from his wounded horse. The chariot of the Persian Monarch is prepared for retreat, while in the foreground a Persian of rank, in order to insure the more speedy escape of the King, who is absorbed in thought at the sight of his expiring General, offers him his horse." We have a colored photograph of this mosaic. There is a good collection here of Egyptian antiquities, a collection, said to be the most extensive extant, of ancient crystal, "showing the numerous ways in which it was used by the ancients;" and an interesting collection of Renaissance works, among which are a bronze Tabernacle, very curious; an altar, with *reliefs* in marble; Indian and Chinese paintings; and various kinds of Asiatic curiosities. There are numerous precious relics, consisting of beautiful cameos, gold and silver jewelry, vases. goblets, and many other objects. A loaf of bread found at Pompeii bears the name of "Q. Cranius," the baker. There is an extensive Picture Gallery, containing some paintings, regarded as masterpieces of the Italian as well as the Neapolitan school, and also a large collection of engravings here, which form an important part of the thousands of interesting objects in this vast Museum.

Everybody knows how beautifully Naples is situated; but it has one serious drawback, from being too nearly on a level with the tide along the southern border skirting the sea. This is an obstacle to a complete drainage, and is no doubt a constant cause of sickness; but it is no good excuse for the dirt and filth one encounters in many of the streets, particularly in the lower parts of the city. We have taken a long walk through some of these streets for the purpose of observation, and much as we have seen of Italy we have nowhere seen so much of squalor as we found here. Many of the inhabitants appear to prefer dirt to cleanliness, and in their dress and all their surroundings they are consistent. Beggars salute you at every turn; and not unfrequently, if refused, they will fling insulting epithets at you. which you are thankful you do not understand. In our perambulations toward evening we met goatherds with their flocks of goats brought in from pasture for the night. Some of these animals yielding milk are taken from house to house, where they are milked and the milk sold on the spot. Were this wholesome regulation applied to some of the milkmen who supply Washington city with milk. there would be a fall in the price of water. It is a sight to see the common laborers and market people, who live in the suburbs or outside of the city, returning toward home at the close of their day's work. Sometimes you may see as many as fifteen or twenty on a single two-wheel cart, drawn by one poor mule or donkey. They not only fill the cart, but cling to the sides and thills, looking not unlike a swarm of bees; and very little mercy is shown to dumb beasts in Naples. In this regard, hackmen and cartmen are alike, and they seem to take delight in cracking their whips over and torturing their poor animals. Go into the street either for a walk or a ride, and if you are not careful you will be run over by hackmen, who, jehu-like, drive up to you, urging you to employ them. Make a bargain with one of them and enter his carriage, a hanger-on stands ready and mounts the seat with the driver, and when you come to alight he is on hand to open the carriage door, for which service you must pay him a fee or receive a measure of his abuse. We have learned to watch for these interlopers, and to let them understand in advance that we will have nothing to do with them. They are evidently on good terms with the drivers, who never object to their company.

The Strada di Roma, running north and south, dividing the city nearly in the center, is the fashionable business street of Naples; and on pleasant afternoons it is alive with beauty and gayety in all the glory of kingly aristocracy. The street is filled with carriages and the sidewalks with pedestrians of both sexes, all out for exercise and in pursuit of pleasure. The Strada di Chiaja and the charming Villa Reale, a beautiful Park between that broad avenue and the seashore, are likewise places of great resort for travelers and the *élite* of the city. This is particularly so on two evenings of the week. when there is excellent music by the band in the Park. The Park is long and narrow, and among its adornings are a number of marble statues, which would be a valuable acquisition to any gallery. It presents a curious contrast to the acres of linen strung on clothes lines in an open space nearer the shore, just to the southwest—a sight which might lead a stranger to suppose that half of the linen of Naples was sent there to dry.

CHAPTER LII.

NAPLES, January 9.—The 7th and 8th of January are days in our traveling experience long to be remembered. Our American party of nine left the city on the morning of the 7th by railroad for Castellamare, seventeen miles, where we hired two coaches, with drivers and a guide, to take us to Sorrento and back the same day. Both of these towns are situated directly on the bay, and the turnpike between them, a distance also of seventeen miles, runs quite near the shore most of the way. The hills and mountains on the east extend, here and there to the sea, and had to be excavated to admit of passage. On a pleasant day no ride could be more delightful; but unfortunately for us, the air was raw, with now and then a flurry of sleet from the mountains, and this was calculated in some degree to chill our enthusiasm. Nevertheless, the trip was novel and highly interesting. At the north, a part of the way much nearer to us than when in Naples, was dark Vesuvius with its endless moving clouds of smoke, and, also in plain sight, were the famous islands of Ischia and Capri, while the Mediterranean, stirred by the winds, continually addressed us in plaintive murmurs. Our road took us through Vico, Equense, Meta, and one or two other small villages; and where the mountains do not intervene there were on either side orange and olive groves, mulberry trees, pomegranates, figs, and aloes, the orange trees being loaded with their golden fruit. On our arrival at Sorrento, our guide led us up a long, muddy lane to the gate of an extensive orange grove, expecting to be admitted; but, much to our regret, he could make no one hear either his vigorous raps or his hallooing, and we were obliged to content ourselves with a look at the tops of the trees over the high walls. Disappointed in this, we turned and walked a mile or more to the top of a high hill on a point of the peninsula, affording a splendid view of Naples and the intervening gulf, as well as of Capri, now only a few miles off; of Ischia; the coast west of Naples to Pozzuoli and Baiæ; and of Mount Vesuvius on the northeast. We next went to see an old mansion in which Tasso was born in 1544, and "where, on his return in 1592, disguised as a shepherd, after a glorious but chequered career, he was received by his attached sister Cornelia." The only things we noted as remarkable about the building were two queer old marble griffins supporting the balcony. After taking some refreshments and purchasing a few articles of carved and inlaid wood, for which Sorrento is famous as well as for its cheap silk goods, we started on our return to Castellamare. It was deemed prudent to make the journey by daylight for two reasons: First, the fear of brigands at night, and secondly, the danger from obstructions by stones falling from the mountains. It was, however, quite dark before we reached Castellamare, where we stopped over night.

The next morning opened finely, and our coachmen having served us reasonably and very satisfactorily the day before, we made another bargain with them to carry us to Naples by the way of Pompeii, stipulating for a stop of four hours at the latter place, four miles from our starting point. We were soon set down at the Hôtel Diomède, a mean public house, which we should advise all travelers to shun, although our guide-book speaks of it as the best in the place. It is situated near the office where we obtained tickets and a guide to see the silent city. And now we were guided from street to street and from house to house, walking over three hours; but this was time sufficient to explore only comparatively a small portion of the ruins. Pompeii, when destroyed, was a town of from twenty to thirty thousand inhabitants. In the year 63 it was visited by a destructive earthquake, and in 79 it was overwhelmed by the eruption of Vesuvius. More than half the city yet remains to be excavated. The streets are paved and in good condition, save that in some places there are ruts six or eight inches deep, worn by the wheels of carriages; and the sidewalks are also generally well paved. In some of the streets the carriage-way is considerably below the level of the sidewalks, and at the crossings are high stepping-stones for foot passengers. Many of the shorter streets are only wide enough for one carriage, and there must have been a regulation requiring approach by carriage always from one and the same direction to avoid meeting. The walls of few of the buildings are standing above the first story, and these are generally either of brick or of small stones and cement. Many of the houses have staircases, showing that they were of more than one story; but as the upper portions have disappeared, it is supposed they were chiefly of wood and were consumed by the red-hot scoriæ of the eruption. The shops are generally distinguishable from the common dwellings and palaces; and many of the shops as well as the palaces bear over their doors the names of their former occupants. In some of the shops the marble counters are still standing, and in one of them we saw large earthen vessels, used for the sale of oil or wine. In a bakery the large oven, in which a batch of bread was found baked to charcoal, still remains intact, and near it are mills for grinding corn. The Basilica and Forum was an immense edifice, the surrounding pillars of which, mostly destroyed nearly to their base, witness its former magnificence. Many of the pillars of the House of Ariadne, the House of the Tragic Poet, the House of Sallust, the House of the Faun, the Temple of Pompeii, the Cascerne, and of other large structures remain standing at full length, but are more or less defaced by the heat of the scoriæ and the ravages of time. With sensations impossible to describe, we walked over and through these ruined Temples, the House of Lucretius, the Temple of Mercurio, the Temple of Augustus, the Temple of Jupiter, the House of Pansa, and along the street of the Tombs into the Villa of Diomedes. Many of the tombs and monuments are in a perfect state of preservation. The Villa of Diomedes is one of the most extensive private residences yet discovered, and according to our recollection one of the best preserved. "Near the garden gate of this Villa were found the skeletons of the owner and his attendant, one holding in his hand the keys of the Villa, the other carrying a purse which contained one hundred gold and silver coins of Nero, Vitellius, Vespasian, and Titus." At the southeast extremity of the town and detached from the other ruins is the Amphitheater, said to have been capable of accommodating twenty thousand spectators. The circles of seats, one above another, are of brick and cement, more or less covered with scattering tufts of grass, and as the ashes and soil on the exterior have not yet been removed, we were enabled to walk over adjacent ground on a level with the top of the wall and look down upon the ruins. There are the ruins, also, of the great Theater, holding five thousand, and the small Theater, made to seat fifteen hundred spectators. Near by are the remains of a building called the Gladiator's Barrack, one chamber of which appears to have been used as a prison, in which were found three skeletons and iron stocks for the feet. It is probable that other apartments of this edifice were likewise so occupied, as there were, in all, the remains of sixty-three bodies discovered on the premises. Here was a spacious bathing house, one section for males and one for females, with their marble basins for both hot and cold baths, their dressing rooms, and every other convenience of such an establishment. These rooms, like those of nearly all the houses and palaces, are ornamented with stucco *reliefs* and fresco paintings on the walls.

In one part of the town we came to a well, still supplied with pure water. Connected with the palaces were beautiful fountains, the marble adornments of which, with their cisterns, are still in a good state of preservation. There is a small Museum here filled with curious relics and models of various objects here brought to light. The most striking are plaster casts of corpses of a number of the ill-fated inhabitants, and a cast of the body of a dog, showing from his contortions that he died in extreme agony. A figure of a young girl has a ring on one of the fingers. These casts were taken by filling with plaster the cavities left by their bodies, which, embedded in the hardened ashes, had decayed. We have a perfect photograph of one of them, showing that the poor sufferer met death lying on her face, doubtless in the hope of avoiding suffocation. The excavation is still going on, but very slowly, we should judge from the comparatively few persons at work when we were present. Most of these were women and children, who carried the soil and ashes in baskets on their heads a short distance to a truck running on a temporary railroad to be conveyed away. Army or other Government officials were superintending the work. Pompeii was a walled city, and we entered through one of the old gateways. We might give many more particulars, but we should leave room for the poet, Rogers:

> "At the fount,
> Just where the three ways meet, I stood and looked,
> ('T was near a noble house, the house of Pansa,)
> And all was still as in the long, long night
> That followed, when the shower of ashes fell,
> When they that sought Pompeii sought in vain!
> It was not to be found. But now a ray,

Bright and yet brighter, on the pavement glanced,
And on the wheel-track worn for centuries,
And on the stepping-stones from side to side,
O'er which the maidens, with their water urns,
Were wont to trip so lightly. Full and clear
The moon was rising, and at once revealed
The name of every dweller, and his craft;
Shining throughout, with an unusual luster,
And lighting up this city of the dead.

" Mark, where within, as though the embers lived,
The ample chimney-vault is dun with smoke.
There dwelt a miller; silent and at rest
His mill-stones now. In old companionship
Still do they stand as on the day he went,
Each ready for its office — but he comes not.
And there, hard by, (where one in idleness
Has stopt to scrawl a ship, an armed man;
And in a tablet on the wall we read
Of shows ere long to be,) a sculptor wrought,
Nor meanly, blocks, half chiseled into life,
Waiting his call. Here long, as yet attests
The trodden floor, an olive merchant drew.
From many an earthen jar, no more supplied;
And here from his a vintner served his guests
Largely, the stain of his o'erflowing cups
Fresh on the marble. On the bench, beneath,
They sat and quaffed and looked on them that passed,
Gravely discussing the last news from Rome."

And now, bidding a last good-bye to the silent city, we mounted our carriages and were speedily conveyed to our lodgings in Naples, wondering why it is that while one city is engulfed by a terrible earthquake and another overwhelmed with burning ashes, others still are exempt from any such awful catastrophe.

CHAPTER LIII.

NAPLES. January 18.—On the 12th our party of nine passed the day in a most interesting trip to Baiæ, about twelve miles on the bay southwest of Naples, and back. The roads run near the sea all the way. From the strada Chiaja we enter the Grotto of Posilipo, a tunnel half a mile in length through a ledge or spur of a mountain. It is supposed to have been constructed in the reign of Agustus. "It is mentioned by Seneca and Petronius, under Nero, as a narrow and gloomy pass. Mediæval superstition attributed it to magic arts practiced by the poet Virgil," whose tomb is on the side hill near its eastern opening. Originally the bed of the road was much higher than at present, and we could see in the sides of the walls, about twenty feet above our heads, where deep grooves had been worn by the hubs of carriage wheels. The height of the grotto varies from twenty to ninety feet, and its width is from twenty-five to thirty feet. At the entrance and in the middle are small chapels, the ledge having been excavated to make room for them; and meek looking monks in their gowns and cowls stood ready to solicit any soldi we might have to spare. At the egress of the grotto we came to the small village of Fuorigrotta, whence we took the road to Pozzuoli, or Puteoli, as it is called in the 28th of Acts. After landing and tarrying three days at Syracuse—this was after his shipwreck—St. Paul says: "And from thence we fetched a compass, and came to Rhegium; and after one day the south wind blew, and we came the next day to Puteoli, where we found brethren and were desired to tarry with them seven days; and so we went toward Rome." We naturally took a lively interest in the place on St. Paul's account; but the only "brethren" who greeted us on our arrival were an army of guides and beggars, from whose importunities we were glad to escape by proceeding as speedily as possible on our journey. On an eminence behind the town there are the ruins of an amphitheater, which some of our party entered while the rest were satisfied with a look at the outside. By excavations made in 1838 a number of subterranean passages and receptacles for the wild beasts and other purposes were discovered. There was also a conduit by means of which the arena "could be laid under water when naval combats were to be represented. The celebrated gladiator combats under Nero, when he received Tiridates. King of Armenia, as a guest at his court, took place here. and even the Emperor himself enlivened the arena." Before going to the amphitheater we went to the crater of Solfatara. It is bowl-shaped, with a level bottom, and about a quarter of a mile in diameter. At one side is a boiling mass of mud, which bubbles and sputters, as one of our party remarked, like hasty-pudding. Near this was a considerable opening in the pumice-stone crust. through which sulphurous vapor and smoke were being emitted in a manner to indicate pretty lively operations directly beneath our feet. The guide led us close to this breathing-hole of the crater, and with a long-handled rake drew out red-hot pieces of porous stones yellow with sulphur, which we brought away with us. The soil is composed mostly of lime and sand, and six inches beneath the surface the sand under our feet was so hot that we could not hold it in our hands. Here the guide raised a heavy stone to his head and let it fall to the ground, producing a reverberating sound from below, indicating plainly that the earth directly beneath was hollow. We declared ourselves satisfied with a single demonstration, nor had we any desire to remain longer in such near juxtaposition to what is undoubtedly a region of fire and brimstone. The latest eruption, attended with an emission of lava, known to have taken place from this crater, occurred in 1198.

Returning to our carriages, we pursued our journey toward Baiæ, stopping to view the ruins of several temples on the way. It was past midday when we reached the end of our route; and here we were again beset by a gang of beggars, men, women, and children, from whom we endeavored, but in vain, to escape. Our landlady had kindly provided for us a bountiful lunch, and that we might enjoy it unmolested, we walked a quarter of a mile away from any dwelling — there were not a half a dozen in the place, one of them being a dirty inn — but the ragged crowd followed us like a herd of hungry wolves. In ancient times, before the fall of the Roman Empire, Baiæ was a great watering-place, and the desolate ruins of splendid baths, palaces, and temples are seen here at various points. On a height overlooking the bay there is a fort, which is the only structure we saw here in good repair. We gathered curious shells and pumice-stones from the seashore, and on our way home we were conveyed along by Lake Avernus, "regarded by the ancients as the entrance to the infernal regions on account of its somber situation and environs. Tradition affirmed that no bird could fly across it and live, owing to the poisonous exhalations, and that the neighboring ravines were the abode of the dismal, sunless Cimmerii, mentioned by Homer, (Odyss. XI.) Virgil, too, represents this as the scene of the descent of Æneas, conducted by the Sibyl, to the infernal regions (Æn. VI., 237.)" We drank of the water of this lake, which is of circular form and about one mile and a half in circumference. All this region round about is volcanic, but there was no taste in the water we drank to indicate that it came from other than a pure fountain. Our whole trip was novel and interesting, and we reached our lodgings in time and with keen appetites for our six o'clock dinner.

Like Turin, Venice, Florence, Rome, and we know not how many other Italian cities, Naples also has her Royal Palace, and this we visited on the 14th. It is not very remarkable for elegance, but the main staircase is grand and beautiful, adorned as it is with statues of the Erbo and Tagus, and the state rooms, which are furnished with many paintings and other objects of art, compare favorably with those of other palaces we have seen in our travels. There is here one unique piece of furniture, a Royal Cradle, which attracted our special attention. It is set up in the style of a swing, and stands in the center of the reception room. It is lined with white satin and has a pillow also covered with white satin. The outside is studded with coral, pearls, and lapis lazuli, and over it hovers a gilded angel. The view from this Palace is very fine. From the windows of the main salon you look out upon the Castle of St. Elmo and the Church and Monastery of St. Martin, high up on the hill in the southwestern part of the city. We have been to this famous Church and Monastery, and they are well worth a visit if only to enjoy the view from the garden and belvidere. This view takes in the city, bay, and the country in one direction as far as the Appenines. Listening from this high eminence, it was curious to hear the mingled sound of carriage wheels, of the tread of man and beast upon the pavement and street, of the voices of the moving multitude, of all the noises of a busy city rising in one ceaseless hum, not unlike the distant moaning of the ocean. The Church contains many paintings, all possessing more or less interest.

We had a jolly time on the 17th in an excursion to Mount Vesuvius. Taking a double carriage, in company with Dr. Merriman, Mr. and Mrs. Lippincott, and Miss Lillian Parker, and being provided by our landlady with a generous lunch, including oranges, mandarins, and *vin ordinaire* in abundance, we were driven along the coast for a few miles through a succession of villages, inhabited principally, we should think, by the lower class of laborers and beggars. Fishing and the manufacture of macaroni appeared to be the leading industries, judging from the number of persons mending their nets and the strings of macaroni hung out in every quarter to dry. The lovers of macaroni would be wise not to give special attention to the secrets of its manufacture. By this caution we are reminded of an incident in the life of Hawthorne, whose humorous side, Mr. James T. Fields says, was not easily or often discoverable, yet that he had seen him marvelously moved to fun, and that he remembers how he writhed with hilarious delight over Professor L——'s account of a butcher who remarked that "Idees had got afloat in the public mind with respect to sassingers." It was a sight to behold the crowd going to and from the city, especially the market people, some carrying their products on their heads, some with carts, and others with donkeys completely covered all but their head and ears by huge panniers, one on either side, reaching nearly to the ground and filled with whatever they had to sell. One of these interesting animals was almost entirely enveloped in golden carrots, impelling the punster of our party, Mr. Lippincott, to remark that "that donkey was more than eighteen carrots fine." That this pun may not be credited either to *vin ordinaire*, or to the genuine "Lachrimæ Christi," a bottle of which was purchased by one of our party at the Hermitage, it is due to our friend to say that he got it off before lunch. Our road took us through the villages of Portici and Resina, situated very near the sea. The latter village has been built over the buried town of Herculaneum, the excavated portions of which are reached by about one hundred steps. Only a small part of the town has been excavated; and having seen Pompeii, and not having sufficient time on this trip to take a look at Herculaneum, we concluded to forego any satisfaction we might have enjoyed in visiting the latter ruins, which, we are informed, present nearly the same general appearance of those at Pompeii. Both towns were destroyed by the same eruption. It is not probable that any part of Herculaneum will ever be uncovered to the sun. Turning now to the left, we were driven on a smooth zig-zag turnpike up the hill, through and over immense lava beds, to a point called the Hermitage, which is at the end of the carriage road. The only buildings here are a tavern, a small chapel, and the observatory. They are situated on a ridge so high that when there is an eruption from Mount Vesuvius the streams of lava flow down on either side. The distance from this point to the base of the cone is about one mile, and persons wishing to ascend the cone ride on mules or walk to the foot thereof at their pleasure. Dr. Merriman was the only one of our party who ascended to the mouth of the crater. the rest of us contenting ourselves with a ramble over the lava beds at the base of the cone, with an examination of the instruments in the observatory used for determining the conditon of the cauldron. and with the splendid view of land and sea afforded by our elevated position. We had a near view, also. of the great clouds of smoke, which come rolling up continually from the mouth of the seething crater. We walked over the identical beds of lava by which a party of tourists were suddenly overwhelmed and lost their lives in 1871. Hard now and immovable. these broad fields of lava, nevertheless, have an angry look, seeming to warn us to beware of a similar catastrophe to ourselves. The lava is of a dark color, like the scoriæ from an iron furnace. and has taken crude shapes, sometimes like coils of ropes. again like roots of dead trees, and then again swelling up into huge heaps. and, in the process of cooling, splitting open on the surface, presenting deep seams, or separating into smaller pieces. Dr. Merriman, in his ascent to the crater, outstripped all others with him, making the ascent unaided in just fifty minutes and the descent in ten minutes. Between Resina and the Hermitage, wherever there is a spot of ground not covered with lava, if no larger than a flower bed, grape vines have been planted. and gardeners were engaged in trimming and nursing them. One pleasant incident of this trip was our first meeting with Professor S. F. Smith, author of the National Hymn, "My Country, 'tis of Thee." at the Hermitage. He is one of the Faculty of the

Baptist Theological Seminary at Newton, Massachusetts. We all returned to our lodgings well satisfied with the day's enjoyment.

CHAPTER LIV.

ROME, FEBRUARY 1.—Our former traveling companion, Mr. Stickney, having joined us again at Naples, he and Dr. Merriman took final leave of us, and embarked for Egypt on the 18th of January. Dr. Parker and family returned on the same day to Rome, while we remained another week to keep company with Mr. and Mrs. Lippincott and finish up a little shopping, as well as to have executed a likeness in shell cameo, which we had just learned we could have done here on very reasonable terms. Naples is the place to buy all kinds of shell work, coral jewelry, and fancy articles in wood; and one can usually make such purchases there for one half or one quarter of the asking price. Having nearly completed our sightseeing there, we devoted the week to rest. We should not, however, forget to speak of a very interesting visit we made to the Aquarium in the Villa Reale. It is said to be the best in Europe. We also spent an hour agreeably in the Church of San Francesco di Paola, and went a second time to the Royal Palace. The Church is built after the style of the Pantheon in Rome. Its high altar is entirely inlaid with jasper and lapis lazuli.

We began now to think about securing our passage home by the Cunard Line, and we sent the company the required £10 pledge for a good state room on the "Bothnia" for the 6th of May. We left Naples at half past two on the afternoon of the 25th of January, and arrived in Rome at half past nine. Finding all the rooms taken at the Hôtel della Pace, where we had previously stopped, we found equally good quarters at the Hôtel du Sud near by, both being under the direction of the same proprietors. We were now again in daily communication with Dr. Parker and family, but Mr. and Mrs. Lippincott remained in Naples, and we have not had the pleasure of seeing them since.

In the Capitoline Museum there is an extensive collection of relics of almost every description, embracing statues innumerable, sarcophagi, bronzes, vases, and an endless variety of other curiosities, besides a large collection of paintings. We saw here the celebrated statues of the "Dying Gladiator," and the "Capitoline Venus." Half a day was barely sufficient for us to take a casual look at what is to be seen here, and it would require a volume to furnish a full description of even the more striking objects of interest in this vast collection. While we were at the Museum, General Garibaldi arrived in a coach at the Capitol, and was carried into the Chamber of Deputies, whence after a few minutes he was brought back in the arms of men, and departed amid the loud acclamations of the people assembled in front of the doorway. We were attracted by the noise, and reached a window just in time to see him reënter his carriage. He is evidently very popular, especially with the common people. From the Museum some of our party went to the Palace Rospiglioso to see the famous fresco painting of "The Aurora," by Guido.

On the 27th ultimo, with Mr. Van Meter as our "guide, philosopher and friend," our whole party took carriages and were shown through many interesting parts of the city, embracing the Palace of the Cæsars, a view from the bell-tower of the Capitol, the Church of St. Augustine, the Ghetto, or Jews' Quarter, and the exterior of the House of Rienzi and of the Cenci Palace. The House of Rienzi "derives its present name from a long inscription over a doorway, which tallies with the bombastic epithets assumed by the 'Last of the Tribunes' in his pompous letter of August 1, 1347, when, in his semi-madness, he summoned Kings and Emperors to appear before his judgment seat." The Cenci Palace — the home of Beatrice Cenci and the "scene of many of the terrible crimes and tragedies which stain the annals of the Cenci family — is of great extent," having a court "supported by columns, and adorned with antique friezes of fine workmanship, and built with balcony over balcony of open work." Both of these buildings are situated in an obscure corner of the city, and near the Ghetto, which was formerly inclosed by walls, outside of which the Jews at one period were prohibited from showing themselves, "unless the men were in yellow hats or the women in yellow veils." It is a pretty rough looking place, and our curiosity was quite satisfied with riding through it. In an open space in front of a little church we observed letter-writers, sitting at their tables, engaged in writing letters for the illiterate. It is a regular trade.

We were particularly pleased with our visit to and view from the Capitol. From the bell-tower Mr. Van Meter pointed out and remarked upon all the points of historical interest within the scope of our vision. Here were the "Seven Hills," all, or nearly all, in sight, with the Capitol, the Roman and Trajan Forums, the Palace of the Cæsars, the Coliseum, and the Pantheon, all on the east side of the Tiber. The names of the "Seven Hills" were given and the separate locations pointed out in their order—the Aventine, Cœlian, Palatine, Esquiline, Viminal, Quirinal, and Capitoline.

The Church of St. Augustine is noted for the "Madonna and Child," a fine piece of sculpture by Andrea Sansovino, before which the credulous Roman Catholic devotees are wont to prostrate themselves in sign of adoration. The figures are "smothered with jewels, votive offerings of those whose prayers the image had heard and answered. All round the image the walls are covered with votive offerings, likewise; some of a similar kind—jewels, watches, valuables of different descriptions." Frederika Bremer relates that long prior to her visit here, the report was spread that one day when a poor woman called upon this image for help it began to speak, and replied, "If I had only something, then I could help thee, but I myself am so poor." This story being circulated, very soon throngs of credulous people, she says, hastened hither to kiss the foot of the Madonna, and to present her with all kinds of gifts. "Candles and lamps burn around, and people pour in, rich and poor, great and small, to kiss, some of them two or three times, the Madonna's foot—a gilt foot, to which the forehead also is devotionally pressed. The marble foot is already worn away with kissing; the Madonna is now rich." We had seen so much of this kind of devotion that we looked on without any new emotion, either of wonder or surprise.

The 28th ultimo was devoted by our party to sight-seeing outside of the city, in the Baths of Caracalla and the Catacombs of St. Calixtus. Our trip took us again on the Appian Way for a short distance, affording us another opportunity to see this exceedingly interesting part of Rome. These Baths take their name from their projector, Caracalla, who began them in the year 212. They were continued by Heliogabalus and finished under Alexander Severus — so our guide-book states. One mile in circumference, they could accommodate sixteen hundred bathers at once. Only a portion of the walls, which are of brick, remain standing, and these are broken and crumbling. Some of the pavements, or ground floors, which are of marble mosaic, are still left, but they are very uneven and more or less covered with sand and dirt. Gibbon states that the walls of the lofty apartments were covered with curious mosaics that imitated the art of the pencil in elegance and design and in the variety of their colors. The nobility and common people alike had access to these baths. "The perpetual stream of hot water," Gibbon continues, "was poured into the capacious basins through so many wide mouths of bright and massy silver; and the meanest Roman could purchase, with a small copper coin, the daily enjoyment of a scene of pomp and luxury which might excite the envy of the Kings of Asia. From these stately palaces issued forth a swarm of dirty and ragged plebians, without shoes and without mantle; who loitered away whole days in the street or Forum to hear news and to hold disputes; who dissipated, in extravagant gaming, the miserable pittance of their wives and children; and spent the hours of the night in the indulgence of gross vulgar sensuality." In these habits of luxury, inertia, and consequent vice, the historian traces the main cause of the decline of the Roman Empire. The ruins of this immense structure, which covered a space of two million six hundred and twenty-five thousand square yards, do not present the appearance of having been unearthed; yet the books speak of numerous works of art, among them the statues of the "Farnese Bull," "Hercules," and "Flora," which have been "discovered" here; and it is presumed, therefore, that the débris in the interior was composed of the fallen roof and crumbling walls, together with light soil and sand conveyed thither by the winds of centuries.

Our descent into the Catacombs was by a long staircase, or a series of staircases, attended by a guide. We carried lighted tapers in our hands, and were careful not to lose sight of our conductor lest we might never find our way out. We were from twenty to forty feet below the surface — a cultivated field. "The galleries are from two to four feet in width, and vary in height according to the nature of the rock in which they are dug. The walls on both sides are pierced with horizontal niches, like shelves in a bookcase or berths in a steamer, and every niche once contained one or more dead bodies." In some of them we saw human bones. These galleries "cross and recross one another, sometimes at short intervals," on different levels, and it is estimated that in all the Roman Catacombs there are not less than three hundred and fifty miles of them. Here and there they open into small chambers, the walls of which are likewise generally pierced with graves, and in some of which are rude scriptural paintings. One of these chambers is called the Chapel of the Popes, many of the earlier Popes having been buried in it. We roamed among these ancient sepulchres for half an hour or more, and came out, glad to see daylight once more, at an opening some distance from the one where we entered.

Learning from Miss Foley, whose sculpture studio we visited yesterday, that William and Mary Howitt were stopping at her house, we called on them last evening and were exceedingly gratified with our short interview with them. Mr. Howitt is a gentleman of medium size, with hair entirely white, and an expression of countenance and manner at once attractive and agreeable. He is over eighty years of age, but still active as a man of sixty-five. Mrs. Howitt, we should judge, is from ten to fifteen years younger. Both in dress and deportment she appeared like an accomplished Quaker lady. Her hair is brown, and with a handsome nose and brilliant eyes, her expression is sweet and winning. For a number of years they have passed their winters in Rome and their summers in the Tyrol. They were gratified to hear us speak of the many friends they have made in the United States by their writings, and mentioning the names of a few of our best authors, they said they had met some of them in Europe. Mrs. Howitt desired to be kindly remembered to "Grace Greenwood," whose acquaintance she said she had the pleasure of making twenty years ago.

Now, having turned our faces homeward, we take our final leave of Rome.

CHAPTER LV.

GENEVA, FEBRUARY 19.—In company still with our friends, Dr. Parker and family, we took our departure from the "Eternal City" at eleven in the forenoon of the first instant, and arrived in Florence at seven in the afternoon, stopping at our old rooms on via Palestro. We left in good time, as we have since learned that a great many travelers were soon prostrated by the Roman fever; nor did some of our party entirely escape from the bad effects of the malaria brought away in our systems. It showed itself in tooth-ache and painful swelling of the gums and in the glands of the face. Another fortnight, now, in Florence enabled us to finish up our sight-seeing there pretty thoroughly, although the weather during most of the time was wet, raw, and disagreeable, inclining us to stay indoors more than we should have done had it been pleasanter. We revisited some of the churches, the Protestant Cemetery, St. Miniato, the Picture Galleries, and other places, in respect to all which we have already written, and notwithstanding the variableness of the weather, we shall always have pleasant recollections of Florence.

A ride of two hours by rail brought us on the 14th to Pisa in time to visit the great Cathedral, Baptistery, and Campo Santo, and to ascend the famous Leaning Tower. Pisa, where we remained over night, is situated on both sides of the Arno, five miles from its mouth, in the Mediterranean. In the thirteenth century it was a city of one hundred and fifty thousand inhabitants; but its present number is stated at not exceeding fifty thousand. The Cathedral was in course of construction from 1063 to 1118. It "is entirely of white marble, with black and colored ornamentation. The most magnificent part is the façade, which in the lower story is adorned with columns and arches attached to the wall, and in the upper parts with four open galleries, gradually diminishing in length. The choir is also imposing." At the end of the nave, suspended by a very long iron rod from the arched ceiling, is the elaborate and beautifully wrought bronze lamp, which suggested to Galileo the idea of a pendulum. We have a fine photograph of it, and also excellent photographs of the Duomo, Baptistery, Leaning Tower, and of parts of the Campo Santo.

The Baptistery, a circular white marble structure with a dome, is remarkable particularly for its beautiful Gothic architecture, its exquisitely carved pulpit, and its wonderful echo. Situated a few rods from the Duomo, its height is about one hundred and ninety feet and its diameter one hundred feet. The pulpit is on pillars near the center, and is entered by a flight of marble steps richly carved. One of the pillars rests on the back of a lion, while others present *reliefs*, representing, we imagine, Saints or Apostles. The panels are in like manner covered with *bas-reliefs* of various descriptions. Near the pulpit is a large baptismal font, adorned with beautifully carved figures in alabaster or marble. The custodian sounded a series of musical notes, and "heavenly echoes burst forth in response. They were of such a tender and exalted rapture that we might well have thought them the voices of young-eyed cherubim singing as they passed through Paradise over that spot of earth where we stood." We called to one after another of our dear friends at home, and their names were echoed back to us, many times repeated, as though they were answering in person.

The Leaning Tower stands across the street from and on the other side of the Duomo. When taken together in a photograph all three structures appear to be connected. We climbed by easy circular stairs to the seventh story of the Tower, from which we had a grand view of the city and surrounding country. In October, 1867, the writer, with his son Henry, ascended one story higher to the top, above the bell deck; but the rain was pouring in torrents, which, of course, obstructed the view. The question whether the oblique position of this Tower was intentional or accidental has been frequently discussed. Some writers hold that the most probable solution is that the foundation settled during the progress of its construction, and that to remedy the defect as much as possible an attempt was made to give a vertical position to the upper part. Our impression is that its leaning position was intentional; and this impression is strengthened by the fact that there is an ancient Leaning Tower at Milan, which we were informed was left unfinished because it could not be carried to its contemplated height on the same oblique line with its base without the danger of its toppling. The work of the Pisa Tower, too, looks very solid; nor could we discover any cracks either in the stone steps or walls. Its height is one hundred and seventy-nine feet, consisting of eight different stages. It is thirteen feet out of the perpendicular. Galileo is said to have availed himself of this position of the Tower in his experiments regarding the laws of gravitation. This structure was completed in 1350. It is supplied with seven bells.

the heaviest of which, weighing six tons, hangs on the side opposite the overhanging wall. To ring these bells the bell-ringer is obliged to stand on the bell deck.

The Campo Santo, or Burial Ground, also near the Cathedral, is well worth a visit. Surrounding the church-yard is a low structure four hundred and fourteen feet in length and one hundred and seventy feet in width, with corridors looking inward. The walls of the corridors are covered with frescoes, representing "The Creation," "The Fall," "Expulsion from Paradise," "Building of the Ark," "The Deluge," and many other scriptural subjects. The pavement is formed of the tombstones of the persons buried here, and there are memorial tablets also in the walls. There is a collection of Roman, Etruscan, and Mediæval sculptures, and some of modern date, among which we observed a fine marble bust of Cavour. On the walls there are two heavy chains, which were used to protect the harbor of Pisa when at war with neighboring principalities. One of them, captured by Florence, was restored in 1848, and the other, captured by the Genoese in 1632, was restored in 1860. That the dead here "might repose in holy ground," the Archbishop, after the loss of the Holy Land in the thirteenth century, caused fifty-three ship loads of earth to be brought hither from Jerusalem.

On the 15th, Dr. Parker and family reached Pisa at half past eleven in the morning, from Florence, and, joining them, we all arrived in Genoa at half past six in the evening, stopping at the London Hotel. We passed near Carrara, where we saw great quantities of white marble, and still nearer Spezzia, which town, situated on the Gulf of Spezzia between two elevated points of land and crowned with forts, was in plain sight. It is a favorite naval station and summer bathing place. Our first experience in Genoa was not very pleasant. On the pretext that his best rooms were all occupied, our landlord put us all in the fourth story, to which, however, we did not particularly object, since our stay was to be short. His office was on the second floor, the lower story being set apart for shops. The dining-room and adjoining reading-room were a few steps above and at some distance from the office. With a few other guests we were all sitting quietly at supper in the dining-room, when suddenly a thick volume of smoke, white with heat, came pouring into the room through the reading-room door, which was open, and it was evident the house was on fire. Now came a race for our lives. Total strangers, it might have been difficult for us readily to find our way to the street even had the halls been lighted; but as soon as the alarm was given, the gas, to avoid explosion, was wisely turned off, and we had hardly more than left the dining-room before we found ourselves in total darkness, groping our way, as we supposed, toward the office as our nearest way out doors. Fortunately we came to a room where two frightened ladies had just lighted a candle, and they gladly joined us in our retreat to the office, which we finally reached in safety, but badly scared. A staircase led immediately from the office to the street, and we no longer feared for our lives. In the moment of doubt whether our lives might not be sacrificed, the thought of the loss of our luggage, all of which was in our room, had not the weight of a feather with us. But as soon as the first danger was over, and we found by a cautious reconnoissance that we might venture to go to our room, we ascended hastily, seized the bulk of our things and as speedily made our way back with them, entirely out of breath. At the same time, Dr. Parker started on a similar errand; as he had not returned when we reached the office. Miss Parker urgently asked us to go to his assistance, but it was half a minute before we could recover our breath to answer. We then proceeded to comply with her request, when, meeting the Doctor coming down, we kept on again to our own room, which was filled with smoke, and secured the rest of our effects. Meantime the servants and others of the hotel had succeeded in subduing the flames by drenching the reading-room, to which the fire was confined, with water, carried in buckets and whatever other vessel was nearest at hand. Had this fire occurred after the inmates had retired to bed, it is more than probable that these "Sketches" never would have been written. As soon as things became a little settled, we all made up our minds to go to another hotel; for, seeing that the fire took from a furnace pipe between the floor and ceiling, we feared it might break out again. This determination did not suit the landlord, who now remembered that he could give us rooms, which he offered us, on a level with the dining room, and we concluded to remain. The next day we all took a good view of the city, going into the principal Cathedral and some other places of interest. There is a handsome monument to Columbus here, and many of the buildings are very elegant. The city is beautifully situated "on a slope rising above the sea in a wide semi-circle," and its harbor is also in the form of a semi-circle, about two miles wide, almost entirely inclosed by the land and a long pier on either side.

We left Genoa about eight o'clock on the morning of the 17th, and arrived at Turin at half past twelve. We spent the afternoon in another survey of portions of the city, embracing occasion to exchange what Italian money we had for gold. While in Italy we sold our gold at from six to eight per cent. for paper. Preferring to travel by the day line, we stopped over night in Turin. The ground here was covered with two or three inches of snow, and the weather was so cold that, although we had a good supply of wood, we found it almost impossible to keep from freezing in our rooms, and were only made comfortable by jugs of hot water in our beds. The rooms of the hotel appear to have been constructed to admit the cold in instead of excluding it; and the fireplaces are sunk as far into the wall as possible, allowing nearly all the heat to go up the chimney. Leaving at nine the next morning, we arrived at Geneva, by the way of the Mont Cenis Tunnel, at half past eight in the evening, happy to be so far toward home.

CHAPTER LVI.

PARIS, MARCH 15.—Now behold us in the grand capital of "La Belle France." We did not hasten hither, because we were comfortably situated at Geneva for recuperation, and we were advised that the season here, owing to almost constant rains, was very unpleasant. Nor, we are bound to say, had Geneva much to brag of in this respect, for during all the time we tarried there, from the 18th of February to the 14th of March, we saw very few fair days. One of these was availed of to visit Coppet, the residence of Madame de Staël, situated on Lake Leman, nine miles northeast of the city. Her house is quite palatial and all its surroundings are charming. Only some half dozen rooms are shown to visitors. In one of these is her portrait and others of her family; and the old furniture is also preserved, just as she left it at her death. Everybody, of course, knows that she was the daughter of Monsieur Necker, the distinguished French statesman, and that she was exiled and otherwise persecuted on account of her opposition to Napoleon Bonaparte. She, however, returned to Paris, where she died on the 14th of July, 1817; and, in accordance with her expressed desire, her remains were brought to Coppet and buried by the side of those of her father, to whom she was devotedly attached. Among her last words, she said to her daughter: "My father is waiting for me in the other world, and I shall soon go to him." Two days before her death, she read and commented on Byron's "Manfred," then just published, and on the morning of her death she pointed to these passages:

"Lo! the spell now works around thee,
And the thankless chain hath bound thee;
O'er this heart and brain together,
Hath the word been passed — now whither?
*   *   *   *   *   *
Oh, that I were
The viewless spirit of a lovely sound,
A living voice, a breathing harmony,
A bodiless enjoyment — born and dying
With the blest tone which made me!"

Before dismissing Geneva, we should not forget to say that this is a good place to get crystals, carved wood, and almost every kind of fancy articles; and Bruel, on rue des Allemands, who deals in these goods, is recommended to us by Mrs. Consul Upton as obliging and honest, and as having always dealt fairly with Americans. For watches, she referred us to Messrs. Patek and Philippe and Mr. Magnin. The Patek firm, she said, have been ever kind and attentive to Americans, rendering the most valuable services at all times.

As in traveling from Turin to Geneva, a long day's ride, we found it desirable to take the first-class cars, so, in starting from Geneva at half past three in the afternoon, to travel all night to Paris, we chose the express train, in which only first-class cars are run. It rained when we started, and the night was raw and cold; but our compartment, warmed by hot water in long flat or partially oval vessels under our feet, was very comfortable. The water in these cylindrical brass or copper vessels, two of which reached across the car, was changed once or twice on the passage. We had it in contemplation to stop at Fontainebleau; but when we reached there about daylight, the weather was so wretchedly uninviting that we decided to go on, and it was half past seven when we arrived at the Grand Hôtel du Louvre, where we staid while in Paris. For miles between Fontainebleau and Paris, we saw a sight such as we have sometimes seen in dreams, but never expected to behold in reality. From the overflow of the Seine, owing to long continued and heavy rains, the country for miles around was under water. What was naturally dry land under cultivation and dotted with dwelling houses was now a broad lake, or series of lakes, the waves of which came rolling up to the railroad track; and but for the scattering trees and buildings in the midst of the waters, a stranger would have had no thought other than that he was journeying along by a permanent lake. The inhabitants were passing from house to house in boats and entering or leaving their dwellings by the windows of the second stories. It was an extraordinary sight indeed.

Before entering upon a hasty view of the great capital, we have a mind to give a brief description of a trip the writer made, with his son Henry, in October, 1867, from Genoa via Nice, Toulon, Marseilles, Arles, Nismes, Lyons, Dijon, and Fontainebleau to Paris. This was before the railroad was built between Spezzia and Nice, and we traveled by diligence over what is called the Conechee Road. It took us along over high hills and mountains and into deep valleys, through endless forests of chestnut trees, literally bowing under their abundance of fruit, and figs also were quite plenty on some portions of the route, selling, dried, at two cents a pound. The chestnuts are twice the size but not nearly so sweet as those of our country. Olives, too, were in abundance. The olive is about the size and shape of an apple tree, and in the shape and size of its branches and leaves much resembles our swamp willow. It was a hard ride from Genoa to Nice, occupying from nine o'clock one evening till the same hour the next evening, twenty-four hours, with only short stops to change horses. On some portions of the way we were near the shore, the waves of the Mediterranean breaking at our feet; but, for the most part, we were high up on the mountains, which, with those also between Genoa and Spezzia, were then being tunneled for a railroad. Not far from the line between Italy and France we were much interested in looking from our high position on the mountains off upon the city of Monaco, the smallest principality in the world. It lies on the Mediterranean, and when we passed early in the evening it was brilliantly illuminated.

We rested over night at Nice, the well known place of winter resort, provided with many elegant hotels and handsome boarding houses. At Toulon we remained over one train for dinner, feasting on fresh sardines, which are nearly as luscious as brook trout. After dinner we took a walk around town, visiting one or two churches, saw the convict hulks in the harbor, and glimpses of many other sights. Fore street was filled with sailors, and everything had the appearance of an active business town.

A ride of about two hours brought us to Marseilles, of which city we obtained a fine view from a high ledge overlooking it, and on which stands the Church of Nôtre Dame de la Garde. In this Church there are many curious paintings, but none possessing very much merit. At the entrance of the harbor are three or four small islands, which appear to be of solid rock, and upon these, as well as upon two hills on the shore, there are strong fortifications, the Château d' If, of Monte Cristo celebrity, being one of them. The rue Prado, a broad street three miles in length, is one of the most magnificent drives imaginable; and the city has good reason to be proud of its many beautiful buildings and its substantial dock.

Arles is a queer old Roman town. We saw here the ruins of an Amphitheater, also the ruins of an old church, in which were open lead coffins containing the bones and ashes of the dead, and near by any number of old Roman sarcophagi, monuments, and other objects of interest. From the cellar of a hotel we were conducted into the catacombs, a loathsome dungeon, extending a long way under the city, and exhibiting here and there heaps of human bones.

We were more interested in Nismes, another old Roman city, in which there is a well preserved Amphitheater, still in use for bull-fights and other exhibitions, and a Museum of most interesting antiquities. Nismes is some twenty miles off the direct route to Paris, and not very far from the boundary of Spain.

At Avignon, where we struck off from the direct line, we also stopped long enough to see the Pope's Palaces, now used as barracks, the tombs of Popes Jean XXII. and Benedictus, and to visit the Museum, where there is an almost endless variety of Roman relics, a large collection of paintings, and other objects of art. We were particularly struck by an ivory crucifix, or figure of Christ, here, made in 1659, which is curious as expressive of extreme suffering when viewed from one side, and of calm

GARDEN AND PALACE AT FONTAINEBLEAU.

resignation when seen from the other side of the face.

At Lyons we spent one night and the better part of a day, going into the Museum, the principal churches, and some of the silk manufactories.

Next we stopped at Dijon, a most interesting city. The most attractive point here is the stately old Palace of the Dukes of Burgundy, now occupied as a Museum, where there is a very large and fine collection of paintings, one or two of which we noted as unusually impressive. One representing "Saul of Tarsus" fallen from his horse, when hearing "a voice from heaven," is remarkably striking. A "Goddess of Beauty" in the act of watering flowers, and several other goddesses in painting as well as in marble, are exquisitely beautiful.

Fontainebleau is about forty miles southeast of Paris. It has very little the appearance of a city, and about the only objects of interest here are the Royal Palace, Garden and Forest Park. After walking through the Palace Garden, which is extensive and beautiful, containing several artificial lakes— one, a mile in length, for boating—we were conducted through forty-one rooms of the Palace. The exterior of the Palace, which is of brick, is not at all imposing; but the interior, both in respect to finish and furniture, is very rich. One large room is set apart for a library. There are two chapels, the smaller being the Queen's Chapel. One room is adorned with porcelain plates from Sèvres. They are set into the walls and are of different dates, going back many years. Several of the apartments were pointed out to us as those occupied in 1812 by Pope Pius VIII., when a prisoner of Napoleon I., and in one of them the Pope's portrait was suspended. This was the Pope by whom Napoleon was crowned. A strange feeling came over us as we stood in the very room in which and by the side of the very table on which Napoleon signed his abdication, prior to his departure for Elba; and sad as we always feel when we think of the cruel decree which separated Josephine from him, it is not strange that this feeling of sorrow was more impressive when we found ourselves in the identical room, with its furniture unchanged, where this fatal decree was pronounced.

CHAPTER LVII.

PARIS, MARCH 30.—In speaking of Paris and of what we have done and seen here, we hardly know where to begin or what to say. We have kept no regular account of our movements here. Dr. Parker and party preceded us here two weeks, taking lodgings at a private boarding house; and shopping being the leading business with the ladies along with us, sight seeing has been secondary with us all, and we have not sought to go much together. Of course, we have paid our respects to Minister Washburne, who received us in the kindest manner, and obtained tickets for us to visit the Legislative Assembly at Versailles. Unfortunately, however, we were one day too late, as on going to Versailles we were disappointed in learning that an adjournment for some weeks had taken place the day before. We made the trip in a two story street railroad carriage, occupying some two hours each way.

We could have gone by steam cars, but chose the former mode because we wished to see the country along the line of the stage road, which runs very near St. Cloud and through the village of Sèvres. We entered the tramway carriage, capable of accommodating thirty or forty persons, near the Louvre and passed along the Seine in the rear of the Palace and Garden of the Tuileries, at the left of the Champs Élysées and at the right of the Champ de Mars, where the great Exposition of 1867 was held, on the opposite side of the river. The trip would have been pleasanter had the day been fair, as we thought when we set out it would be; but we were served with all kinds of weather—sunshine, rain, hail, and a flurry of snow in the course of the day. The Field of Mars is a large open space, bare as the Desert of Sahara of vegetation, and used as a military parade ground. Some of the private residences along the country road are quite elegant. Arriving at Versailles, we at once made our way to the Palace, an immense edifice, with a façade over one quarter of a mile in extent. Two of the larger halls of the Palace are now used, one for the Senate and the other for the Chamber of Deputies. The larger of these two halls was constructed for a Theater. These we were permitted to enter, but the principal interest centered in the more private apartments abounding in works of art. These are magnificent in every respect, and are designated by various names, such as the Salle de Constantine, the Salle des Croisades, the Salle des États Généraux, the Salle de l' Abondance, the Salon de Venus, the Salon de Diane, the Salon d' Apollon, or Throne Room, the Grand Galerie de Louis XIV., etc. In the Gallery of Statuary are many excellent works, including a

368 SKETCHES OF TRAVEL.

PALACE OF VERSAILLES, REAR VIEW FROM THE GARDEN.

beautiful statue of "Joan of Arc," which is much admired. In several of the rooms there are many historical paintings, mostly modern. One of these, very striking, represents "The Storming of Malakoff at Sevastopol." In the Hall of the Crusades are pictures descriptive of battles fought by the Crusaders in their efforts to regain possession of the Holy Land. In the Salle du Sacre is David's famous picture of "The Coronation of Napoleon," which cost, it is said, twenty thousand dollars. In the same or another room is an equally grand picture, a most striking representation of "The Crowning of Josephine by the Emperor" at the Church of Nôtre Dame in Paris on the 2d of December, 1804. Josephine is kneeling, attended by two Maids of Honor bearing her long train, and Napoleon, standing by her and holding the crown up with both hands, is about to place it upon her head. Officers of the Church in their robes and other insignia of office, many of the nobility of both sexes, the foreign ministers, and others are in attendance, as interested spectators, the portraits of many of them being painted from life. One of these was pointed out to us as that of General Armstrong, the American Minister. The Napoleon family is largely represented here by busts, statues, and paintings, nor are they alone in this respect, great numbers of other distinguished men and women of France being in like manner remembered. We paused to look with more than common interest upon the Chambre à Coucher of Marie Antoinette, as on a former occasion the writer entered her little prison in Paris. It was in this room that she lay asleep on the night of the 5th of October, 1789, when the mob broke into the Palace. "She made her escape through a small corridor leading to the grand antechamber of the King." In one of the rooms we saw portraits of Washington, Daniel Webster, Henry Clay, Andrew Jackson, and James K. Polk.

Nothing can be more charming than the Palace grounds, adorned as they are with innumerable statues, a magnificent staircase, splendid fountains, flower beds, and shady groves. In the Grand Trianon, at the further end of the Park, a building "erected for Madamé Maintenon, a favorite mistress of Louis XIV.," there are some fine apartments, in one of which, the Cabinet de la Reine, is the bed formerly occupied by Josephine. On the whole, we were amply compensated by our visit to Versailles.

Another day was devoted to St. Cloud and Sèvres. The glory of St. Cloud had departed, leaving only a mass of ruins. Its beautiful Palace was entirely destroyed during the late war — set on fire, it is said, by French shells in an endeavor to dislodge the Germans on the 13th of October, 1870. The surrounding grounds are still beautiful, but their magnificent Cascade was silent on the day of our visit. A short walk took us to the Imperial Manufactory of Porcelain at Sèvres, just out of the village. The building is of the commonest character of a workshop. We were kindly received and shown through the entire establishment, from the molding and painting rooms to the ovens. None but accomplished workmen and artists could turn out such works as go from this famous manufactory. We were charmed with some of the portraits and other pictures on porcelain we saw here. We do not wonder that they bring a high price.

Beautiful as are the surroundings of Paris, much the greater interest, of course, centers in the city.

which, of itself, is one of the wonders of the world. At first view, and especially if we enter it before seeing other European cities, we feel a sense of oppression from the overwhelming number of novel things to be seen everywhere around us; and we are sometimes startled at the thought whether, after all, we are not dreaming! The Garden of the Tuileries, the Champs Élysées, and the many broad boulevards and streets, with their blocks of high, substantial brick and stone edifices, not omitting the Tuileries, the Louvre, the Palais Royal, the Hôtel des Invalides, the Columns of Vendôme, St. Jacques, and July, the Arc de Triomphe, and many other monuments, the Seine, with its twenty-seven beautiful bridges, and the one hundred or more churches of the city, not further to specify, all go to form a grand spectacle nowhere else to be seen.

There are omnibus lines in all directions, and their management is very systematic. At all the prominent stations there are ticket offices, and the passenger purchases his ticket, which is numbered, and he is received only in the order of his number. He may alight where he pleases; but the omnibus stops for passengers only at fixed stations. The fare is six sous inside and three sous outside, on top, the seats being arranged lengthwise. When the seats are all taken, a card, bearing the word "*Complet,*" is displayed on the rear end of the omnibus as a notice that no more passengers will be admitted.

We have attended services at several of the churches, among them the Church of St. Étienne du Mont, built in 1121, the Nôtre Dame, and the Madeleine, three perhaps the most beautiful. The Church of Nôtre Dame is considered one of the finest monuments of its particular style of architecture in

France. It is provided with an enormous bell, requiring the strength of eight men to ring it. The Church of the Madeleine is probably the more admired. Commenced in 1764, it was only finished in the reign of Louis Philippe. The work upon it was suspended during the Revolution of 1789. By an Imperial decree rendered at Posen, the 2d of December, 1806, Napoleon ordered it transformed into a Greek Temple, and that this inscription, "The Emperor Napoleon to the Soldiers of the Grand Army," should be borne on its front. Another article of that decree provided that, every year, on the anniversaries of the battles of Austerlitz and Jena, this monument should be illuminated, that a concert should then be given, preceded by a discourse on the duties of the soldier and a eulogy on those who fell in those sanguinary battles. It was expressly forbidden to mention the Emperor in these discourses. If this decree was carried out, it was probably abrogated after the final abdication of Napoleon; as we see that in 1815 Louis XVIII. ordered that the church be converted into a chapel in honor ot Louis XVI and his consort, Marie Antoinette, and this failing, it was at length completed in its present form by Louis Philippe. "It is surrounded by fifty-two Corinthian pillars, ornamented by a splendid façade. The interior is most magnificently ornamented with rich gilding, paintings, and statuary, and is lighted by three domes, which are most beautifully painted."

We have passed many hours in the Art Galleries of the Louvre, connected with the Palace of the Tuileries, the northwest wing of which is in ruins. These buildings are just across the rue de Rivoli from the Grand Hôtel du Louvre, where we have our lodgings. To describe what we have seen in the Galleries of the Louvre would be little more than a repetition of what we have spoken of seeing in other galleries; but we should not forget to mention the "Venus of Milo," the original of which we saw here. We were disappointed in not being allowed to see the large collection of most interesting Napoleon relics, which the writer saw here in 1867, when France was in her glory under Napoleon III. The cases containing these are all locked up, and republican France deems it prudent not to allow the old cocked hat, the boots and spurs, the army saddle and pistols of the great Emperor to be exhibited at the present crisis. These are only a few of the many speaking objects here, telling of the reign and power of Napoleon. Even the marble cast of his face, taken after his death, possesses an almost irresistible attraction. It is a wonder that the authorities do not consider it necessary, also, to debar all entrance to his superbly grand tomb in the Hôtel des Invalides; but this is still accessible. Over the entrance to this tomb, so often described, are his words,—"I desire that my ashes may repose on the banks of the Seine, in the midst of the French people, whom I have ever loved." In a recess adjoining the crypt stands a statue of him as Emperor, dressed in his imperial robes, and here also are other insignia of his which he wore on state occasions, together with the sword he carried at the battle of Austerlitz. We were present one Sunday when all the old invalids, officers and soldiers, filed in line on either side of the main aisle of the Chapel, in another part of this vast building, to hear the twelve o'clock Mass. It was a novel sight—one or two hundred old veterans,

HÔTEL DES INVALIDES.

crippled, scarred, and otherwise debilitated, some of whom had, no doubt, served under the great Napoleon, all in their uniforms, and parading in military order. They stood during the whole service, but some of them appeared to give little attention to the religious ceremonies, at the conclusion of which they all retired, keeping step to the martial music, and were dismissed in the court.

CHAPTER LVIII.

PARIS, APRIL 10.—We have been almost daily in the Place de la Concorde, which lies between the Garden of the Tuileries and the Champs Élysées. It is a handsome square, adorned by colossal statues and fountains, and in its center stands the obelisk of the Luxor, a column seventy-two feet in height, covered on its four tapering sides with Egyptian hieroglyphics. It was presented to the French Government by the Pasha of Egypt, and transported from Thebes, where it formerly stood in front of the Temple. It dates back fifteen hundred years before the Christian Era. It was in this square that the guillotine was erected, and where, during the reign of terror in 1793-'4, nearly three thousand victims were beheaded, among them Louis XVI., his unfortunate wife, Marie Antoinette, Beauharnais, the husband of Josephine, the Duke of Orleans, Robespierre, and many other noted persons.

The Place du Carousal and Place Napoleon are formed out of large portions of the space bordered by the Palace of the Tuileries and the Louvre. The former is said to have derived its name from a tournament held there by Louis XIV. in 1662, and the latter is understood to have been so named in honor of Napoleon III. Originally, the whole space was probably intended for the Palace Court.

The Place Vendôme is an octagon, four hundred and fifty by four hundred and twenty feet in extent, surrounded by handsome dwelling houses, including one or two hotels. The rue de la Paix passes through it, and is the direct street leading from the Boulevard des Capuchins into the rue Castiglione.

PLACE VENDÔME.

which ends at rue de Rivoli, in front of the Garden of the Tuileries. There is a constant stream of people passing and repassing through this great channel of communication; and every stranger, of course, stops to view, if not to ascend, the grand column of Vendôme which stands, surrounded by an iron railing, in the center of the square. This column was raised by order of Napoleon I., in honor of the French armies. It is one hundred and thirty-five feet in height, surmounted by his statue. The exterior is of bronze, covered with *bas-reliefs*, representing the victories of the French armies in the German campaign of 1805. As is well known, it was leveled to the earth by the Communists in 1871;

but we could not discover any marks of this destruction. It is a splendid column, much resembling the Trajan column in Rome.

The Column of July, in the Place de la Bastile, is constructed entirely of bronze, except its base, which is of white marble. It stands on the site of the old Bastile, the key of which is at Mount Vernon, and bronze *bas-reliefs* inserted in the sides of the marble base indicate that it was erected in commemoration of those who fell in the French Revolution of July, 1830, and whose bodies, as well as the bodies of the combatants of February, 1848, were here buried. Over a colonnade near the top of this monument there is a large gilt globe, surmounted by the figure of a winged angel, representing "The Genius of Liberty." While standing on this colonnade in a smart breeze one day, we were made so dizzy from the swaying of the column to and fro that, splendid as was the view from that point of observation, we took counsel from our fears speedily to descend to a more stable foundation. There is a railing around this monument, but the rest of the ground forming this irregular open space, where several streets and boulevards concentrate, is inclosed only by the adjacent buildings.

The Place du Trône, also the intersection of many streets and avenues, in the extreme eastern part of the city, is in circular form, and its principal ornaments are columns surmounted by statues of "St. Louis" and "Philippe Auguste." There are numerous other squares under various names, all of which are more or less beautified by fountains, statues, etc.

The Champs Élysées, through which runs the grand avenue of that name, from the Place de la Concorde to the Arc de Triomphe, is the promenade most frequented by the aristocracy of Paris; and in fine weather it is the rendezvous of all the world. It is of great extent, affording ample space not only for gardens of flowers, shady groves, splendid fountains, and magnificent statues, but on one side of it is the Palace of Industry, an immense building filled with statuary and paintings, mostly by living artists, and which is used for agricultural and other fairs; near this is a circular building for panoramic exhibitions; and then there are cafés and pavilions for outdoor concerts, and room always for Punch and Judy shows, not to mention other entertainments known only to the gay Parisians and the more penetrating visitors at the grand capital. In the circular building, which covers perhaps half an acre, we have seen a wonderful panorama representing "The Siege of Paris." It is a picture of nature and art combined. The spectator stands on a raised platform in the center, around which there is a railing, and outside of this stands a French soldier on the natural soil, which forms the foreground of the picture. Bedecked with medals, conferred, no doubt, for meritorious services, he points out the positions of the contending forces and gives any other required explanation. In the foreground lie real broken guns, gun-carriages, knapsacks, and other débris, and beyond is the painting of field, forest, houses, fortifications, officers, soldiers, and all the attendants, save the noise, of a fierce bombardment. So ingeniously is the painting united to the real landscape that we found it impossible to determine the division line with any certainty.

Fronting the Palace of Industry, on the opposite side of the Champs Élysées, is the Palais de l'Élysée Napoleon. It was built in 1718, and at one time owned and occupied by Madame Pompadour, but finally purchased by the Government. It is said to have been a favorite residence of Napoleon I., and Napoleon III. occupied it while President of the Republic. It was here that the former signed his final abdication, and here, doubtless, the latter planned his *coup d' état*, by which he, too, became Emperor, only ere long to suffer a similar mortification. In the invasion of 1814-'15, the English soldiers pitched their tents in the Champs Élysées, and in March, 1871, the Prussians encamped there for two days. No less than eight avenues diverge from the circular Place, in the center of which stands the magnificent Arc de Triomphe. One of these is the Avenue de l' Impératrice, leading to the Bois de Boulogne, and it is a grand sight indeed to behold the gorgeous equipages that almost any pleasant day may be seen in this great channel, flowing in an endless stream from every quarter, but especially from and into the Champs Élysées, crowded with countless thousands on foot as well as in carriages.

The Arc de Triomphe de l' Étoile, erected to commemorate the victories of the French armies, cannot fail to arrest the attention and command admiration. As its name indicates, this is an arched monument, having one high, broad arch through the center from east to west, with lower transverse arches from north to south. Its height is one hundred and fifty-two feet, with a breadth of one hundred and thirty-seven feet, and a depth of sixty-eight feet. It was commenced under the auspices of Napoleon in 1806, but not completed until 1836. The eastern and western sides are embellished by four magnificent groups of statuary, the first representing "The Departure of 1792," the second " Resistance, or War," the third "Peace," and the fourth "The Triumph of 1810." In the "Departure" for the defense of the country, the Genius of War is encouraging to action, and all the actors appear to be intensely animated as if stirred by the Marseillaise—"*Marchons! marchons!*" In "Resistance," "a young man, guided by a Genius flitting over his head and attended by his father and his wife holding a dead child in her arms, rushes to the defense of his country; a warrior is falling from his horse, and Genius is encouraging them to action." In "Peace," "a warrior sheathing his sword stands between his wife and children, while another is taming a bull for purposes of agriculture; and the Genius of Peace, crowned with laurels, sheds over them her protecting influence." In "The Triumph," Napoleon is represented as about to receive the crown from Victory, while History records the event, and Fame, on angelic wings over their heads, is blowing her trumpet. On other parts of the monument are *bas-relief* and *alto-relievo* representations of the different battles in which Napoleon and other distinguished French Generals had been engaged.

Porte St. Denis and Porte St. Martin, on the boulevards of the same names, are also triumphal arches. The first was erected in 1672, in recognition of the rapid conquests of Louis XIV. in Germany, and the latter, raised in 1674, is likewise commemorative of the achievements of the French—one of its *bas-reliefs* representing the "Taking of Besançon and the Triple Alliance," and another the "Taking of Limbourg and the Defeat of the Germans." Both bear the Latin inscription, "Ludovico Magno," to Louis the Great.

The Tour de Saint Jacques de la Boucherie, is

TOUR DE ST. JACQUES DE LA BOUCHERIE.

a handsome structure situated on rue de Rivoli, a short distance east of the Louvre, and the most prominent object in that vicinity, being one hundred and eighty-seven feet high. It is the bell-tower of the church of that name, erected in 1508-'22, and which was demolished, leaving only this tower standing, in 1789. More than two hundred thousand dollars have been expended by the Government in its repair. It is regarded as one of the finest relics of Gothic architecture extant. "It is square, with an engaged turret at the northwestern angle, graceful pointed windows, elaborate tracery, niches with statues of saints, and a perforated balustrade at the summit, adorned with the statues of 'St. John the Baptist' and the animals attributed to the Evangelists. Under the arch of the ground floor stands the statue of Pascal, who here performed his first experiments to ascertain the weight of the atmosphere."

The Palais Royal, originally called l' Hôtel de Richelieu, has a long and interesting history—too long to be given here. It was first constructed by Richelieu out of the Hôtels of Mercœur and Rambouillet, the latter of which is celebrated in the literary annals of the sixteenth century. Richelieu died here on the 4th of December, 1642. The Palace has since been greatly remodeled and enlarged, but we are not advised whether the private apartments are at present occupied or not. We are inclined to think its latest occupants were Prince Napoleon and the Princess Clotilde. The southern section was set on fire in May, 1871, by the Commune and greatly damaged, but has been repaired. The garden, entirely surrounded by the Palace and an arcade, is seven hundred feet long by three hundred feet wide, and is handsomely adorned by a fountain, statuary, shade trees, and flowers. The arcade and glass covered galleries in other sections are lined with the finest shops, particularly for jewelry, watches, opera-glasses, and the thousand and one other smaller articles that the French know so well how to display. Here, also, are some of the best restaurants, or cafés, in the city. It was in this Palace garden that, on the 13th of July,

1789. Camille Desmoulins, mounting upon a table, called to arms the crowd that pressed around him and invited them to seize upon a green cockade as a sign of hope. They at once formed cockades of the green leaves of trees, but these were soon replaced by the tri-colored cockade, and the Revolution was begun.

CHAPTER LIX.

PARIS. APRIL 20.—It is sad to see the ruins of the Hôtel de Ville, the Tuileries, and of several other large Government buildings in the heart of the city, some on one side of the Seine and some on the other. The Tuileries is the only one of four or five immense buildings, all within a short distance of one another, that was not entirely destroyed by fire during the Communist insurrection in May, 1871, following the bombardment of the city by the German forces. Nearly the entire west front of the Palace of the Tuileries, looking upon its beautiful garden, is either razed to the ground or in such a wrecked condition that it cannot be repaired; but the other sections of the building were less damaged, although no part of it, we think, is now habitable. What a contrast between the present period, or 1870-'71, and the year 1867, when the writer saw the Emperor of Russia and King William of Prussia in the same coach with Napoleon III., as a few months later he also saw the Emperor of Austria by the side of Napoleon enter the city in proud array! The smooth concrete carriage-way of the Boulevard

Italien was not nice enough for the grand cavalcade without being covered with clean, moist sand, which was spread upon it by hundreds of laborers, working with their might to keep ahead of the procession. The display was still more grand, if possible, on the occasion of the military review in the Bois de Boulogne, in honor of the Emperor of Russia and King of Prussia. This was one of the wonderful sights with which we were favored in the time of the Exposition, enhanced as it was not only by a near view of those sovereigns, but also of the Emperor Napoleon, the Empress Eugénie, the young Prince Napoleon, and many other distinguished personages, with their brilliant equipages. All the world, with all its horses and carriages, appeared to be present, with no limit to the number of spectators on foot. Never before had we seen anything of the kind half as extensive. It was while returning from this review that a demented Pole fired a pistol shot at the Emperor Alexander, but fortunately failed to hit him, and was immediately arrested. We heard the report of the pistol and witnessed the confusion, and the next day we were present in the Legislative Assembly when a resolution was passed, followed by loud applause, congratulatory of the Emperor's escape. In the evening there was a grand ball at the Tuileries and a general illumination of the city in honor of the distinguished guests. The whole city appeared to be in a blaze of glory. Besides the lights in the windows there were continuous rows of gas jets from the tubes running along the second story at the foot of the balconies of dwelling houses and shops; the walks of the Garden of the Tuileries were festooned on either side by gas lights protected by glass globes, the *jets d' eaux* were illuminated by rays of calcium light, more brilliant if possible than the sun, and of variegated colors, while the trees were hung with thousands of Chinese lanterns — the whole presenting a scene which could not have failed to command the admiration even of dwellers in fairyland.

Now that we have gone back again to our first European trip, we may as well remain a little longer. Although not enjoying the honor of attending the great ball, not having solicited tickets of invitation, we nevertheless saw the rooms in which it was held, as well as most of the other rooms of the Tuileries, and one Sunday were admitted to the Emperor's Chapel by tickets kindly sent us by General Dix, then our Minister; and here we had a good view of the Emperor and Empress of France, who occupied seats in the gallery fronting the altar. There were a few ladies and gentlemen, supposed to be members of the family, in the side galleries, but the Emperor and Empress were the only occupants of the front gallery. Upon their entrance from an adjoining chamber, but before they came in sight of the audience below, an officer at the altar cried out,—"L'Empereur!" and they immediately came forward and kneeled, when the priest proceeded with the services. Napoleon was in plain citizens' dress and the Empress was habited like any other lady. We confess we paid little attention to the religious ceremonies, for we went there, as most strangers did, to see the Emperor and his beautiful spouse, and our eyes were almost constantly on them until they retired. We thought the Emperor looked weary and somewhat broken. Soon after the services were concluded, he entered a carriage at the door, smoking a cigar.

and, in company with the Empress, took his departure to spend the afternoon probably in a drive either to St. Cloud or Versailles.

Now, alas, how changed! The Emperor defeated, made prisoner, the witness of a humiliating treaty of peace, dead, and the Empress and Prince in exile!

> "What is glory? what is fame?
> The echo of a long lost name;
> A breath, an idle hour's brief talk;
> The shadow of an arrant naught;
> A flower that blossoms for a day,
>   Dying next morrow;
> A stream that hurries on its way,
>   Singing of sorrow."

Père La Chaise, the Cemetery made famous by the writings of Lamartine ere special attention had been directed to the embellishment of burial places in the United States, is situated on an eminence in the eastern suburbs of the city, corresponding somewhat with our Congressional Cemetery, while the Arc de Triomphe, on the western side, may, in point of location, be regarded as somewhat corresponding with our White House, or more nearly with the Heights of Georgetown. The great bulk of the city lies principally on lower ground, between Père La Chaise and the Arc de Triomphe, extending to the north and south of the Seine, which, in its course through the city, separates and forms two considerable islands just east of the Louvre. We entered Père La Chaise from a narrow street lined for one or two squares with small shops filled with flowers wrought into crosses, wreaths, etc., as *immortelles* to be laid upon the graves or hung upon the railings around the tombs, as in 1867 the iron railing around the Column Vendôme was hung with these wreaths.

supposed to be in remembrance of Napoleon I., since none are seen there at present. Père La Chaise is not remarkably beautiful, but its walks are well laid out, and it is sheltered by shade trees and adorned by growing vines and flowers. Among the twenty thousand or more tombs here, the one most visited, probably, is that of Abélard and Héloïse, which is quite imposing. When we were there, it was surrounded by a staging and undergoing repairs. There are monuments, also, to La Fontaine, Molière, La Place, Arago, Béranger, and to many others whose names are familiar to us; but Abélard and Héloïse, whose memory has been kept fresh for more than seven hundred years, may survive them all on the tablet of the ages. Naughty as they both were, they nevertheless command the admiration of mankind on account of their undying love for each other. He was born in the village of Palais near Nantes, in the year 1079, and in one of the churches there a lamp, lighted at his demise, has been kept burning ever since in commemoration of his virtues. He early devoted himself to the study of philosophy and the sciences, and for some years was at the head of a school of rhetoric, first at Melun and Corbiel, and later at Paris, where he lectured on rhetoric, philosophy, and theology. He was twice the age of Héloïse, niece of Fulbert, a canon of Paris, when he became acquainted and finally infatuated with her. A girl of seventeen, she is said to have been radiant with beauty, intelligence, and genius, and on her part was equally entranced with the famous scholar. Obtaining permission to give her instruction at her uncle's, he subsequently became a resident at Fulbert's house, where "for several months the lovers indulged in a wild dream of passion." This resulted most unfortunately for both, but it did not weaken their love for each other, and by the consent of all concerned they were married. Héloïse desired to keep the marriage a secret; but this did not please the canon, who, thinking that her husband intended to force her to take the veil, caused him to be seized and ignominiously punished. Abélard now became a monk, and, tired of the world, Héloïse voluntarily took the veil. They were now separated for eleven years, when they again came together at St. Gildas de Ruys, of which monastery he had been appointed Abbot. He died in 1142, at the age of sixty-four. Héloïse, requesting to be buried at his side, survived him only a few years.

The Jardin des Plantes, originally intended only for a Botanical Garden, is a Zoölogical and Ornithological Garden as well, and connected with it are a Museum and Library of Natural History, a Museum of Comparative Anatomy, and a Conservatory of Agriculture, Commerce, and Industry. We have found much to interest us here, especially the birds and animals, of which there is an extensive collection, and one or more of almost every kind.

Returning from the Jardin des Plantes, we visited the Pantheon, a fine church, the portico of which is modeled after the Pantheon in Rome. It is in the form of a Greek cross, and "the interior consists of three naves, surmounted by the dome and separated by a range of one hundred and thirty fluted Corinthian columns." Among the distinguished persons buried here were Voltaire, Rosseau, Marshal Lannes, and the Duke de Montebello.

The Church of Saint Roche, founded in 1653, is rather plain on the exterior, but finished in the interior in a costly style, and it is adorned by a profusion of sculptures, fine statues, and many paintings of marked excellence. It stands on rue St. Honoré, in the heart and one of the richest quarters of the city. It was from the steps of this church that Napoleon I. leveled his cannon on the insurgents at the time of the National Convention; and from its sacred altar Marie Antoinette was led to the guillotine in the Place de la Concorde.

The Palace and Garden of the Luxembourg well repay many a visit. The Garden is large and beautifully laid out, and the Palace is a complete Museum of Art. The painting here which most strongly fixed our attention represents a large number of the victims of the Reign of Terror in prison, waiting, one after another, to be led to execution, neither knowing whose turn might come first. We have a graphic photograph of this famous picture. The Palace has on several occasions been used as a prison for distinguished persons charged with political offences.

The Hôtel de Cluny is a curious old building of the fifteenth century, and it is filled with an endless collection of Roman and other antiquities. We have taken much more pleasure there, in the Louvre, and in other museums of art, than in going to the theater, which we have visited once only, or to the Bourse, where we have been once, to see how crazy men may become in the pursuit of gain, or, in fact, to witness any single sight in Paris. We have not been to the opera, contenting ourselves with an exterior view of the new opera building, which is very grand and beautiful. After all, it is impossible to tell of half the things that strike our attention as we go from place to place

390 SKETCHES OF TRAVEL.

LUXEMBOURG PALACE.

in the city. The vast whole—*le tout ensemble*—of Paris is, we repeat, one of the wonders of the world.

CHAPTER LX.

Home, home again, from a foreign shore.
—*Ballad.*

WE had tarried in Paris about five weeks, and it was now time to prepare for a decisive movement homeward. With the smaller purchases of photographs and various trinkets, which we had collected on our journey after leaving London, together with some larger acquisitions in Paris, we filled a good-sized chest, or box, provided with hinges and locks, which we had purchased for the sum of twelve francs; and for fifteen francs the agent of the Cunard Line took charge of and sent it direct by water to the steamship "Bothnia," on which vessel we had engaged passage from Liverpool. This was quite a relief, as it not only saved the trouble of looking after it on the way through London and Liverpool, but it also avoided all examination by the English Custom House. Our arrangements completed, we left Paris at seven o'clock on the morning of the 22d of April for London, still in company with Dr. Parker and party, who had taken passage in the "Scythia," to sail on the 27th of May. Our route was by the way of Boulogne and Folkstone. The day was pleasant, and all Nature was beaming with the brightness of spring. The fields, laid off into patches, some for one kind of grain or plant and some for another, presented a picturesque appearance; and long rows of the Lombard poplar, trimmed nearly to their tops, skirted the lanes and highways, ready to throw out another set of twigs for fagots, which, tied up in bundles and dried, form in some parts of Europe no inconsiderable amount of fuel. So, likewise, on rough land along the railroads and in swampy places not fit for tillage, we observed that willows, alder, and other bushes of rapid growth are cultivated and cut annually, or less frequently, for the same purpose. Most remarkable to relate, we had a perfectly smooth passage across the Channel. Our boat was crowded with passengers, but we do not remember to have seen a single one who suffered from seasickness. Among the passengers we were happy to meet the Hon. Russell Gurney, who was the Commissioner on the part of Great Britain in the settlement of war claims against the United States, under the Treaty of Washington.

We reached London at five in the afternoon, and at once proceeded to our former lodgings in Queen's Road, Bayswater, West. As the "Bothnia" was not to sail until the 6th of May, we now had ten days more in London, affording us another opportunity to revisit places of interest there, to see some things we had not seen before, and meet again our esteemed English friends. We have heretofore spoken of what most interested us in London. It was a rest to find ourselves here again after a long and tedious journey, occupying nine months, and especially coming as we did directly from noisy Paris, where Sunday is perhaps the noisiest day of the week. We enjoy a quiet Sabbath; and in this respect, as well as on other accounts, London seems like home. We like its solid character, its

Hyde Park, its grand old Abbey, its St. Paul's, its wonderful Museums, and its Westminster Hall. The Thames, too, with its grand bridges, superb embankment and majestic current, holds its proud place in the picture. The apostrophe to it by Sir John Denham (born 1615) is good:

> "Thames! the most lov'd of all the Ocean's sons
> By his old sire, to his embraces runs,
> Hasting to pay his tribute to the sea,
> Like mortal life to meet eternity.
> O could I flow like thee! and make thy stream
> My great example, as it is my theme;
> Tho' deep yet clear, tho' gentle yet not dull;
> Strong without rage, without o'erflowing full."

We took leave of London at noon on the 4th of May, 1876, and arrived in Liverpool at five o'clock in the afternoon, putting up at the Northwestern Hotel. On the following day we visited various parts of the city, and also called on our Consul, General Fairchild, who had kindly selected for us a good stateroom on the "Bothnia." There is nothing remarkable about the city, except its beautiful Park and its river docks, which are noted for their magnificence, being "constructed on a stupendous scale, covering. with the dry docks, two hundred acres, with fifteen miles of quays." The city is situated on the northeastern banks of the Mersey, which are uneven and in some parts quite steep. The public buildings are imposing, and there are several monuments, among them a column to Lord Nelson and an equestrian statue of George III. Passing along one of the business streets, we observed two shop windows which were completely lined with Confederate bank notes. It would, no doubt, be interesting to know their history. The seceding States found hosts of sympathizers in Liverpool during the war, and, encouraged by leading British statesmen to believe that the South would ultimately succeed in establishing and maintaining its independence, many of them, no doubt, cast their fortunes on that side, and lost. Far better would it have been both for England and the Confedeaacy had no such encouragement been given; and the act of Queen Victoria in declining to sanction any measures unfriendly to the United States is a bright jewel in her crown.

Our heart-throbs quickened as we drew near the hour—two o'clock on the afternoon of Saturday, the 6th—when we were to go on board the tender which was to take us to the "Bothnia," Captain McMickan, Commander. We were promptly on hand, and our little steamer soon cast off and was on her accustomed way toward the ocean. While in Italy we responded affirmatively to a letter from Mrs. Tipton, wife of Mr. Thomas C. Tipton, of Washington, asking if she might place herself and her son Frankie, two years old, under our charge in crossing the ocean; and we were happy, on reaching the tender, to find them ready to accompany us. She is an accomplished English lady, and had been on a visit of a year at her old home in Bradford. Her father and two sisters came along to see her safely off. The younger sister had become very strongly attached to Frankie, who was a splendid little fellow, and hard, as it undoubtedly was, to part with her married sister, it seemed almost to break her heart to give him up, and she wept bitterly. Poor girl! we felt for her most keenly. General Fairchild was on board ready to render any advice or assistance; and by half past three o'clock the passengers were all transferred to the great ship, when the final greetings of friends, now to be separated, took place, and the tender with those who had come to see us on board, returned to her dock. It was five o'clock when we set sail. And now—

> "How swift we mount these watery hills!
> As light as horse or hound;
> Our good ship knows as on she goes
> That she is homeward bound —
> That she is homeward bound, my hearts,
> That she is homeward bound;
> For every gale that swells her sail
> Sings —We are homeward bound!"

It was one o'clock in the afternoon of the next day when our vessel made the harbor of Queenstown, where we waited till half past three for the mail. Thus far the passage had been comparatively smooth, and it continued so until Monday morning, when we found quite a different state of things. The waves did not run very high, but they were very active and irregular, and it was impossible to adjust one's self to the motion of the ship, which, huge as she is, jumped about like the small steamers crossing the British Channel in a gale. The result was that many of the passengers were compelled to remain in their berths, or at least in their staterooms; but we, with a few others, chose the deck for our performance—a sort of *contre-danse*, in which there was a good deal of *chassez-ing* between our seats and the side railing of the vessel. Knowing that in our rather bilious condition the exercise was pretty sure to prove beneficial, we were not in the least averse to taking part in it, although we cannot say we were proud of the figure we cut before quiet spectators. Indeed, it would have been a relief if those only who engaged in the *danse* had been present. The two following days were pleasant, the sea had quieted down, and everything on deck wore a cheerful aspect. We were now several hundred miles from "where the broad ocean leans against the land," and yet a flock of sea-gulls, as if to cheer us on our solitary course, followed gaily in our wake. What a wonderful bird! and well may we ask —

> "Wanderer, whence? From earth, or air, or ocean?
> Hast thou thy home 'mid clouds or on the billow?
> Or from some northern crag by sea-bird haunted,
> Hangs thy wild eyrie?"

Among our two hundred saloon passengers there were less than a dozen whom we had ever met before. Some of these were Mr. W. D. Washburne, of Minnesota, and family, Mrs. Tipton, and Mr. and Mrs. William H. Ferry, Jr. We formed a slight acquaintance with a few other pleasant people; for instance, Mr. and Mrs. Fred. James, Rodney House, Clifton, England; Dr. James B. Gould, of Rome; Mr. T. R. Gould and son, sculptors, Florence; Hon. Mr. Stanley, cousin of Dean Stanley, and wife; and Hon. J. Lowthian Bell, M. P. Mr. Bell, with Sir Charles Reed, F. S. A., Colonel Rich, R. E., Henry Laird, son of the great shipbuilder, and other English gentlemen, were on their way to our Centennial Exposition, some of them to act as judges.

We cannot say we are fond of being on the ocean, yet there is a fascination about it when once at sea, and particularly in fair weather, when the waves run not too high, that it is difficult either to fully comprehend or describe. It is at such times that we seek to find expression to our feelings in language more eloquent and stirring than commonplace prose.

"What is the theme entrancing and eternal
   The wild waves sing?
What is the message fraught with life supernal
   Their voices bring?

"Men change and cease to be,
   And empires rise, and grow, and fall;
But the weird music of the sea
   Lives, and outlives them all."

It is because of our apparently helpless condition on the ocean, doubtless—only a single plank, as it were, between us and the world beyond—that, while thus situated, we feel a livelier and more child-like dependence on the Great Source of all power than we usually experience in the busy walks of life on land. Stopping to contemplate, we lose ourselves in a vain effort to comprehend the vastness of creation and the mysteries of our being. Here before us rolls "the round ocean girdled with the sky," and we stretch our mental vision, alas how feebly! in trying to obtain the least glimpse of what there is beyond. The expanse of the great ocean alone is amazing:

"Dark-heaving—boundless, endless, and sublime—
The image of eternity—the throne
Of the Invisible.
   *   *   *   *   *   *
Time writes no wrinkles on thy azure brow;
Such as creation's dawn beheld, thou rollest now."

We can only gaze in wonder, striving with our might to reach after infinity, and then, seeing that all is in vain, sink back hopeless into utter nothingness. "Be still, my soul, and trust."

We move rapidly on, sometimes at the rate of three hundred miles, a little more or a little less, every twenty-four hours. The 11th was rough and disagreeable—the night foggy and dark, and the fearful screech of the warning steam whistle was heard above the roaring billows every three minutes until after midnight. Except a few hours toward evening on the 12th, there was a high sea, with more or less fog, until Sunday afternoon, the 14th, when the weather cleared off and continued pleasant the rest of the way. On our first Sunday, owing to interruptions consequent upon stopping at Queenstown, formal religious ceremonies were omitted; but on the second and last Sunday the customary Episcopal services were held in the dining saloon, most of the passengers being present. All day on the 15th there was scarcely a ripple on the face of the great deep. It was like oil. The sun shone brightly, and we were favored with the sight of three or four whales, spouting and disporting on either side of the ship as if for our amusement. We had spoken one steamship on her way to Liverpool; and we began now to meet or overtake an occasional sailing vessel. These are always cheerful sights at sea. About nine on the morning of the 16th, much to our delight, a pilot boat appeared in the distance and the pilot soon came aboard. Two hours and a half later we espied land—a joyous sight indeed. By two o'clock a tugboat, bringing custom officials, came alongside, and with them a cherished relative to welcome us home. We cannot express the joy and thankfulness that took possession of our being at this hour.

And, now, kind readers—you who have followed us in our long ramblings, among whom we recognize many dear friends, who have cheered us by flattering words of encouragement—good-bye and farewell,—

"Farewell! a word that must be, and has been —
A sound which makes us linger; yet, farewell!"

www.ingramcontent.com/pod-product-compliance
Lightning Source LLC
Chambersburg PA
CBHW050846300426
44111CB00010B/1145